IMAGES
of America

THORNVILLE AND THORN TOWNSHIP

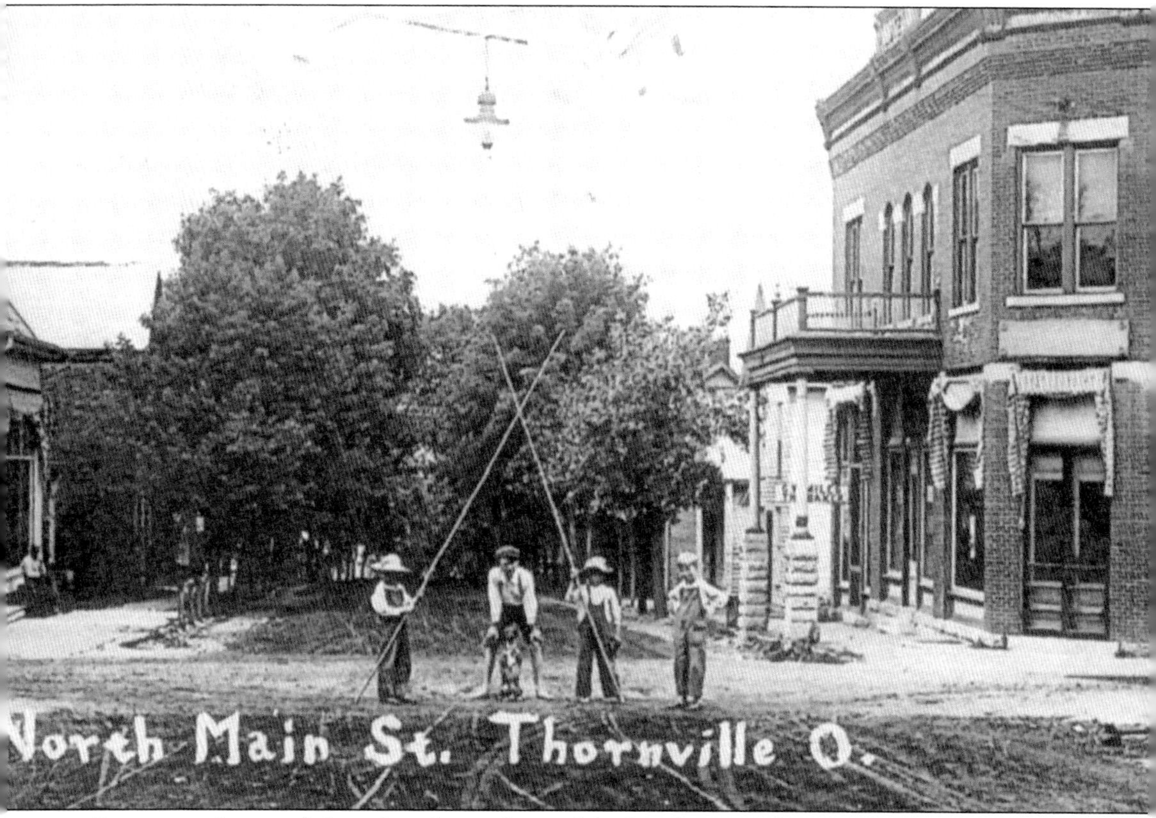

Four young boys and their dog play in front of the hotel on North Main Street in Thornville. This was prior to Shelly Company since the road was dirt, and instead of a stoplight, a gaslight was lit each evening. (Courtesy of the Historical Society of Perry County.)

On the Cover: Eli Long was born in 1823 and, after having lived 90 years in Thornville, died in 1914. He married Emily Packer in 1850, and together they had three sons: Charles, Samuel, and Frank. Emily died in 1866, and Eli married Elizabeth Murdock in 1870. This particular Long homestead sat across from Coop's Corner; Jockey Hollow, where townspeople and school students would socialize in a parklike setting, was nearby. A spring and bucket-lift contraption furnished water for the home. Later, Frank Taylor owned the property and sold used car parts there. Dick Shelly purchased the property and demolished all the buildings. Consequently, today, visitors traveling up the hill into Thornville from Route 13 see a striking landscape where this home once stood. (Courtesy of Helen George.)

IMAGES
of America

THORNVILLE AND THORN TOWNSHIP

Historical Society of Perry County

ARCADIA
PUBLISHING

ISBN 978-0-7385-8858-2

Published by Arcadia Publishing
Charleston, South Carolina

Printed in the United States of America

Library of Congress Control Number: 2011941159

For all general information, please contact Arcadia Publishing:
Telephone 843-853-2070
Fax 843-853-0044
E-mail sales@arcadiapublishing.com
For customer service and orders:
Toll-Free 1-888-313-2665

Visit us on the Internet at www.arcadiapublishing.com

This book is dedicated to the men and women of Thorn Township who chose to make their homes here and raise their children; without them, the pages in this book would be empty.

Contents

Acknowledgments

The following people generously contributed photographs, information, and assistance for this book: Mary Jane Bugh Gordon, Thelma Crader, Bob Combs, Ruth White, Judy McGaughey, Luann Cooperrider, Ann Starr, Lester Anspach, John Ridenour, Charles Williams, Lena K. Bowman, Beth Patrick, Jackie Fisher, Charlene Roberts, Tom Johnson, John McGaughey, Vesta Skinner, Larry Roberts, Bonnie Goldsberry, Judy Berrara, Barb Packer, Ann Wilson, Becky Krumlauf, Shirley Packer, Patty Ridenour, Connie Foster, and Judy and Chuck Cupp. Helen Long George has been one of the township historians for most of her 92 years; she has been a treasure trove of information and has been a significant part of this endeavor.

Unless stated otherwise, all photographs are from the Historical Society of Perry County. The author's portion of the profits from the sale of this book will go to the Historical Society of Perry County.

INTRODUCTION

Thorn Township lies along the northern edge of Perry County and borders Fairfield County on the west and Licking County on the north. Because the glacier ended here, this township, unlike the hilly southern half of the county, is relatively flat with rich black soil. Before pioneers arrived around 1800, this area was heavily forested, and where Buckeye Lake is now was a swamp where Native Americans hunted.

The first settlers came from Pennsylvania and Virginia, and most were of German descent. Joseph McMullen and John Feidler bought 21 acres from Andrew Foster for $50 and platted a village on a hill overlooking the swamp in 1811. They named it Lebanon. It was a great location since it was not far from the National Road or Zane's Trace and was high above the swamp. In 1820, the name was changed to Thornville because there was already a Lebanon in Warren County. In 1877, Thornville officially became a village with elected officials. The first mayor was D.D. Avery.

In 1833, digging was completed on the Ohio Canal, and Buckeye Lake was dug to supply water for the canal, which would go south to Millersport, Lancaster, and Nelsonville and north to Newark and Cleveland. Until 1880, Thornville was a center of trade, with tailors, blacksmiths, shoemakers, a wagon factory, and tin shops. Thornport became a thriving metropolis with two large grain warehouses, hotels, restaurants, and bait shops. Grain from miles around was brought to Thornport to be put on canal boats and sent north to Cleveland. Returning boats brought groceries, dry goods, hardware, salt, and lumber. Canal boats gave Perry County an avenue to the world.

In 1871, the Newark, Somerset & Straitsville Railroad began operating with a depot in Thornport. Railroads replaced the canals as the primary transportation system for both products and people. Cattle could now be moved by rail instead of being driven overland along the National Road.

The 20th century saw the advent of automobiles and paved roads, mechanization of farm equipment, improved schools, and increased population. The people of Thorn Township experienced depressions and sent sons and daughters to wars. The community spirit endured, and Thornville celebrated a centennial in 1911, a sesquicentennial in 1961, and a bicentennial in 2011. Our children and grandchildren will be organizing a celebration in 50 years to party again and hopefully keep the spirit living.

One

Long Ago

What the settlers found when they came into Thorn Township were forests with trails made by animals and Native Americans. To produce a shelter, the settlers had to chop down trees, cut them into four-inch poplar planks, mortar them, and then attach them to vertical posts, which produced a "cabin in the clearing." Those residents provided their families with food by growing gardens, from which they preserved vegetables by drying and canning; picking wild berries for making jelly and jam; collecting wild honey for sweetening; butchering animals in the fall; and grinding corn and wheat to make bread. Soaps were produced from mixing animal lard and lye. After sawmills were organized, the wood for homes was much more manageable, and the homes became larger and more ornate. Later, they found that Perry County clay made great bricks, so kilns were built, and consequently, there are some very beautiful 19th-century brick homes in the township.

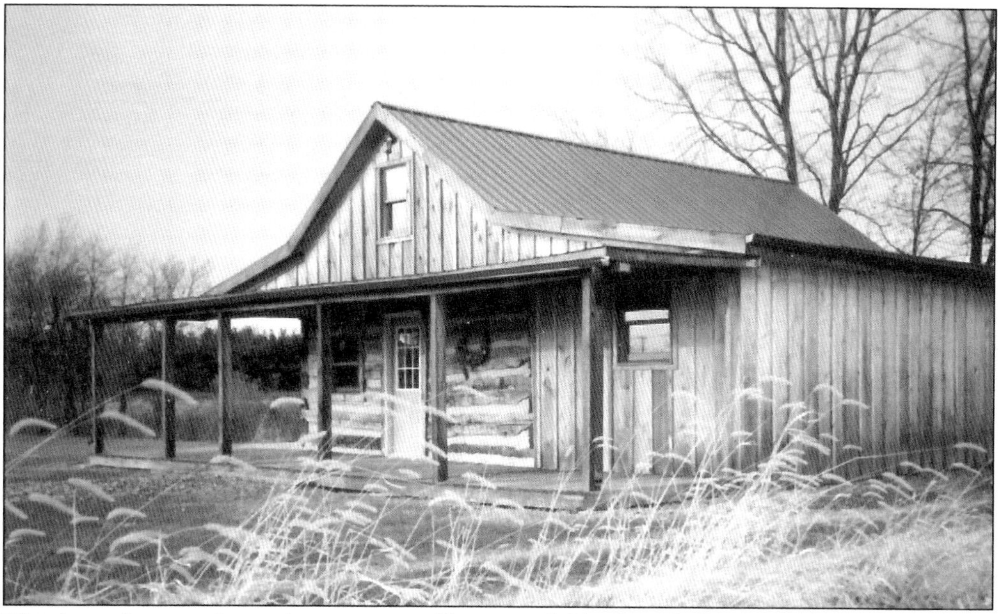

This log cabin stands on the property of Larry and Charlene Roberts on Route 204 west of Thornville. Original owners included William Hamilton, John Dent, Daniel and Mary Alspach, Henry Alspach, Albert Alspach, Harry Roberts, and Ralph and Juanita Roberts. Larry and Charlene have owned the land since 1960. It is unknown when the cabin was last used as a home. (Courtesy of Larry Roberts.)

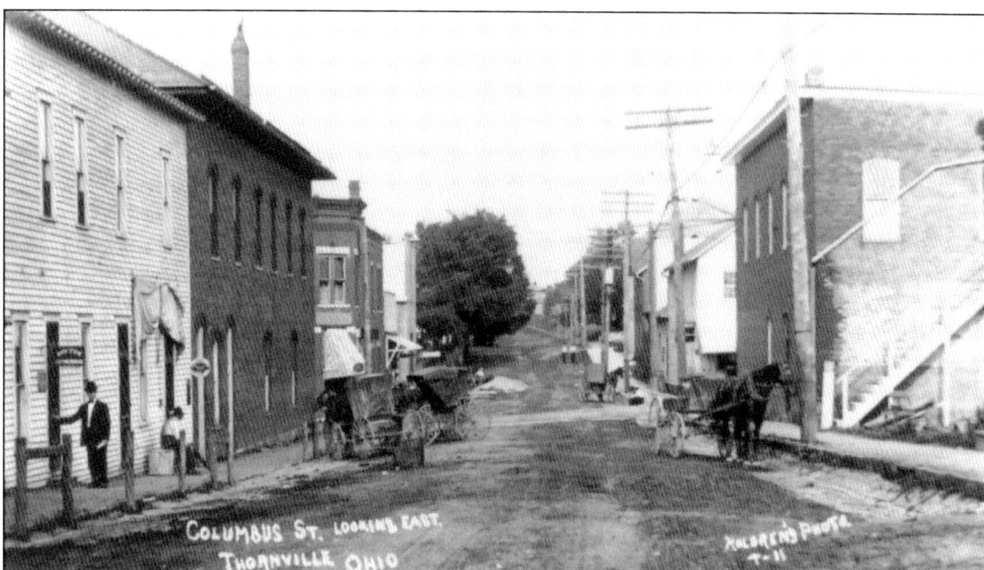

This view of Thornville is looking east along Columbus Street. Roads were unpaved, and transportation included riding horses, horse-drawn buggies, and walking. Women spent their days growing and processing food, sewing, mending, darning socks, washing and ironing clothes, baking bread, making butter, and cooking.

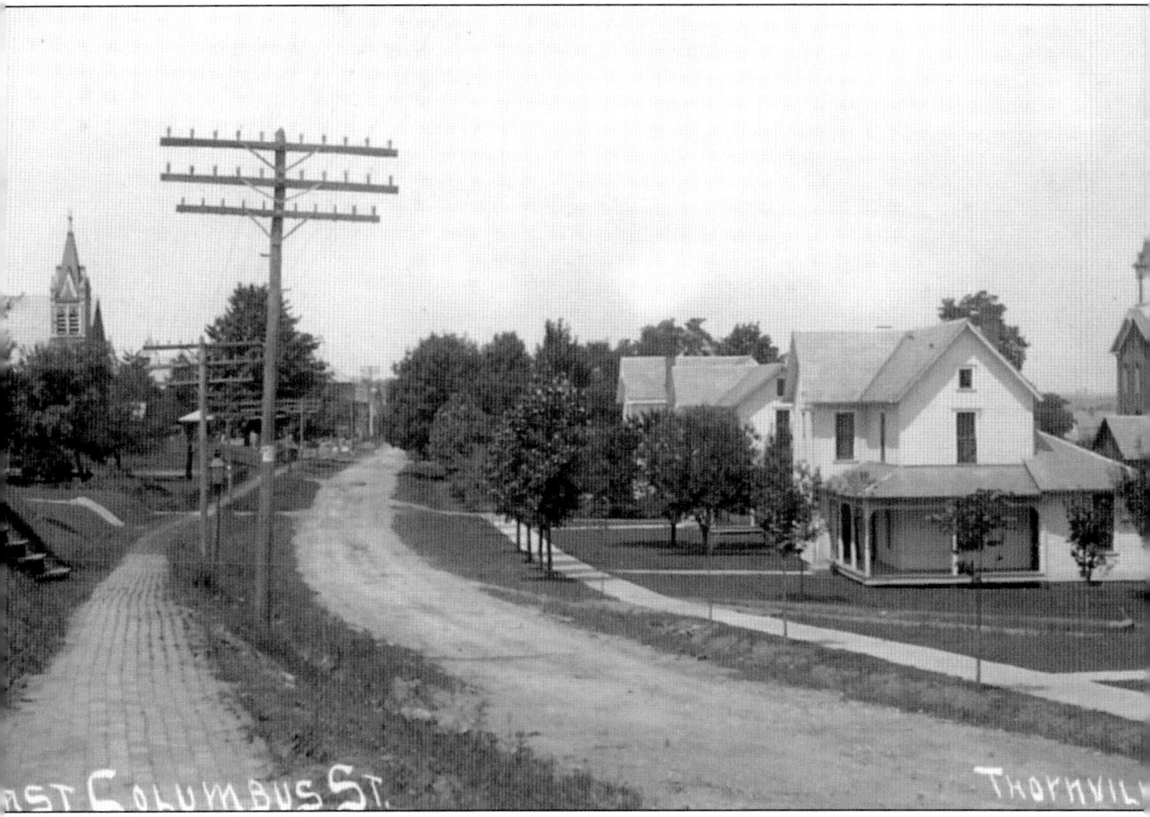

East Columbus Street had brick sidewalks, but the roads were still unpaved. Grace Lutheran Church and the school are in the distance. Residents did have accessibility to telephones. With the advent of satellites and cellular phones, how much longer will telephone poles be needed?

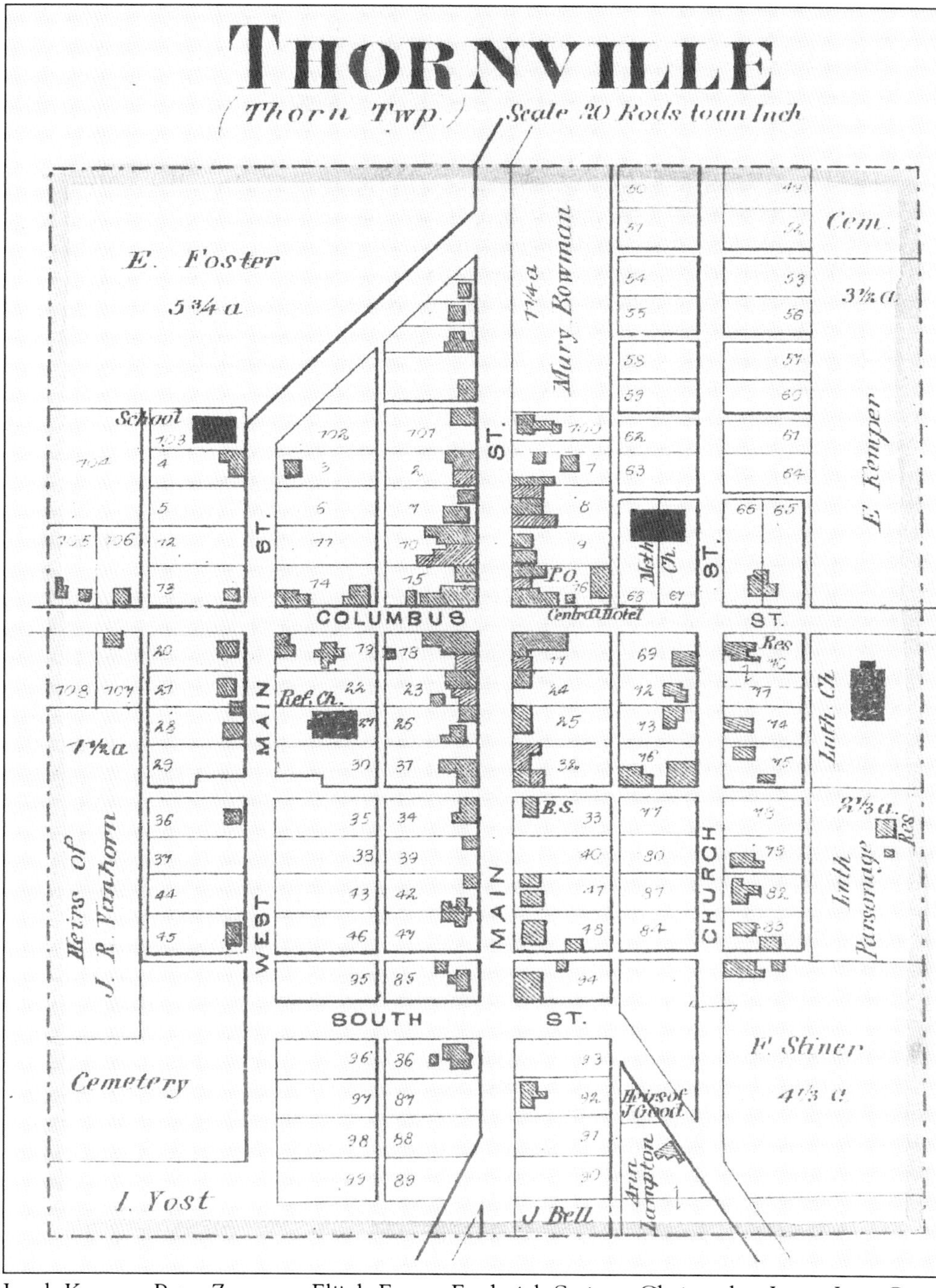

Jacob Kemper, Peter Zartman, Elijah Foster, Frederick Steiner, Christopher Long, Levi Crist, David Long, C.V. Clum, Robert Foster, and Lester Anspach all contributed land to the village of Thornville over the years, as depicted on this map.

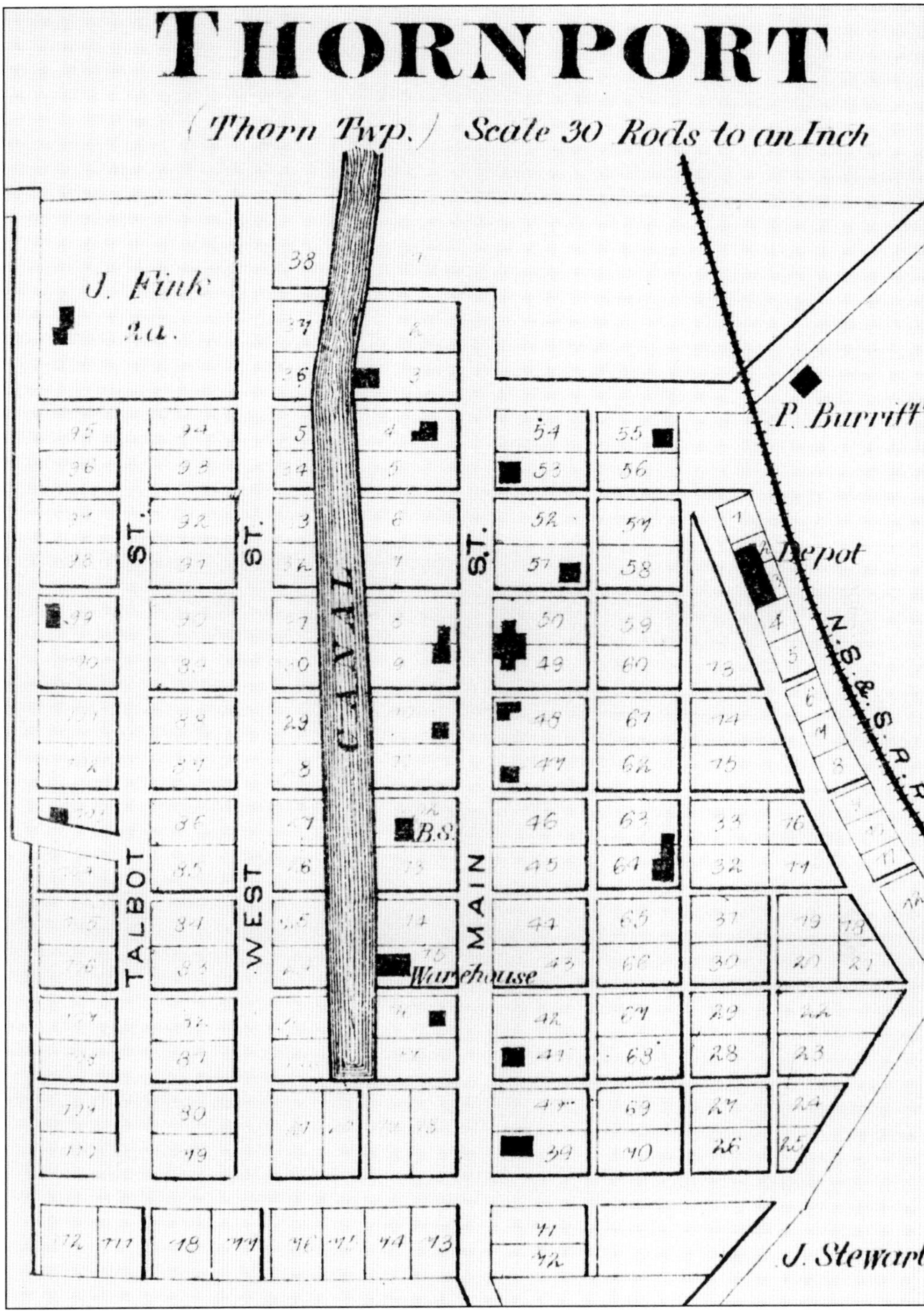

Thornport was platted by Jacob Talbot in 1839, and by 1850, the community was thriving. The canals, and then the railroads, brought travelers and goods to and from Perry County by way of Thornport.

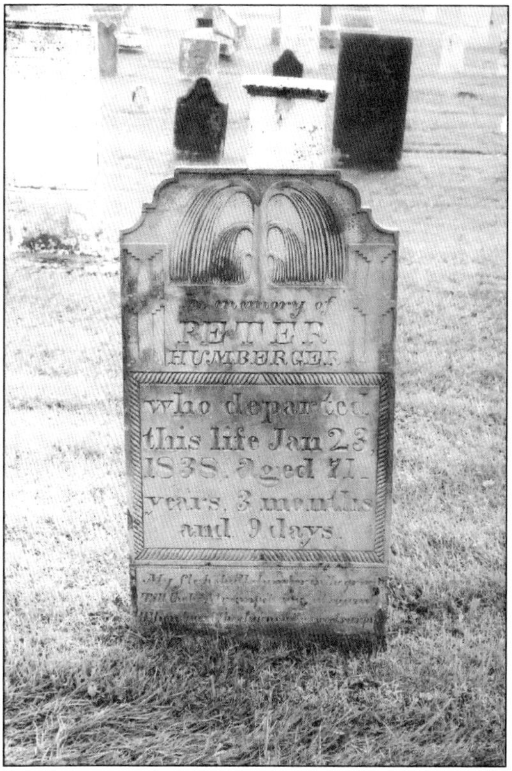

Peter Humberger moved his family to Perry County in 1802 and was soon followed by his brothers John and Henry. Peter and his sons were well-known gunsmiths—Humberger rifles are highly sought after by today's collectors. Peter died January 23, 1838, at the age of 71 and is buried in the Zion Reformed Cemetery. (Courtesy of Lena K. Bowman.)

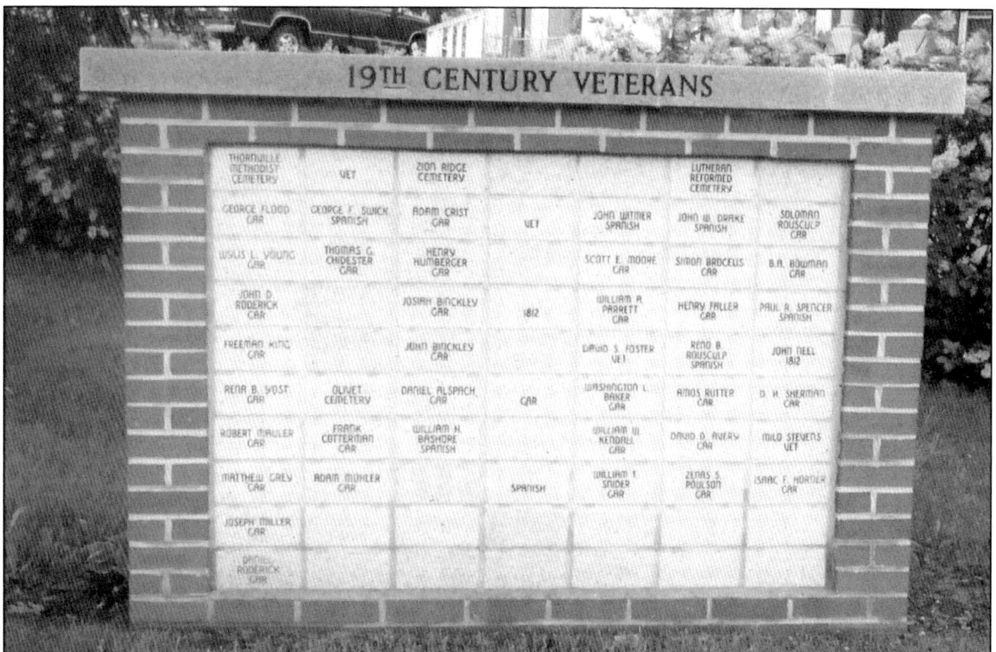

Erected by Andy Fry and Bob Combs, this monument dedicated to 19th-century veterans stands in Veteran's Park behind the town hall on West Columbus Street. A Veteran's Park committee made up of township residents cares for the monuments.

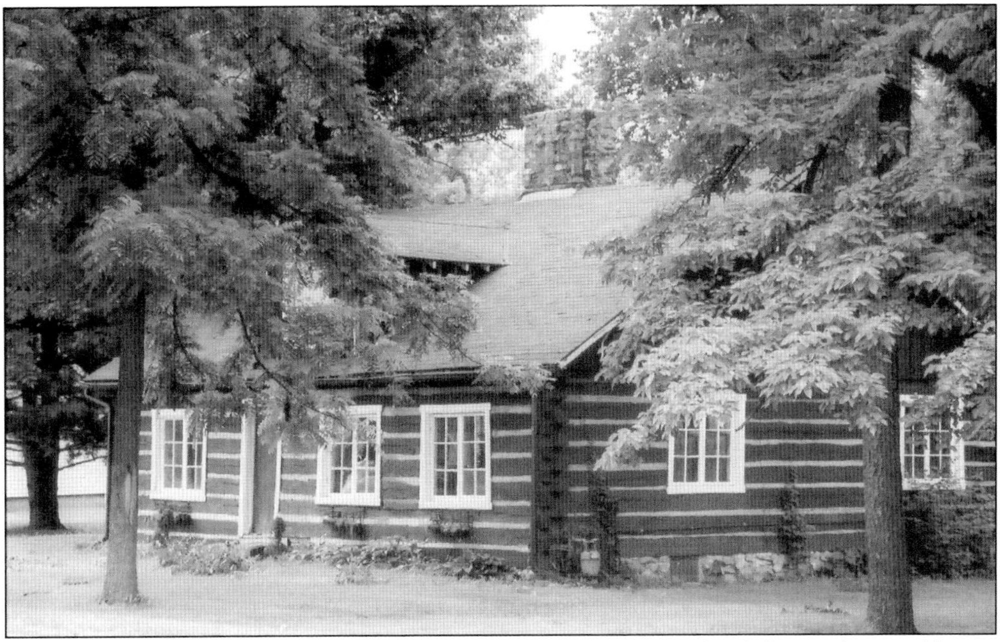

The Culbertson Warehouse in Thornport stored grain until it was loaded onto the canal boats. After the canal closed, H.G. Roberts stored wool in the warehouse. Later, it was torn down, and the logs were used to build this house, which still stands in Thornport. (Courtesy of Lena K. Bowman.)

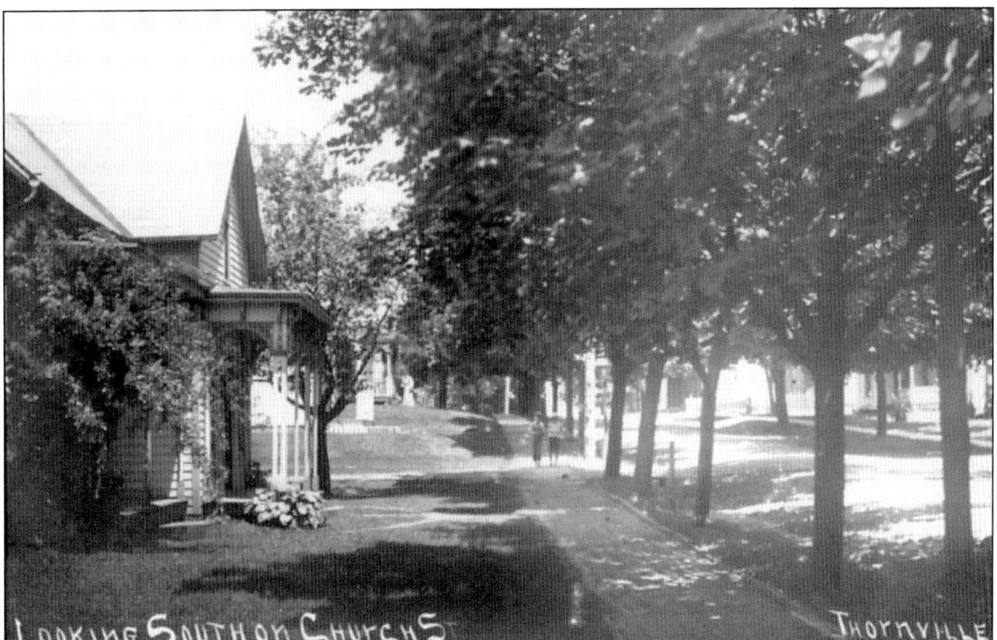

This view of Thornville looks south on Church Street. Today, one might see young people walking to the gymnastics center at the top of the hill or to the baseball field, the pool, or the bowling alley, which are all located along South Church Street.

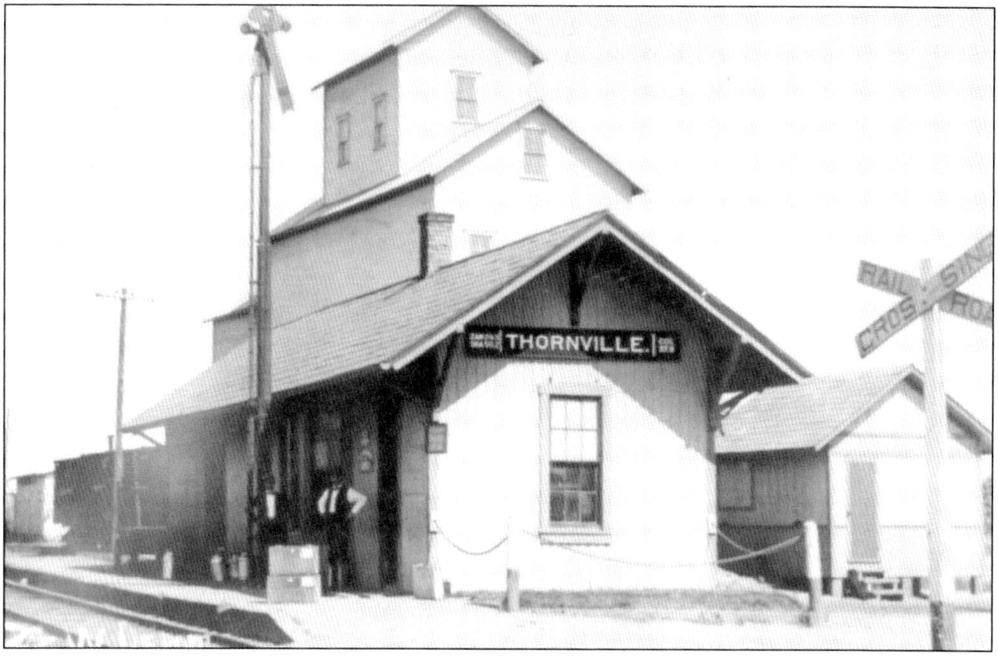

During the 19th century, the railroad ran from Newark, around Buckeye Lake, and south through Perry County, bringing visitors and goods. The depot and nearby grain elevators were located in Thornport.

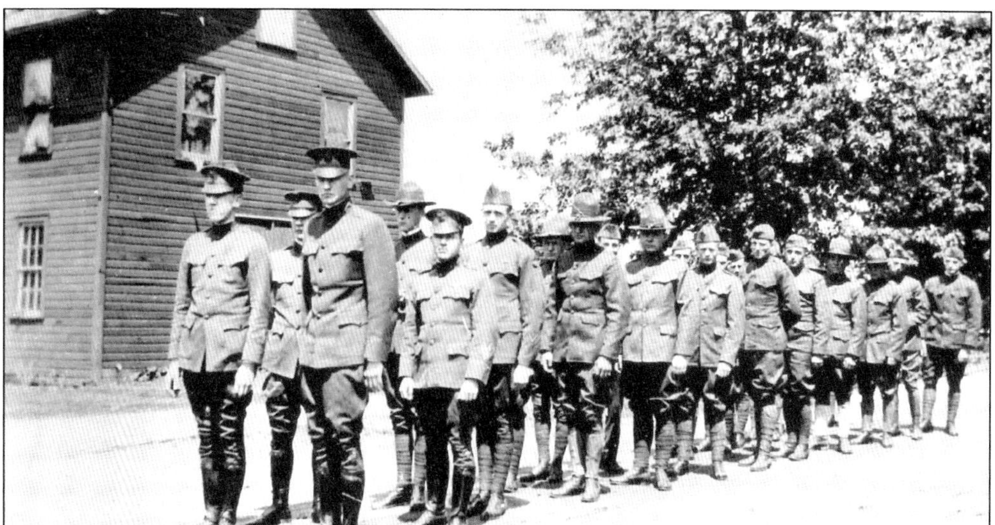

The Ewing Guards were organized and first appeared in the Fourth of July parade in 1876. They were later called the New Lexington Guards. In 1877, they camped in Thornport. Behind them in this image is the Culbertson grain warehouse, which was built in 1845. (Courtesy of Helen George.)

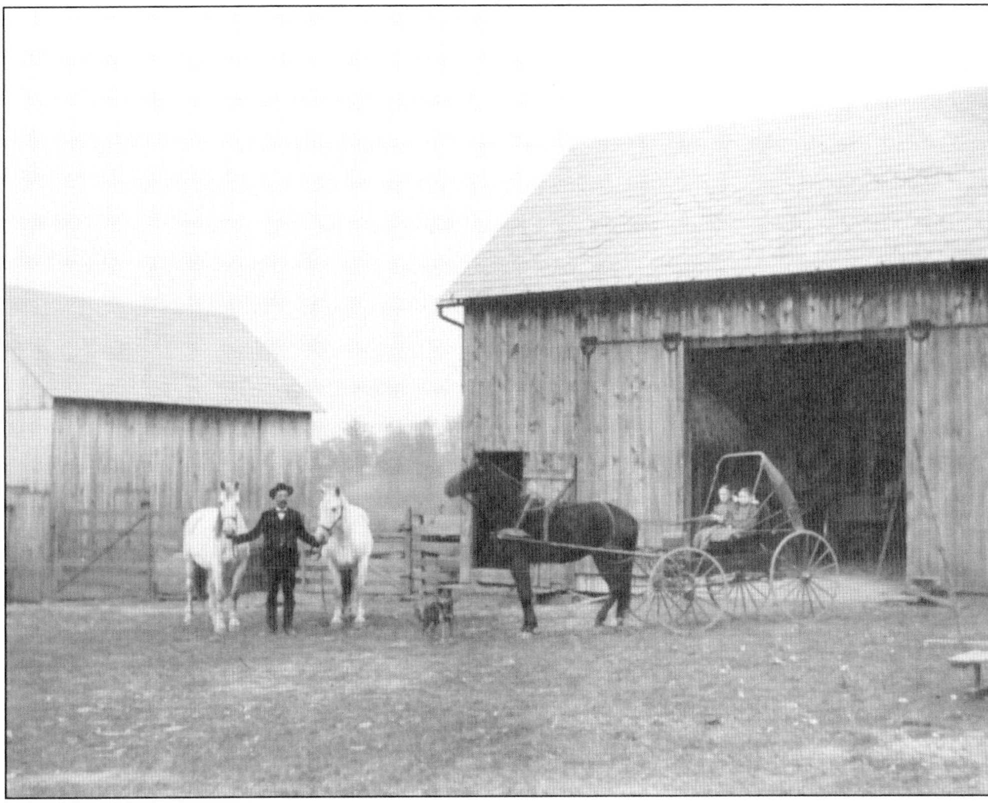

Elmer Zartman (left) was Helen George's grandfather; his home was at 11430 Zion Road. Evelyn and Minta Zartman, Elmer's children, are sitting in the buggy. (Courtesy of Helen George.)

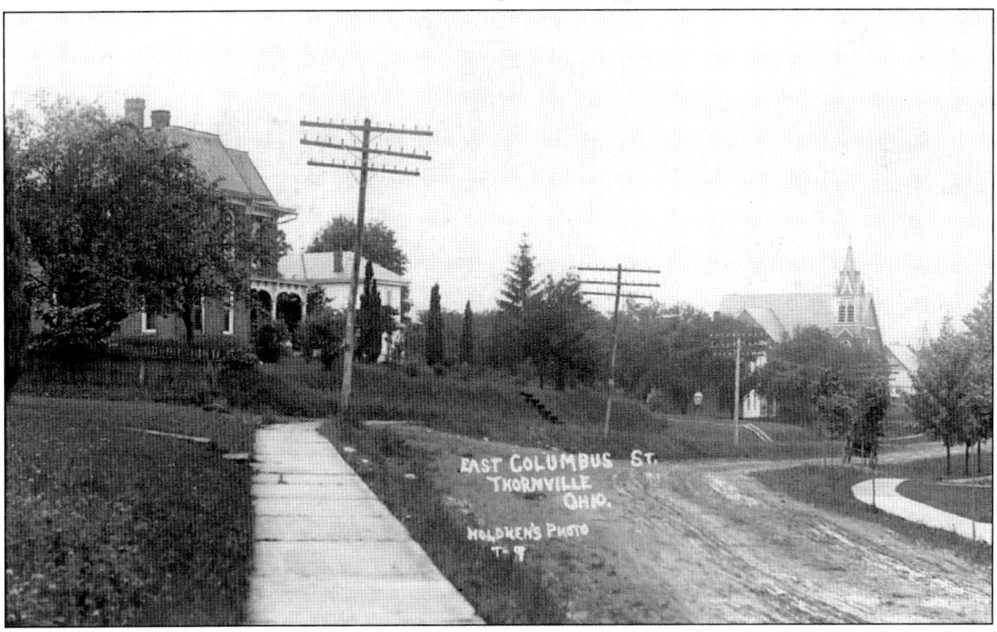

This view of Thornville looks west down Columbus Street. Grace Lutheran Church sits in the distance. Some of the first homes in Thornville were constructed in the east end of the village.

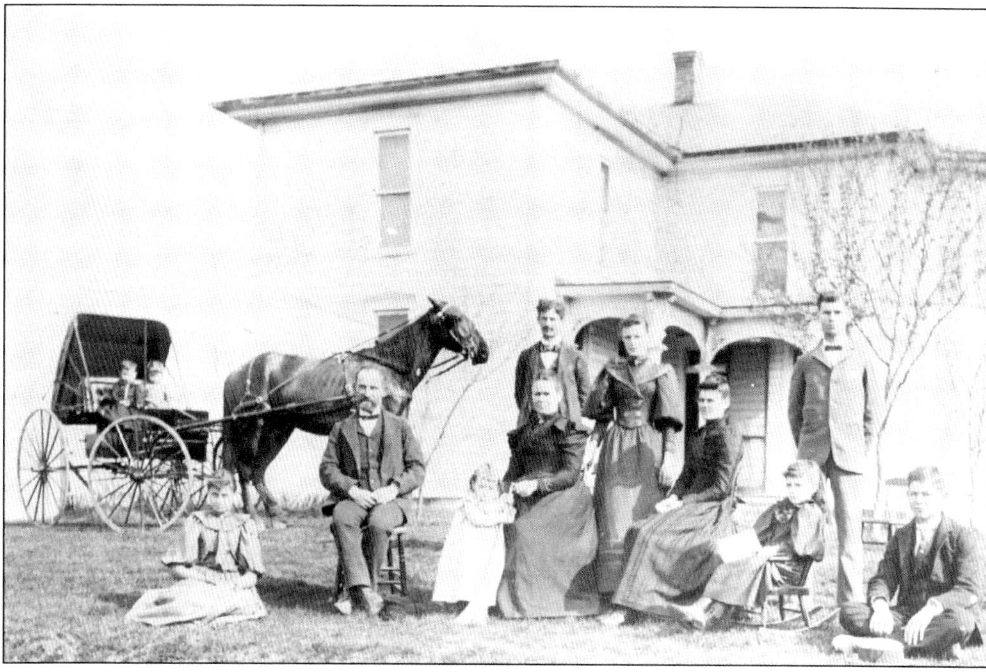

Jonathon Bope and Elizabeth Alspach lived here with their 10 children. This farm was located near Point Beautiful Road. Augustine Wherle, who owned the Newark Stove Company, bought the property, and the farm eventually became Heron Bay. (Courtesy of Helen George.)

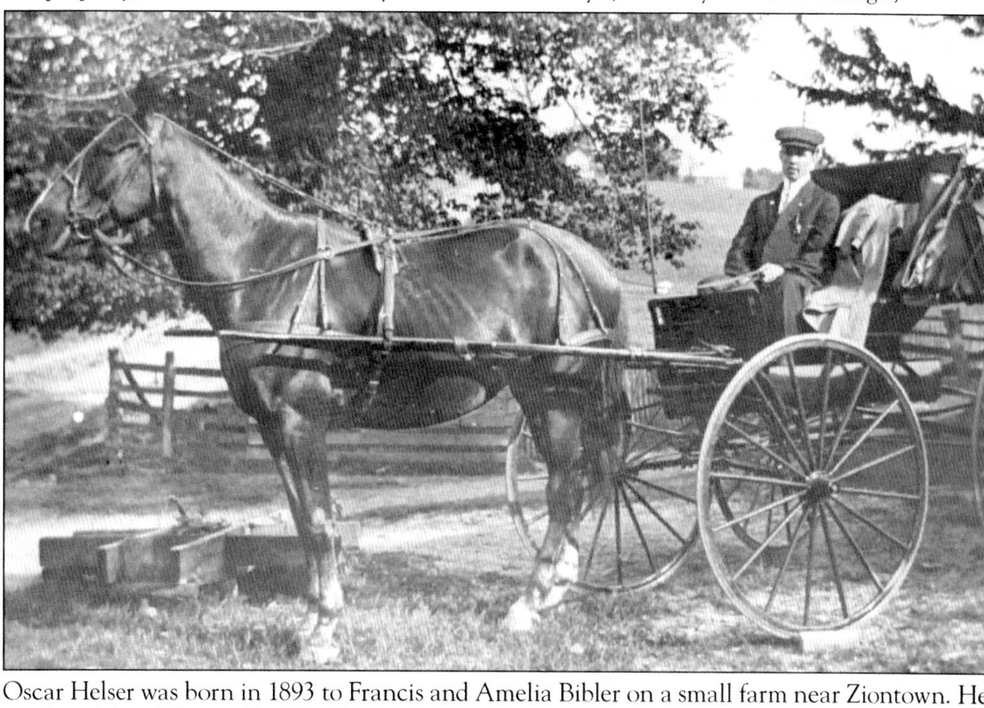

Oscar Helser was born in 1893 to Francis and Amelia Bibler on a small farm near Ziontown. He graduated from Thornville School in 1912 and taught at Goods School. He married Laura Miller, and they and son Eugene had a grocery store behind what is now T.C. Market. Oscar had a filling station, sold used automobiles, and drove a school bus. (Courtesy of Helen George.)

Augustine Wherle purchased the 280-acre Bope farm along the south shore of Buckeye Lake in 1924 and built this Elizabethan-style home with a greenhouse, boathouse, and barns. The 32-room home was constructed of stucco and brick, with a red tile roof, wine cellar in the basement, solid cherry doors, teakwood floors, stained-glass windows, and four fireplaces. One of the fireplaces was made of flint from Flint Ridge. Part of the Wherle estate was sold for the Robinwood Estates development. The remainder was sold to Andrew Wolfe, who began the development of Heron Bay. The Wherle mansion still stands among the homes of Heron Bay. (Courtesy of Thelma Crader.)

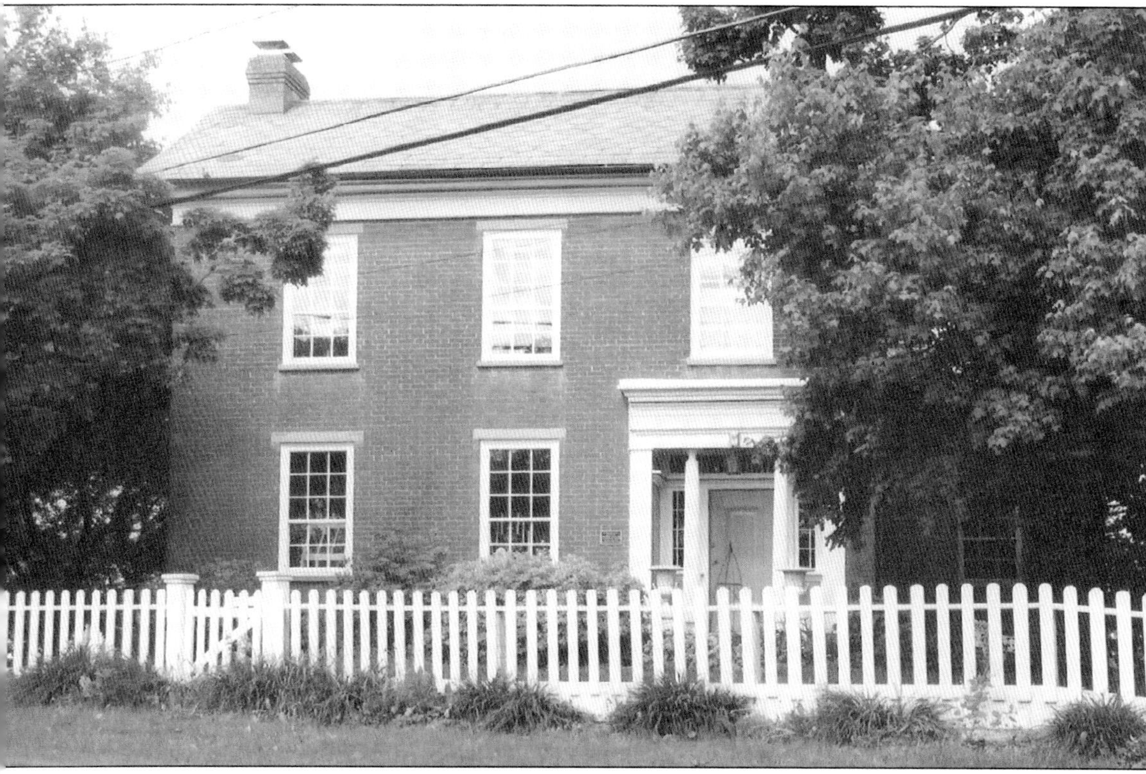

Solomon Whitmer (also spelled Witmer) served in the Revolutionary War and came to Thorn Township from Pennsylvania to build this brick home on Zion Road between Thornville and Thornport. The bricks were fired in kilns east of Thornville and carried to the site by horse and wagon. The woodwork inside is black walnut. The house is of Federal and Greek Revival styles and is the only building in Thorn Township on the National Register of Historic Places. Dr. Charles Bope was a great-grandson of Solomon Whitmer. (Courtesy of Lena K. Bowman.)

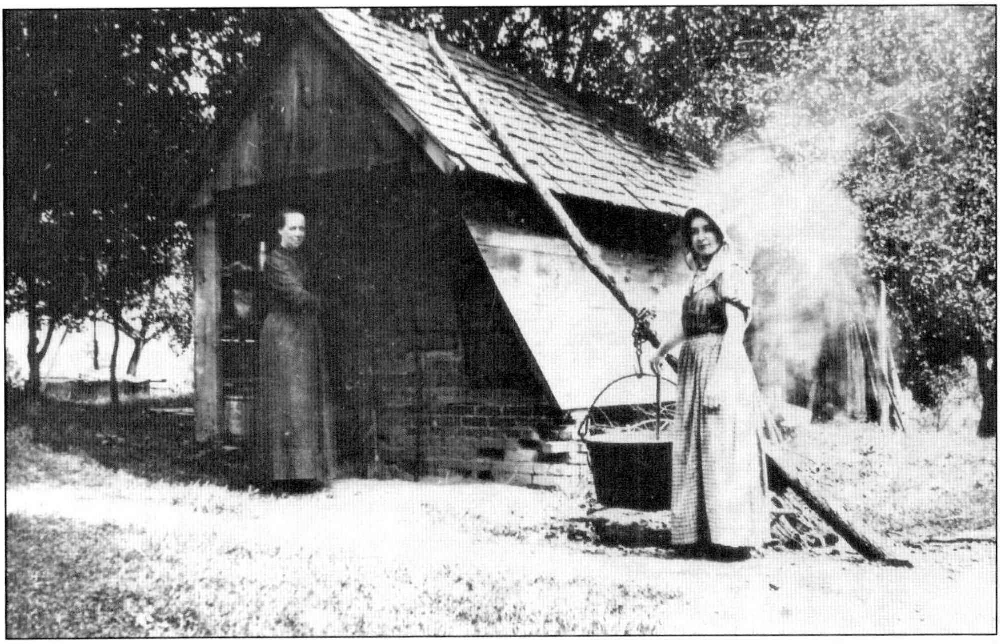

Cassie Long was born in 1856, and her sister Mary was born in 1861. During the summer and fall, food, including wild berries and garden vegetables, was preserved for the winter and spring months. Animals were butchered in the fall and salted down, beans and potatoes were dried, and hickory nuts and walnuts were collected. The building in the image was used for baking bread. Homes often had outside kitchens due to the risk of fire, which also kept the homes cooler during the summer months. (Courtesy of Helen George.)

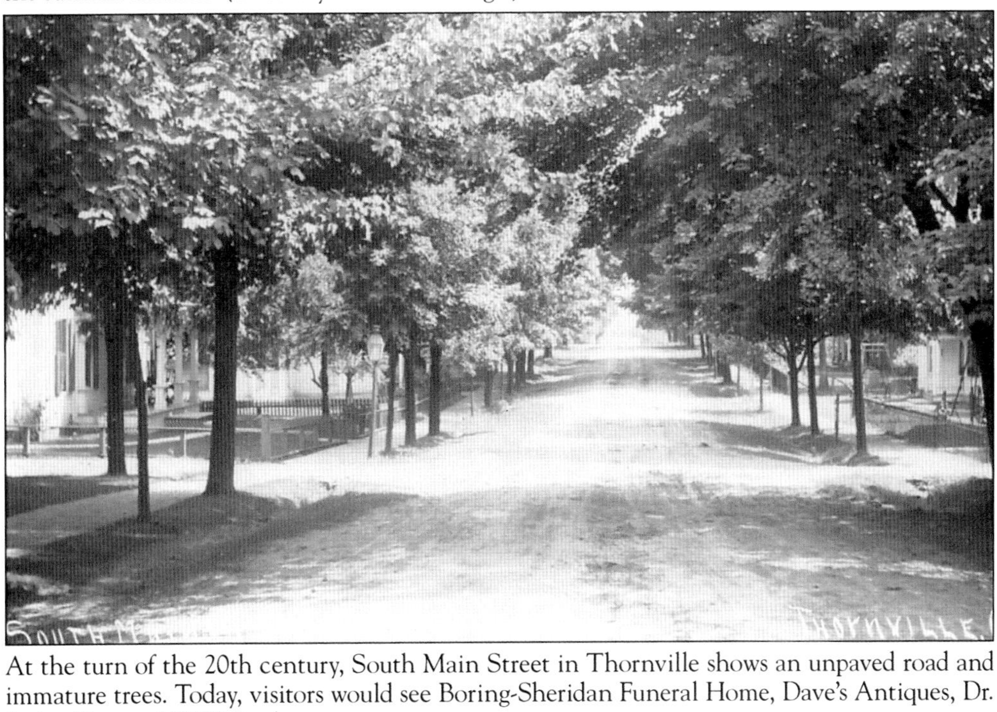

At the turn of the 20th century, South Main Street in Thornville shows an unpaved road and immature trees. Today, visitors would see Boring-Sheridan Funeral Home, Dave's Antiques, Dr. Joy's office, and PNC Bank.

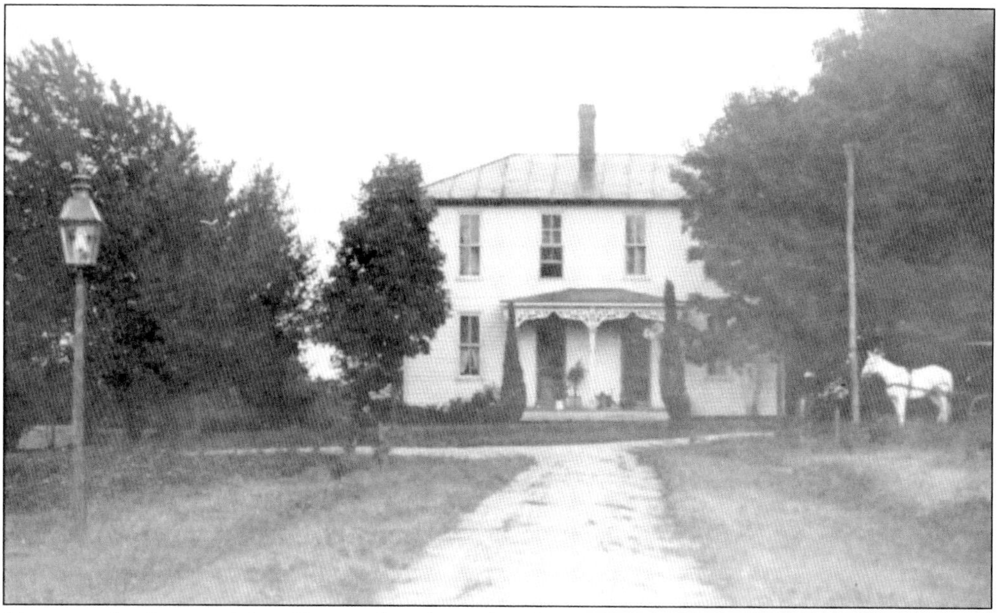

This was the home of the Christopher Long family on the southeast end of Thornville. Son Henry Long was blind, and this white horse was trained to take him anywhere in Thornville. A loom was placed in the home, and the family took turns weaving carpets, which were then sold in Thornville. Eventually, the farm became part of East Columbus Street, the water tower, Shelly maintenance and office, Clark apartments, and the Shelly home. Note the gaslight in front of the house. (Courtesy of Helen George.)

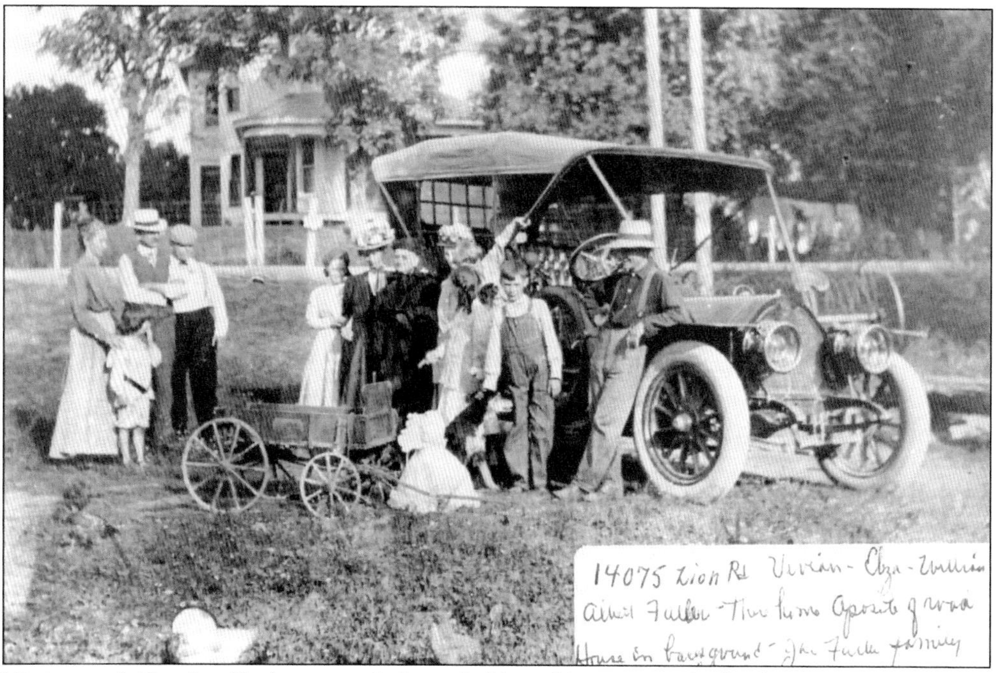

Vivian and Charles Skidmore and their children Virginia and Charles visit with Albert, Elisa, and Phyllis Faller at 14075 Zion Road between Thornville and Thornport. (Courtesy of Helen George.)

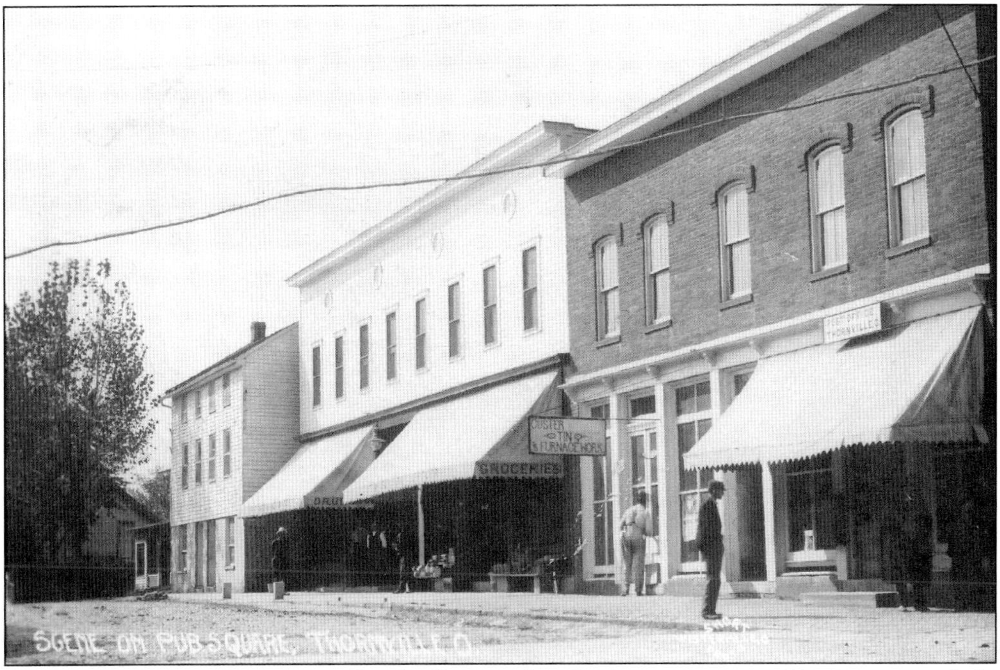

In 1877, Thornville became an official village, with D.D. Avery as mayor, N.L. Stevens as clerk, and Jacob Dunwoody as marshal. Council members included A.W. Thomas, W.H. Schneck, Nathan Dodd, J.D. Stevens, S.K. Zartman, and C.E. Hite.

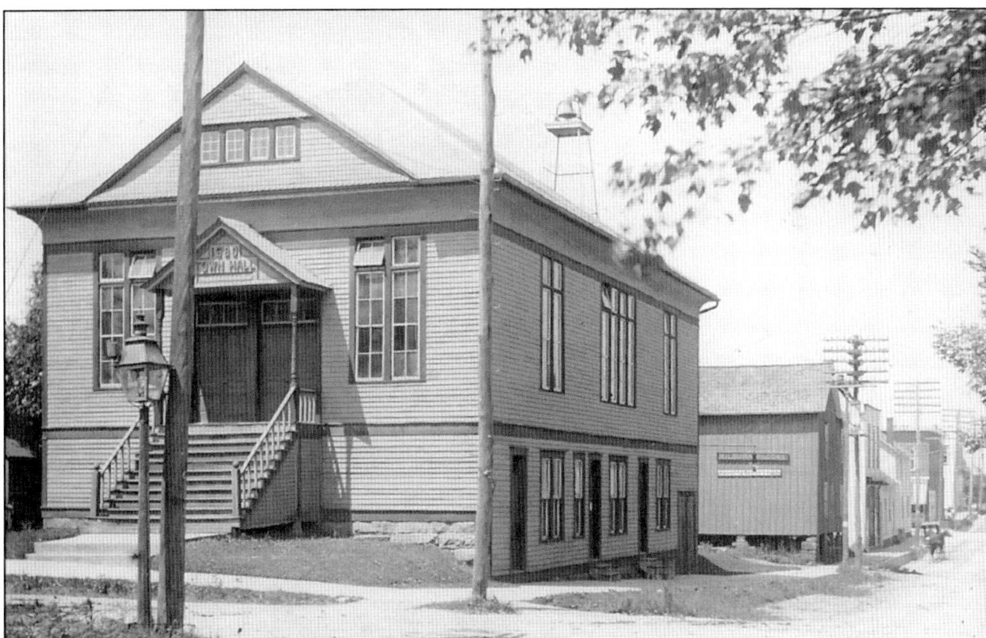

The town hall was not only the seat of government for the village but also the venue for entertainment in the area. Residents attended silent movies, vaudeville acts, minstrels, concerts, basketball games, and lectures there.

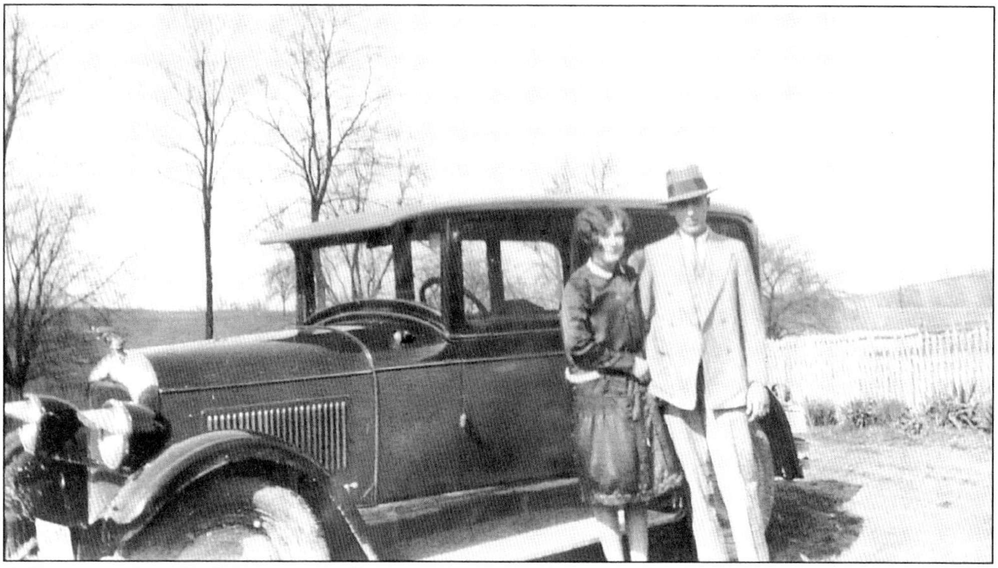

Affectionately called O.J., Dr. Letherman was one of the first people in the township to own a car. Because the roads were unpaved and the first automobiles did not have heaters or tops, they were only driven during the summertime. In the wintertime, they were jacked up to save the tires from wearing. O.J. served in World War I and practiced medicine in Thornville for 37 years. His home still stands north of the post office. (Courtesy of John Ridenour.)

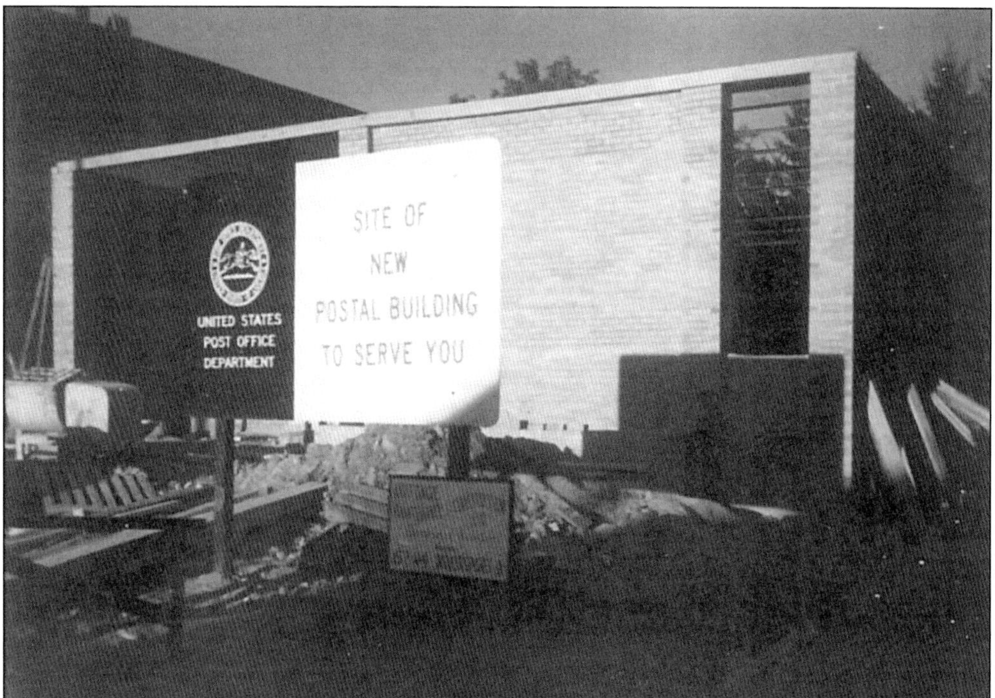

The Thornville Post Office had more than one home; this is the present building being constructed across from Thornville Pharmacy on North Main Street. (Courtesy of Chet Erwin.)

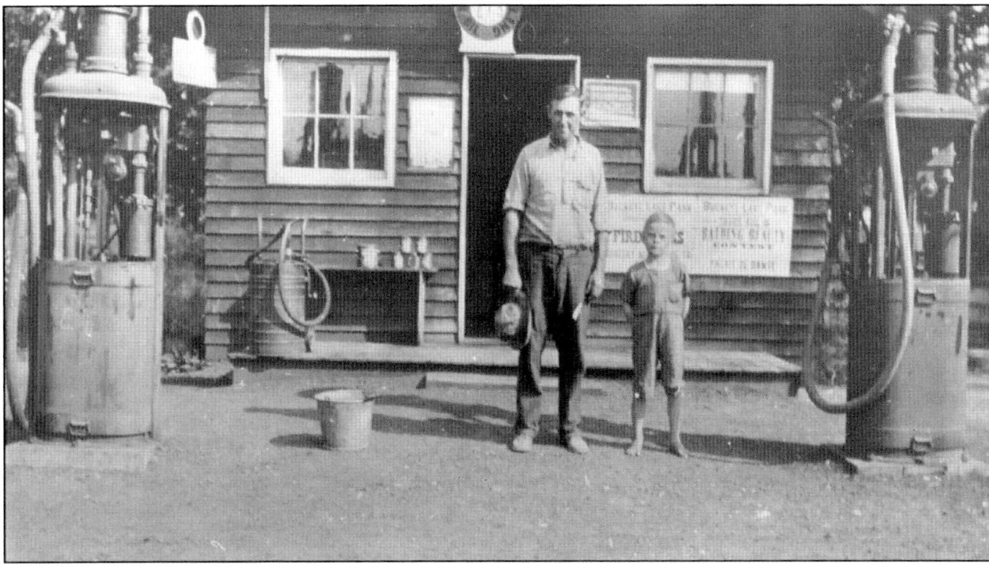

Quickly following the addition of automobiles to the township were filling stations, which provided gasoline, tires, and repairs. Although Coop's Corner is the only one still in existence, there have been several filling stations in the township over the years.

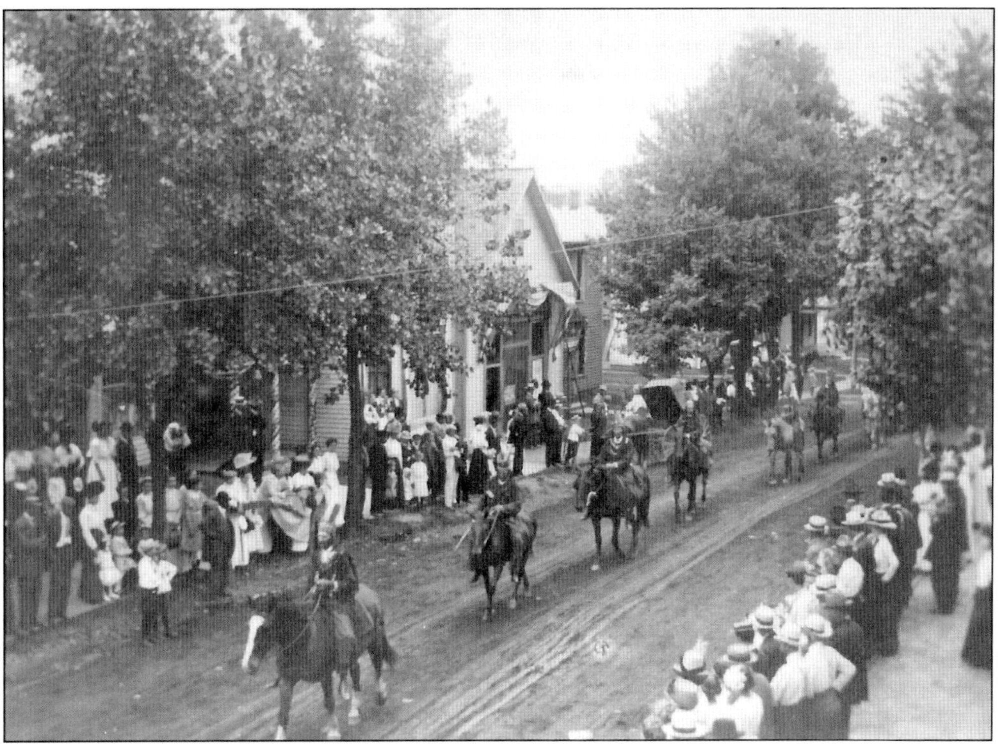

In 1911, Thornville celebrated its centennial with a parade through the village. A group of Native Americans rode horses down Main Street for residents who turned out to celebrate the village's 100th birthday.

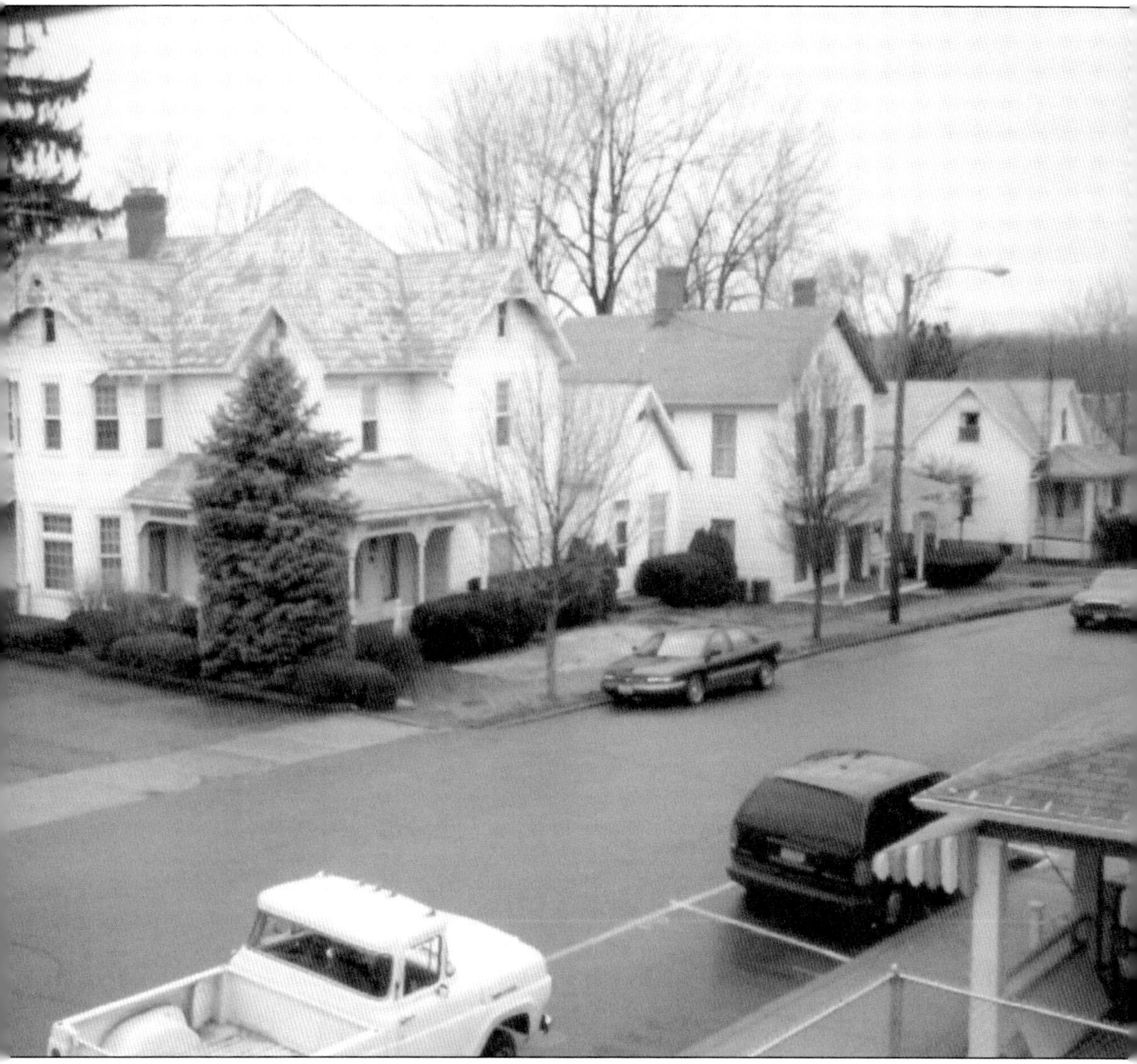

The large house beside the present post office on North Main Street was the home of Dr. Omie Joe Letherman; his wife, Emma; and daughter Mary. The small building beside it served as his medical office. He purchased the home before he married and practiced there for 38 years. Dr. Letherman died in 1941 at the age of 59 after a heart attack. Mary and Gavin Reiner purchased the property around 2009. (Courtesy of Thelma Crader.)

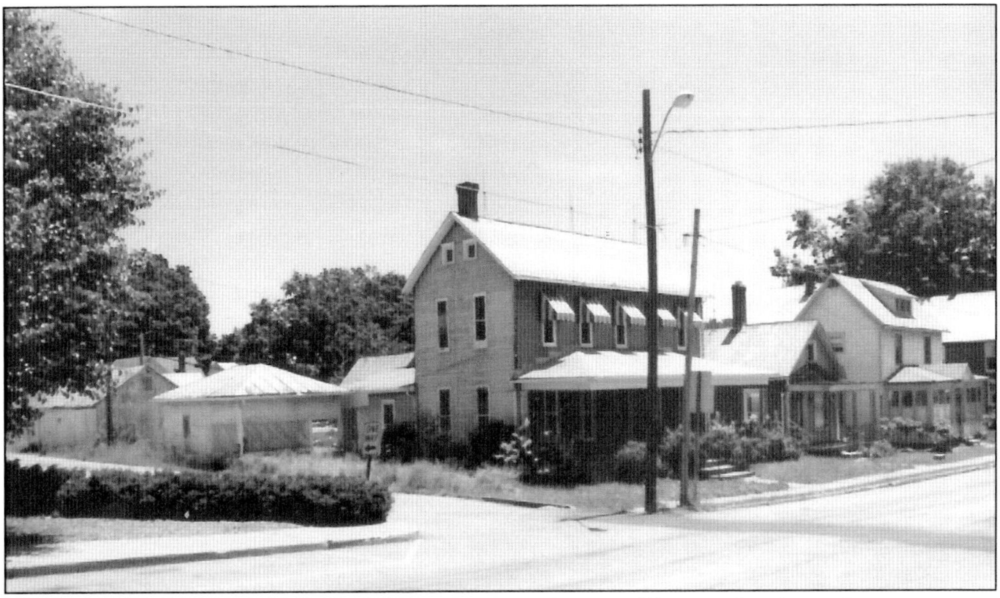

Dr. Frank R. Clemson, who served the community for over 50 years, lived in a large two-story home at 30 South Main Street, with a small office building beside it. In 1990, both buildings were torn down, and today, Dr. Joy Stovcik has her dental office on that site.

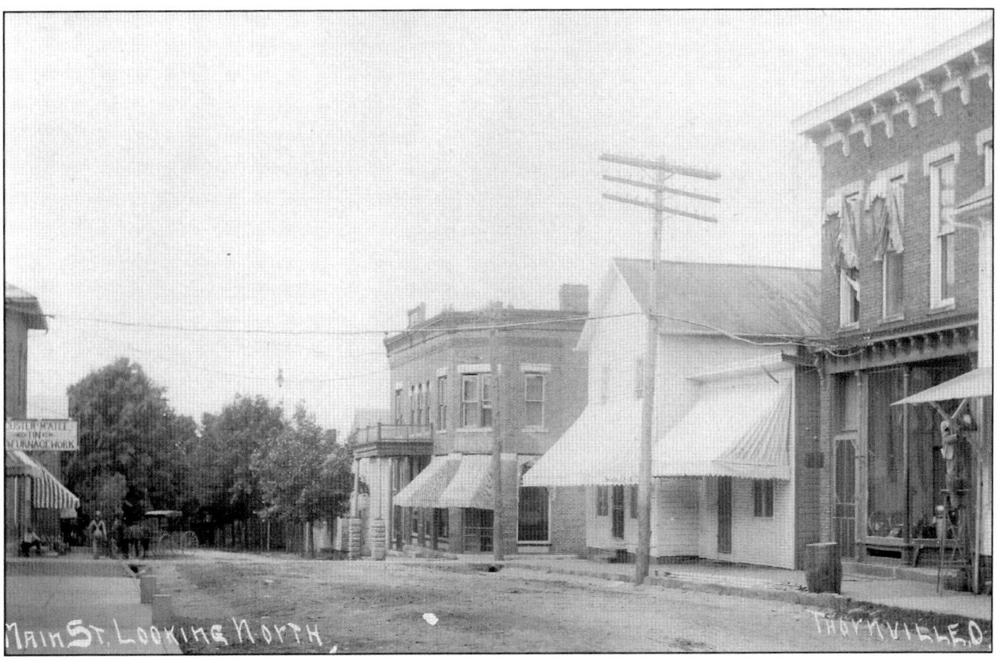

Looking north on Main Street, the hardware store is on the right. Today, it is condemned and slated for demolition.

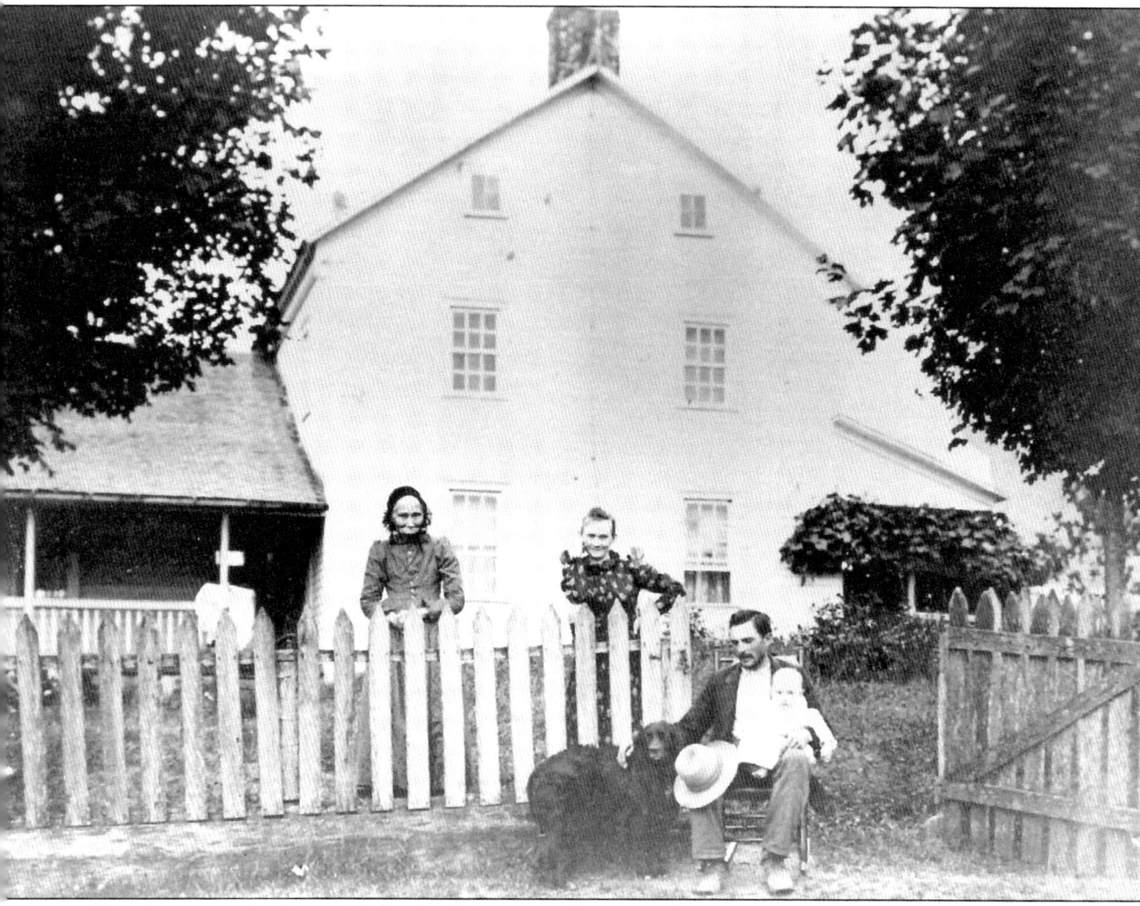

This home was built in 1860 by Jacob Ream and is located on Township Road 85. It was the home of Guy and Nellie Williams. (Courtesy of Helen George.)

Two

Churches

When the early pioneers brought their families into Thorn Township in the early 1800s, they also brought their strong religious values. There are five Protestant churches in Thorn Township, and although there is no Baptist church currently, Baptists congregate at the Athletic Zone in Thornport. The churches have not only been places to worship but also to hold community events, such as breakfasts, dinners, ice cream socials, workshops, quilting bees, and concerts.

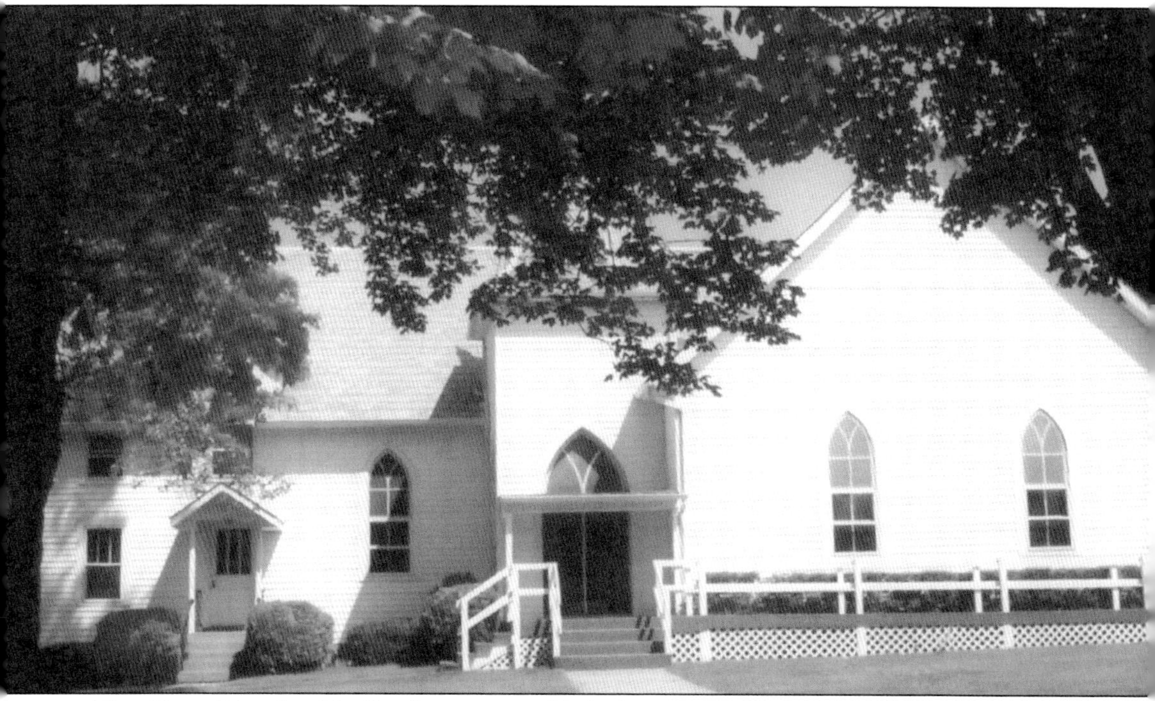

The Olivet Church of the Brethren was established in 1844 in Ziontown as the Jonathan Creek congregation of the German Baptist Brethren Church. The first meetinghouse built at Ziontown in 1855 was called the Helser Meetinghouse. In 1904, the members decided to build a new church, and A.W. Dupler named it Olivet. Charles Cupp served as pastor from 1965 to 1974; he and his wife, Judy, were very active in Thornville activities. Judy retired as an elementary teacher in the Northern Local Schools. David Helser is the current minister. (Courtesy of Lena K. Bowman.)

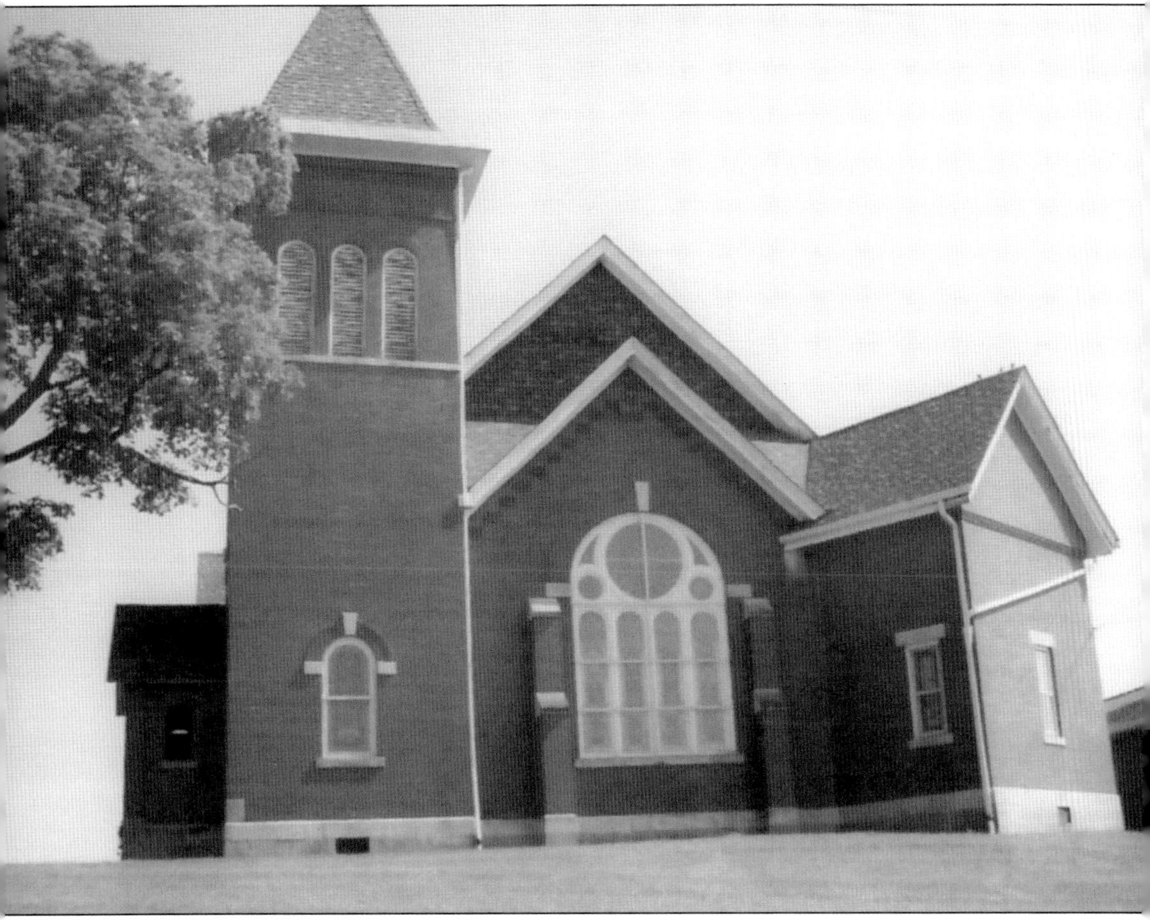

The Trinity Church of Christ alternated between German and English services during the 1830s. Rev. Sam S. Richly became the minister in 1844 and later founded Heidelberg College in Tiffin, Ohio. The parishioners celebrated its 100th birthday in 1937.

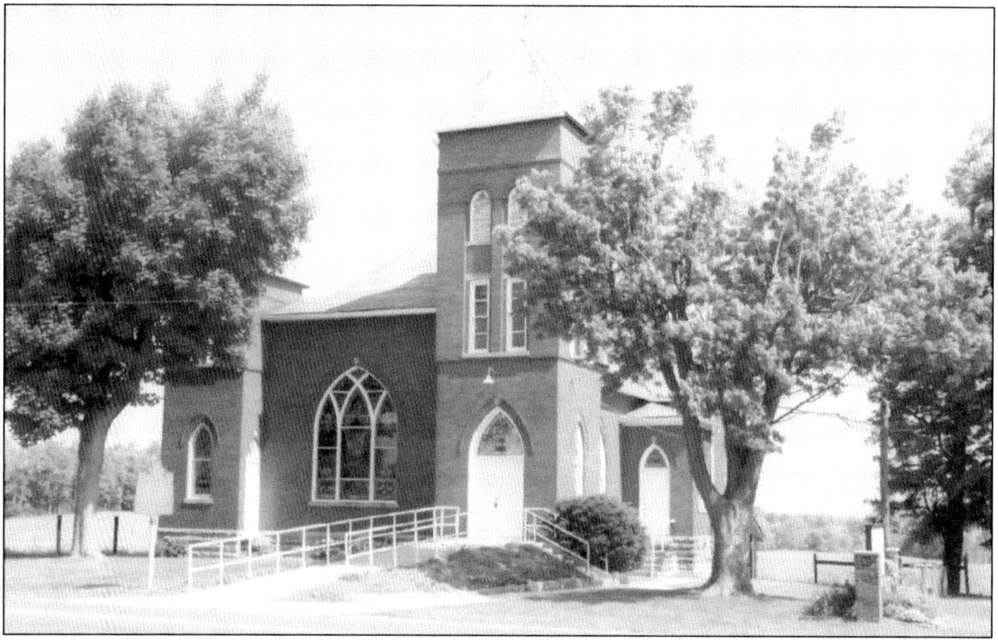

The Zion Reformed Church is the second oldest church in Perry County and stands at the corner of Route 13 and Zion Road. Henry Humberger, a well-known gunsmith who died in 1838, was a founding member and is interred in that cemetery.

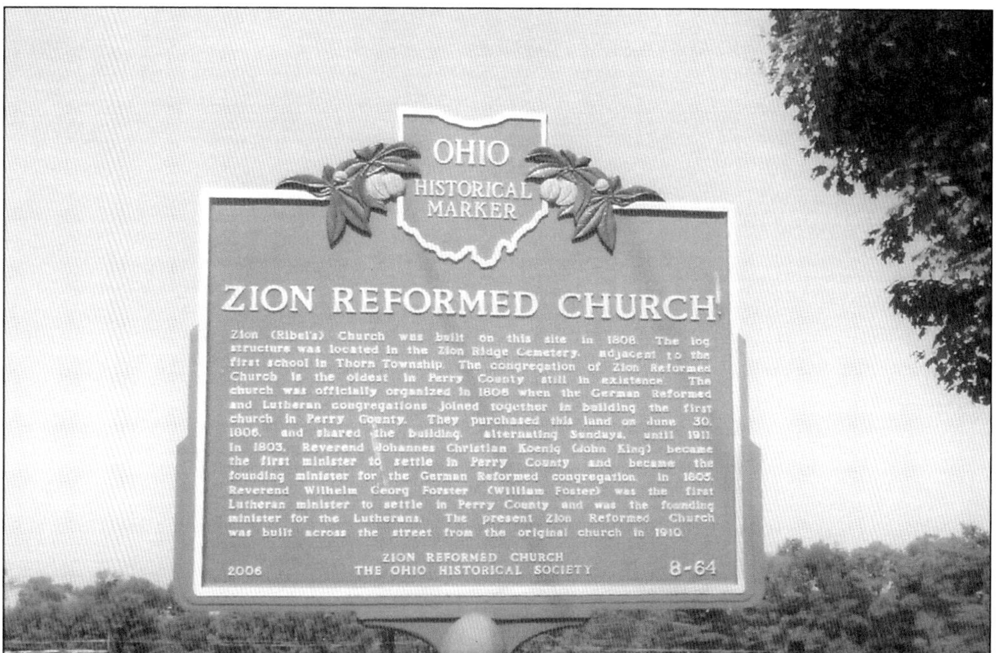

This Ohio Historical Society plaque sits at the site of Ribel's Church, which was organized in 1808. Adjacent to the church was the first school in Thorn Township. The present Zion Reformed Church was built across the street.

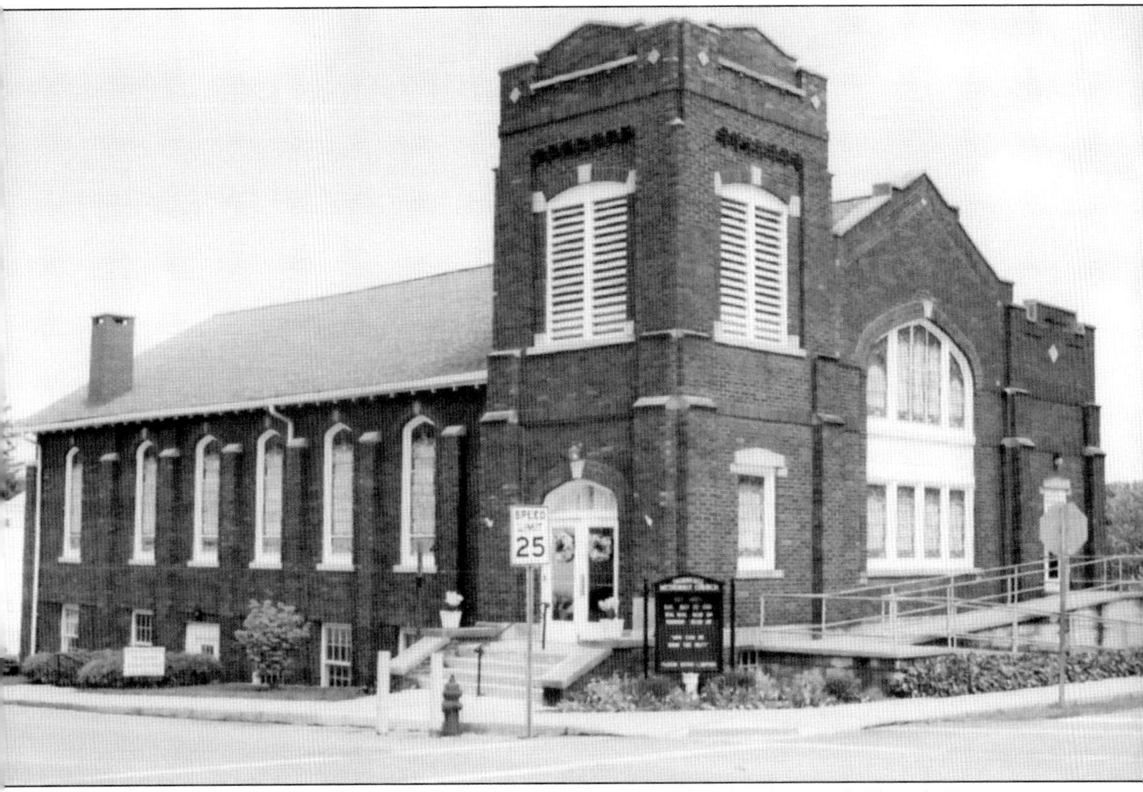

The Thornville United Methodist Church at the corner of Columbus and Church Streets was built in 1920 under the pastorate of Rev. E.F. Andree. With the help of circuit riders serving as pastors, Methodists were worshiping in Thorn Township as early as 1807. This church celebrated its bicentennial in 2007. Jerri Lampton serves the congregation today as minister. (Courtesy of Charles Williams.)

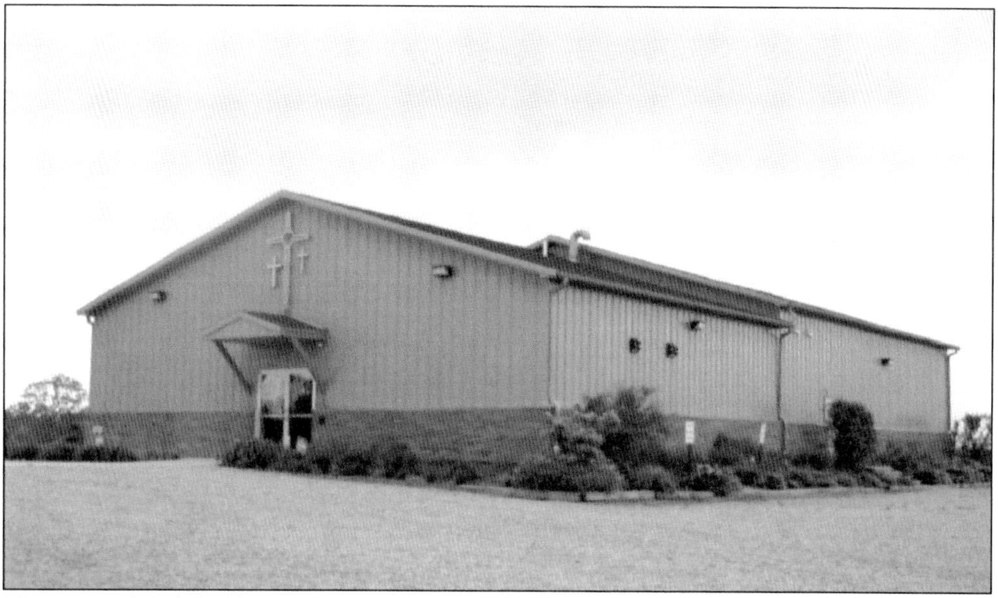

The newest church building in the township is South Shore Ministries, which is nondenominational, with Doug Lynn as the pastor. Formerly, churches were constructed of wood, stone, brick, or cement. Today, more of them are being built of metal, and most new ones are only one story high.

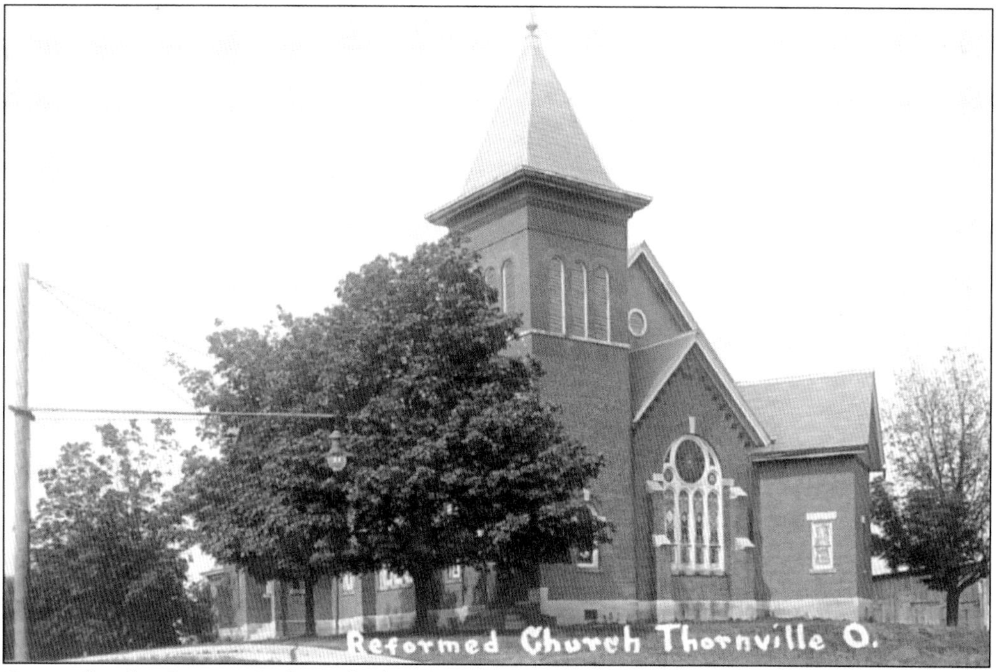

Originally, the German Reformed Church and the Lutheran Church shared the same building until 1910, when the present Trinity Reformed Church was constructed in Thornville. The Lutherans moved their congregation into Thornville.

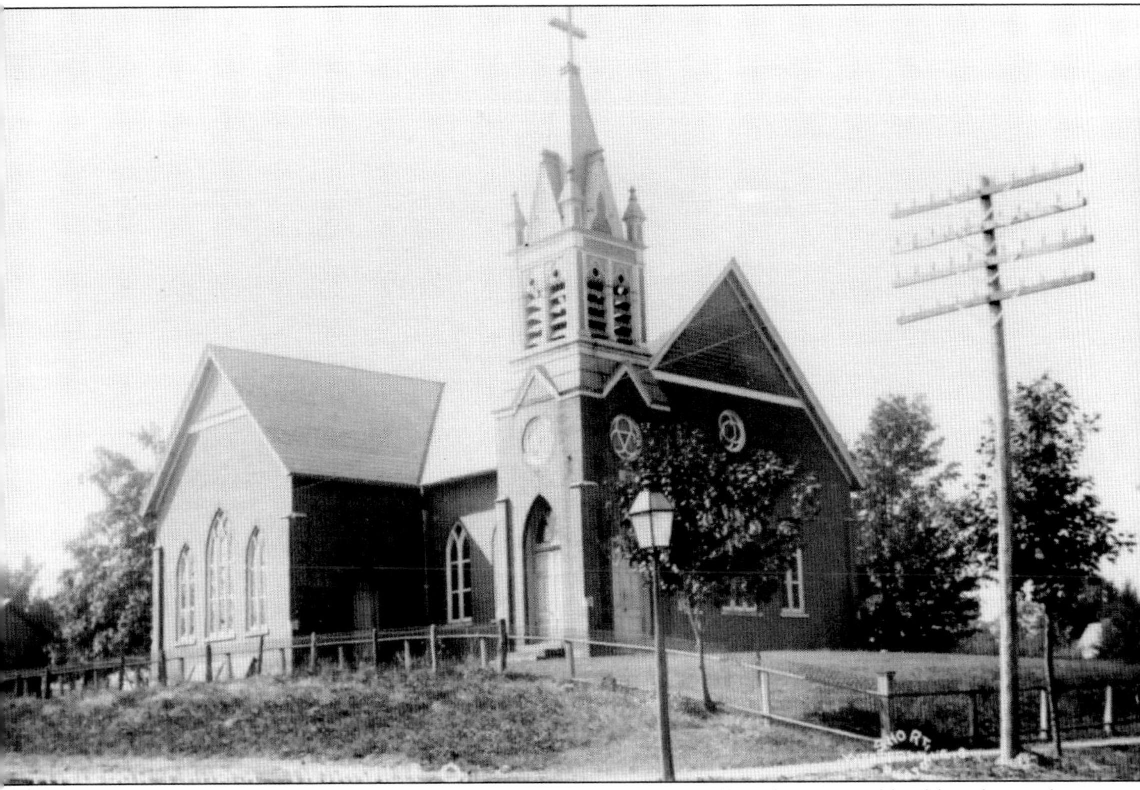

Grace Lutheran Church stands on Columbus Road in Thornville. The original building burned, and the present church was erected in 1889. Over the years, improvements were made, including the remodeled kitchen and the addition of restrooms in 1956. Pastors Jeff and Patti Morlock serve the congregation.

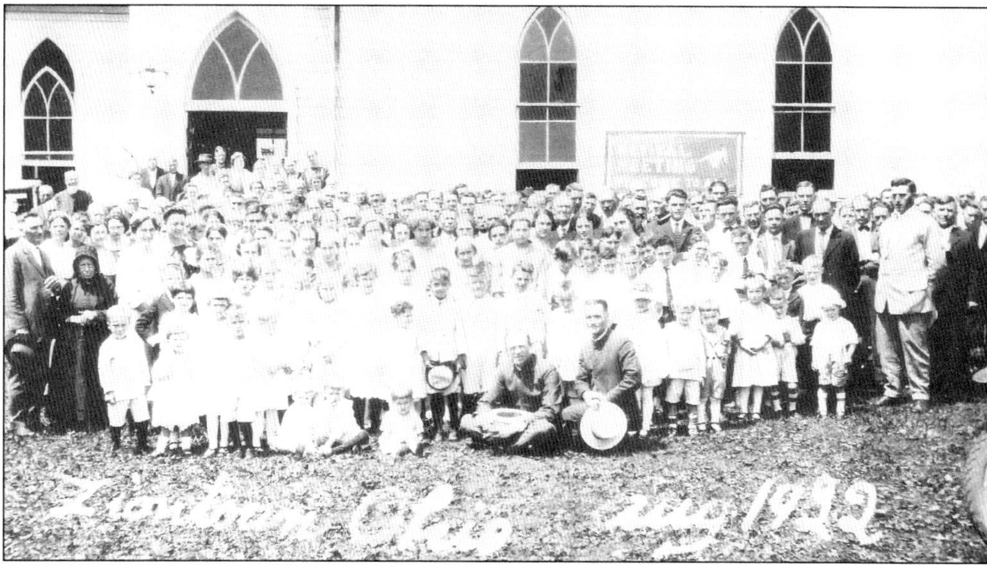

Led by Pastor Frank Meyers, a group of parishioners gather at the Olivet Church of the Brethren in Ziontown in August 1922 following a revival meeting.

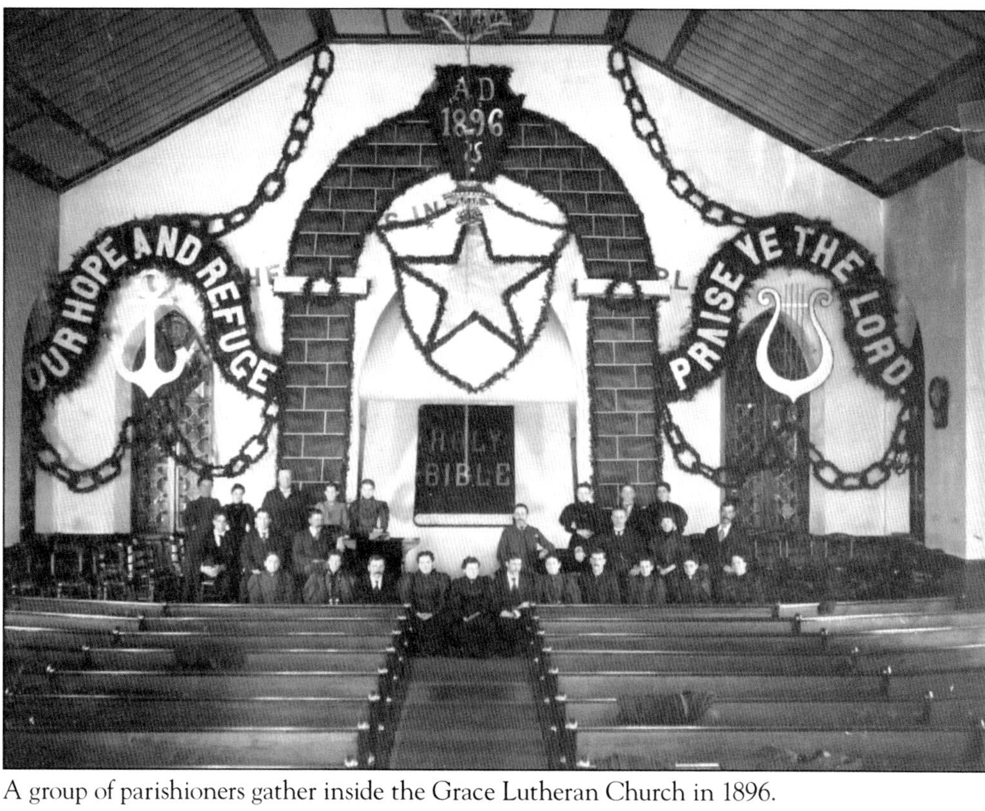

A group of parishioners gather inside the Grace Lutheran Church in 1896.

Three

Business and Agriculture

People who moved west from Pennsylvania and Virginia in the early 1800s did so primarily because they had worn out the soil where they lived. They not only brought farming methods but also knowledge in business, mechanics, and education. Carpenters, blacksmiths, bakers, teachers, and bankers set up shops in Thorn Township. Travelers required lodging and food, thus, hotels and restaurants were built. As the population grew, so did the stores selling everything from buttons to plows. Some of the businesses that have come and gone include King's Kandy Kitchen, C.L. Brown Undertaking, Wolverton Barbershop, Fairmont Cream Station, Cotterman Bakery, Pickerington Creamery, Kelsey and Son Meats, Harpster and Zollinger Autos, Cooperrider Hauling, Urick Hotel, Lake Lumber, Scrantons Market, Donsan's Dance Hall, City Drugstore, Saum Ford Sales, Hayes Produce and Dairy Bar, Bank Head Sawmill, Culp's Ice House, Weekly's Barbershop, Lamb and Eckenrode Insurance, Shelly's Clothing, and Mosher's Union 76.

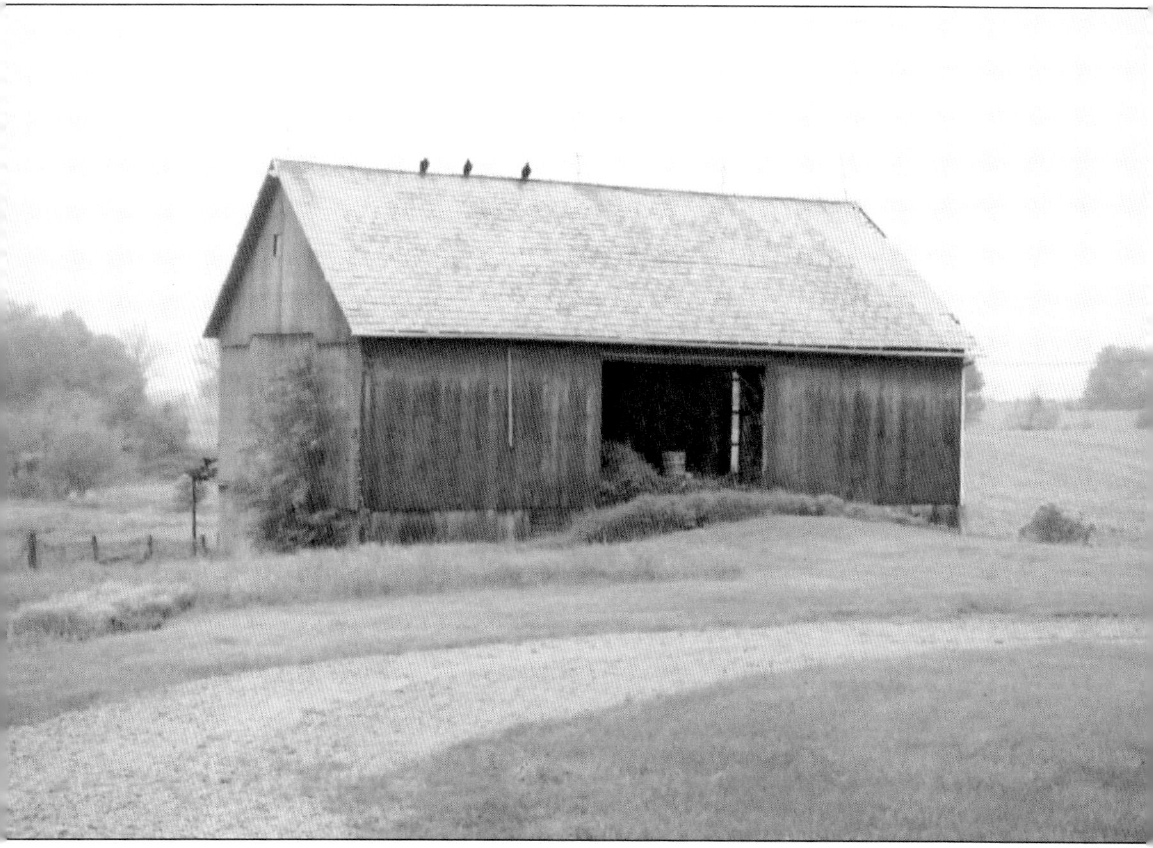

When the first Pennsylvania German farmers arrived in Thorn Township, they brought with them an architectural style for barns that other farmers soon copied—these barns are prevalent throughout the area. Usually two stories high, they have an earthen bridge to access the upper floor where hay and feed were stored. On the first floor, either at the side or rear, there was an overhang where livestock could shelter. This particular barn is located on the farm of Jake and Polly Walker, who came from Kansas to farm in Thorn Township. Polly is well known in the community for having been employed as a nurse by Drs. Clouse, Bope, and Cowan. (Courtesy of Lena K. Bowman.)

Farmers relied on mules, horses, and oxen to supply the heavy labor to operate their farms. Children also helped their parents with planting, weeding, and harvesting. Charles (left) and James Williams take a wagon of hay to the barn for winter storage. (Courtesy of Charles Williams.)

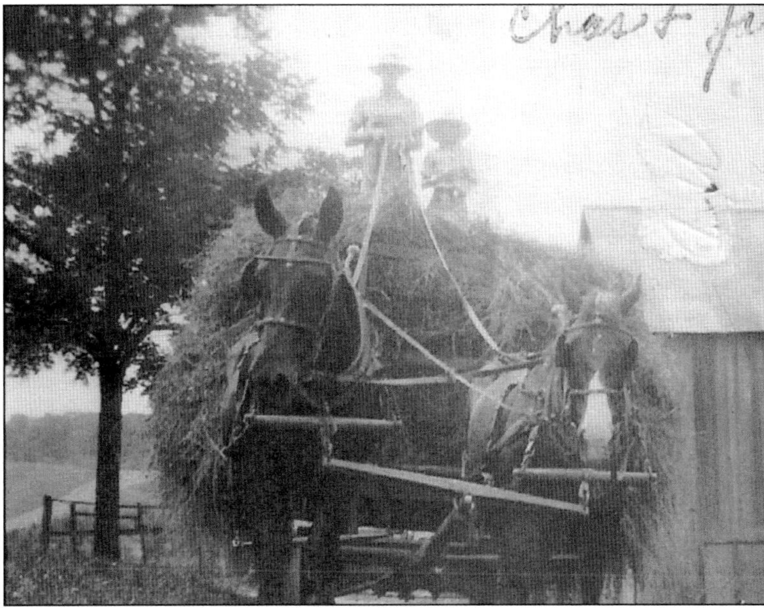

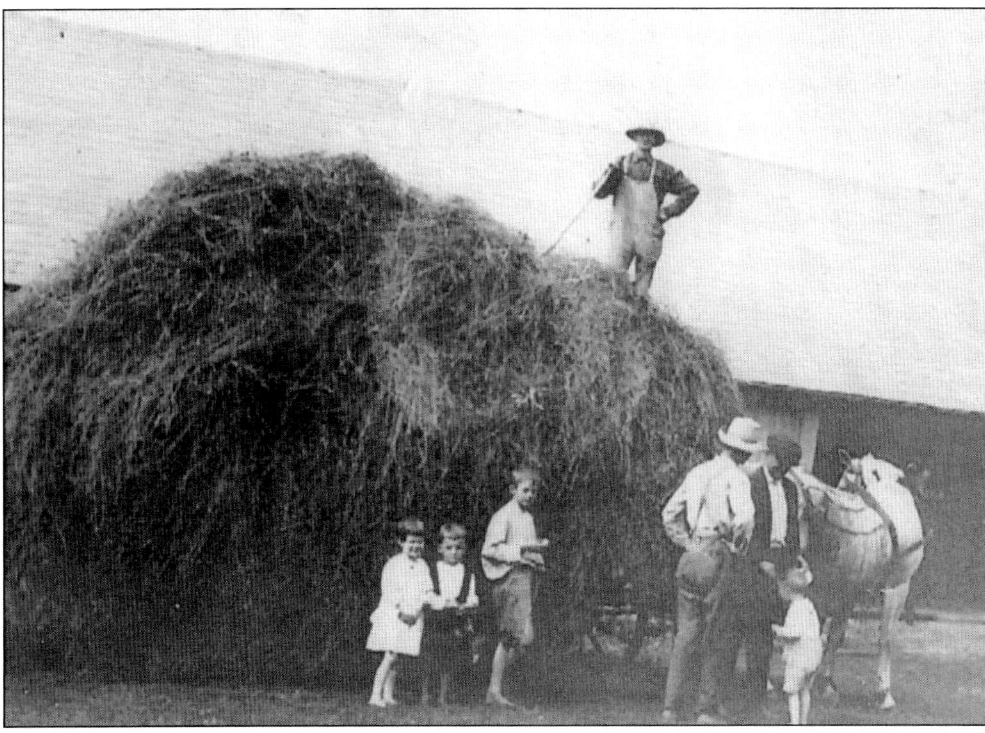

Farming methods have changed greatly over the past 200 years. Early farmers arrived in Thorn Township with a horse, a hoe, and a pitchfork. Hay that was required for the winter sustenance of livestock was cut by scythes, allowed to dry in the field, and then thrown, with the aid of a pitchfork and strong muscles, around a pole to form a haystack. Hay was also carried by wagon to the barn and stacked on the upper floor. (Courtesy of Charles Williams.)

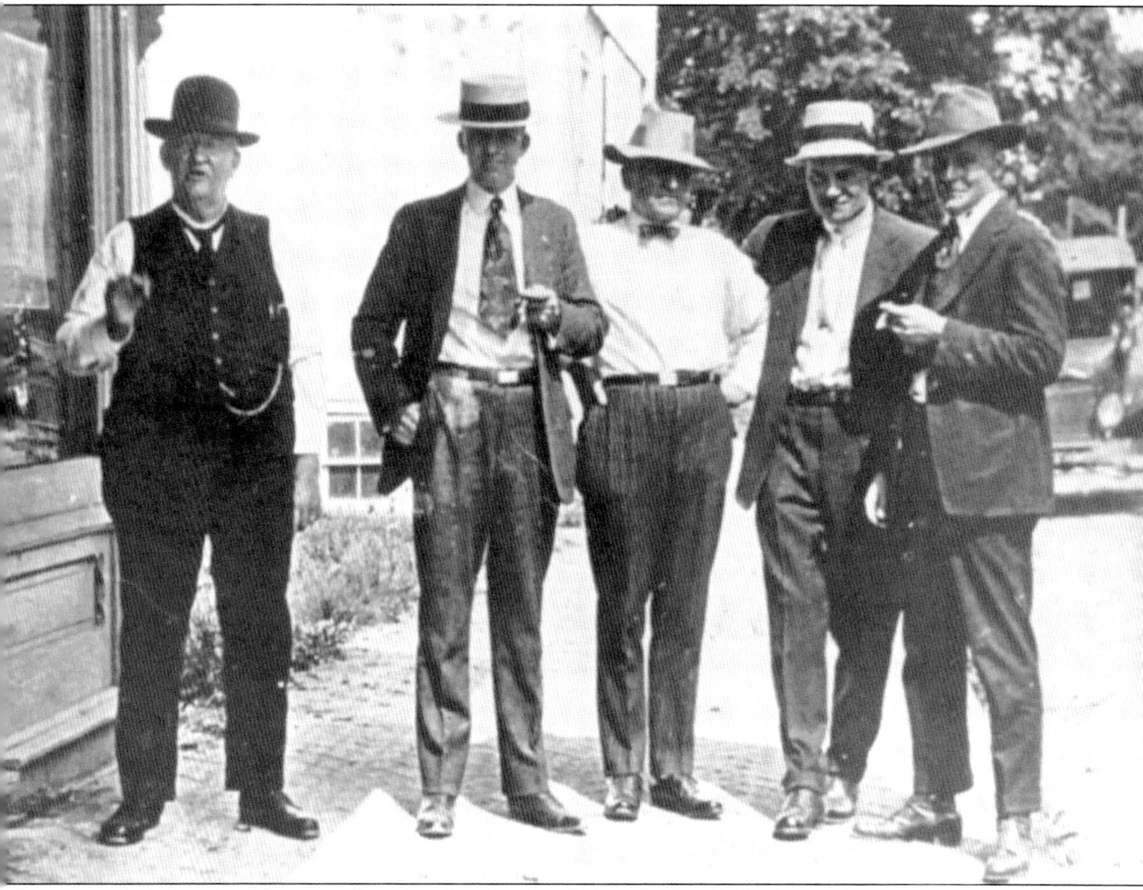

Seen here, from left to right, Charles "Banty" Rarick was the village hack driver; Tim Smith was a plumber; Fred Anspach owned a feed store and creamery; Stan Lynn sold automobiles; and Rollow Swartz ran the filling station and delivered mail. (Courtesy of Helen George.)

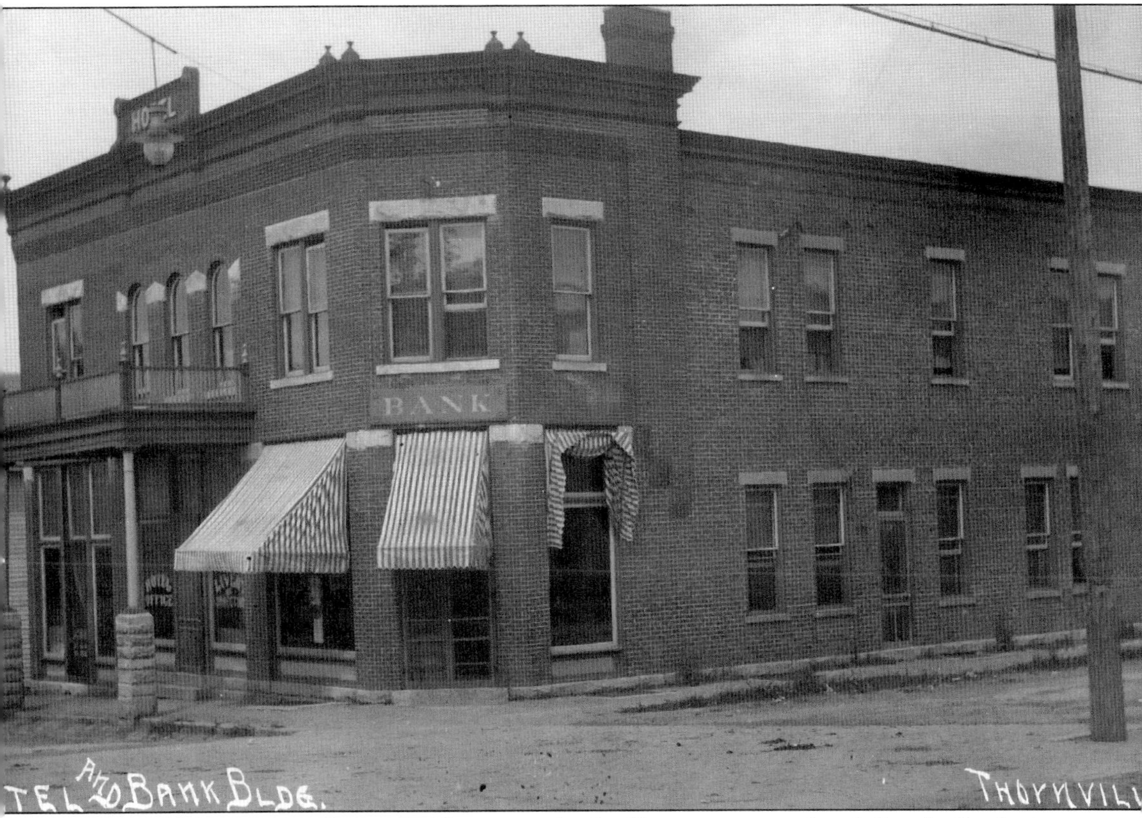

The site of the current Thornville Pharmacy, this building was once a hotel. Peoples Bank also operated here from 1911 to 1974. John and Vesta Skinner purchased the building and opened a pharmacy. In 1983, Dave Whetstone bought it and has served the people of the township as their pharmacist since then.

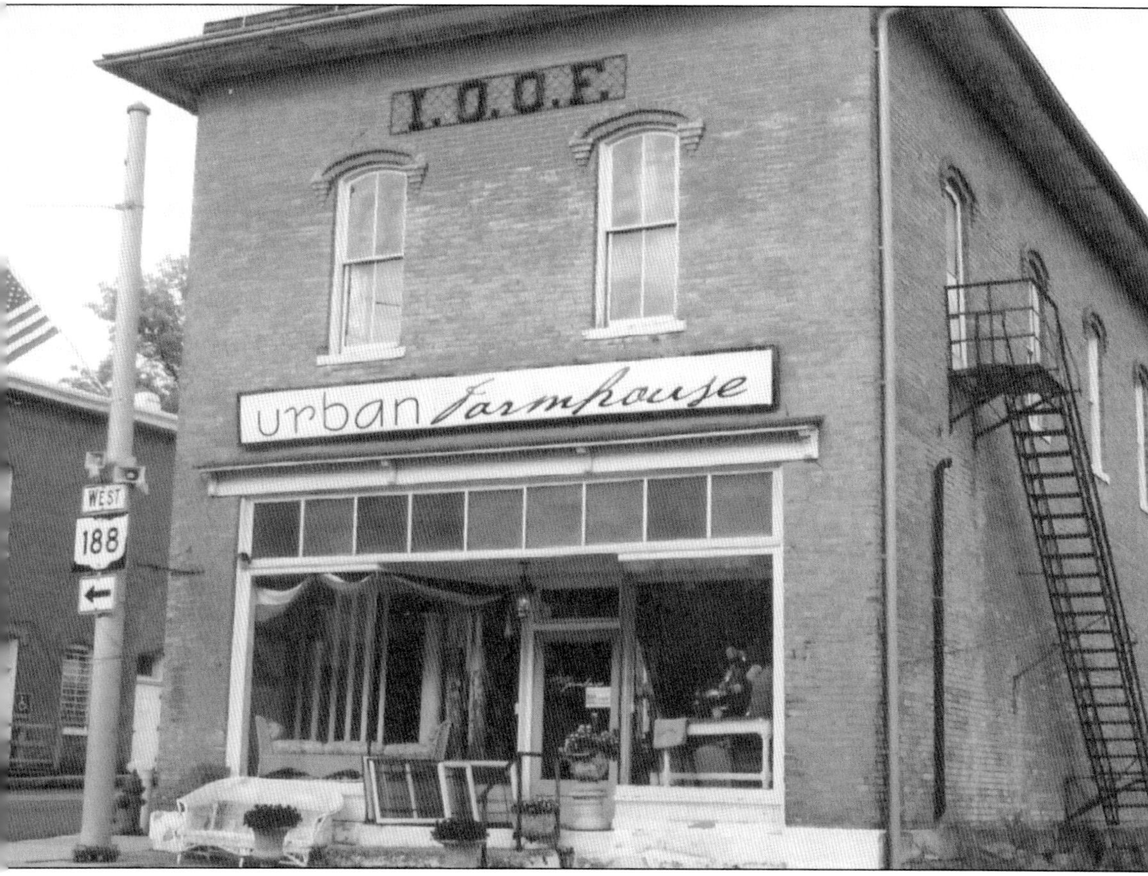

On the corner of Routes 188 and 204 stands a redbrick building, which was built by the Fraternal Order of Odd Fellows. The organization met monthly on the second floor. Once a general store for many years, it was run by Ivan Hansbarger, Charlie and Fred Johnston, Harry Lamb, and Dick Neel. From 1913 to 1947, it was the Padgett and Watson Store. Later owners included John and Jane Reichelderfer and George and Gwen Lewis. Following them, Mike Clum and Don Noyes operated the Heritage Auction House there. Gene and Kathy Launder then opened the Thornville Country Store. Today, it is the Urban Farmhouse. (Courtesy of Lena K. Bowman.)

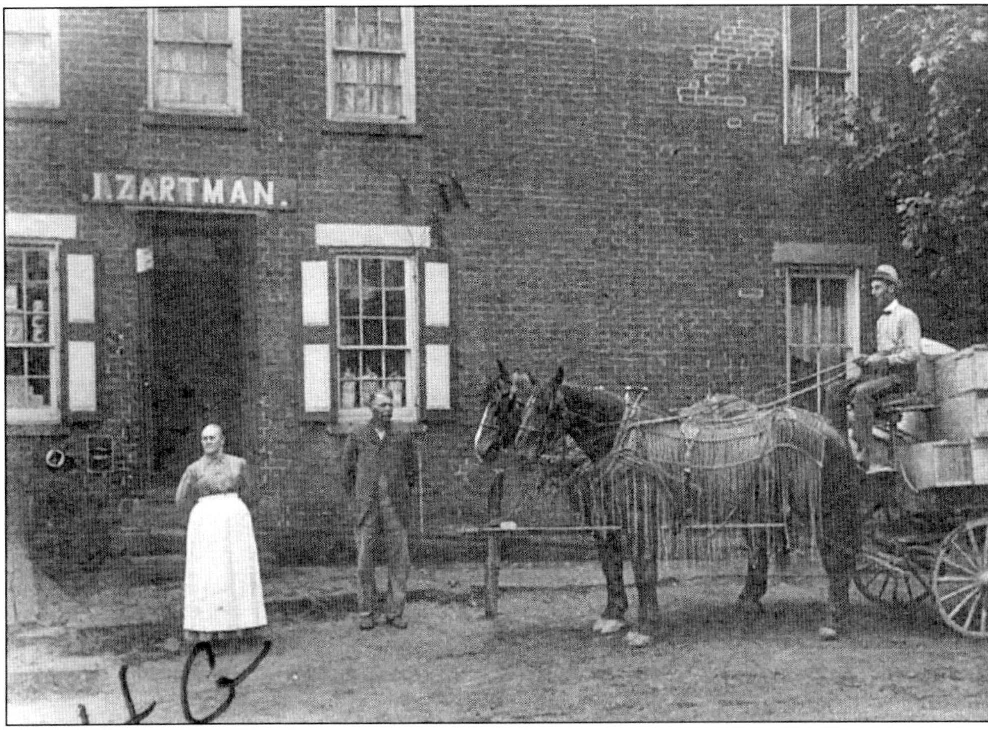

Isaac Zartman, who was born in 1850, was a teacher, tax assessor, and justice of the peace. He and his wife, Sarah Jane Person, opened this general store in Ziontown and furnished the area residents with food, kerosene for lamps, and clothing. After his death in 1921, his son Thornton operated the store. (Courtesy of Helen George.)

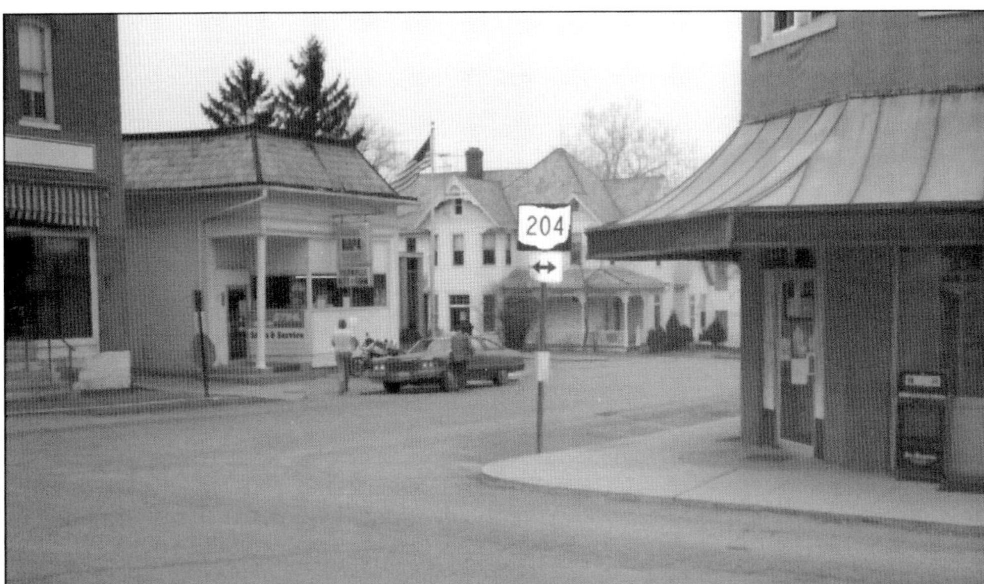

The NAPA auto parts store was originally beside the Odd Fellows building on North Main Street until it moved to Thornport. This building was demolished.

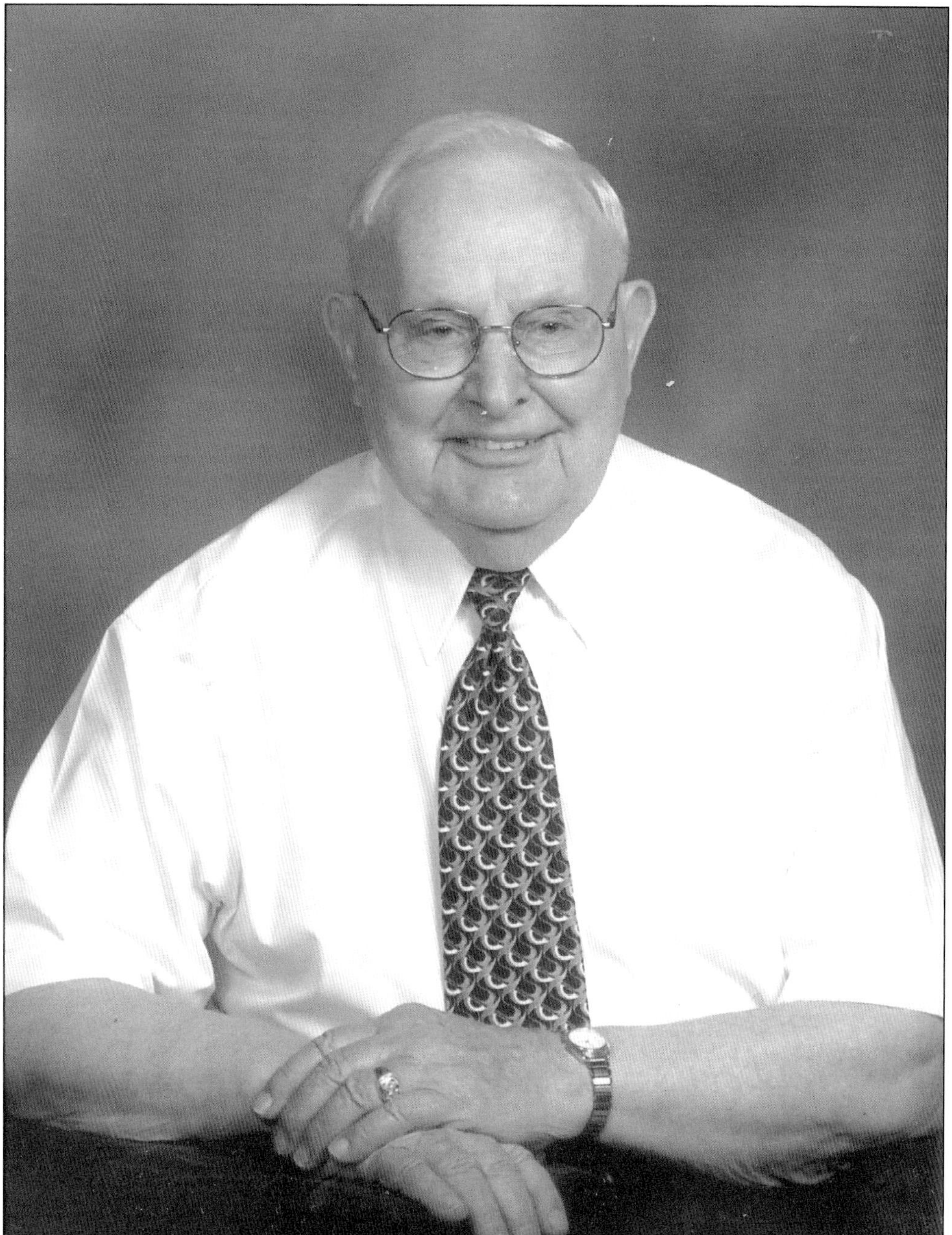

Jerry Blackstone was operator of the elevator and hardware store. He was very active in community events, participating in the Lions Club and the school board. Married to Carrie Cooperrider, their children are daughter Ann, a Thornville Elementary teacher, and son Wayne. (Courtesy of Ann Wilson.)

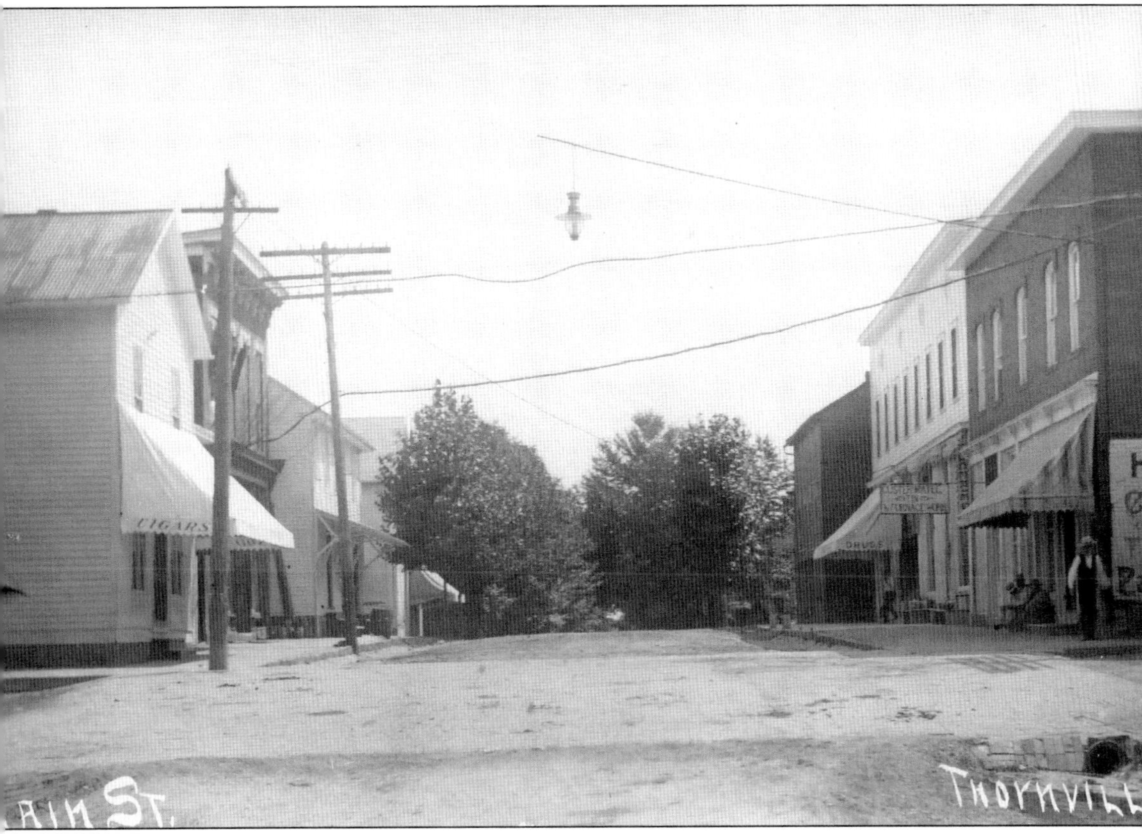

Buxton's Grocery and ice cream parlor was a very popular destination on Main Street in Thornville. Other businesses that were in Thornville at one time included *Thornville News*, Cream and Egg Station, William Hite Law Office, Tysinger Cream Station, Shelly Men's Clothing Store, Shriders Red and White Grocery, Noah Long Funeral Home, and Livery Barn.

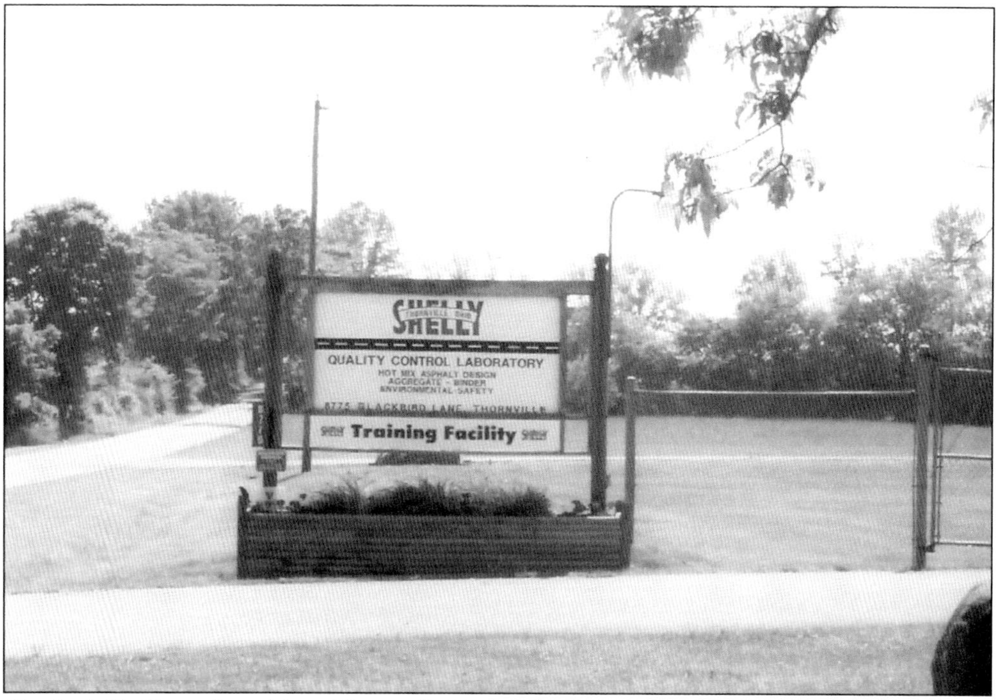

Charles J. Shelly graduated from Thornville High School in 1921 and later from Denison College. The Shelly Company was organized in 1938 and is involved in surface treating, oiling roads, asphalt plants, sand and gravel plants, and stone quarries. Its main office at 80 Park Drive was built in 1956. This company has provided employment for many area residents, and during the summer months, college-bound students in the county are also hired. Shelly Company is well known for its civic pride and contributions to Thorn Township. (Courtesy of Charles Williams.)

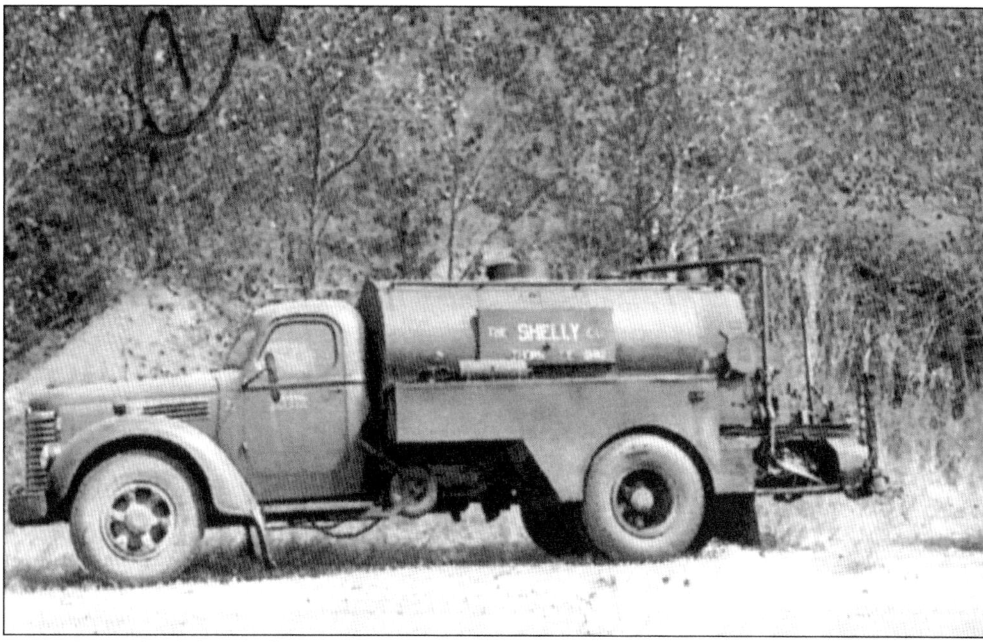

An early truck of the Shelly Company is seen here.

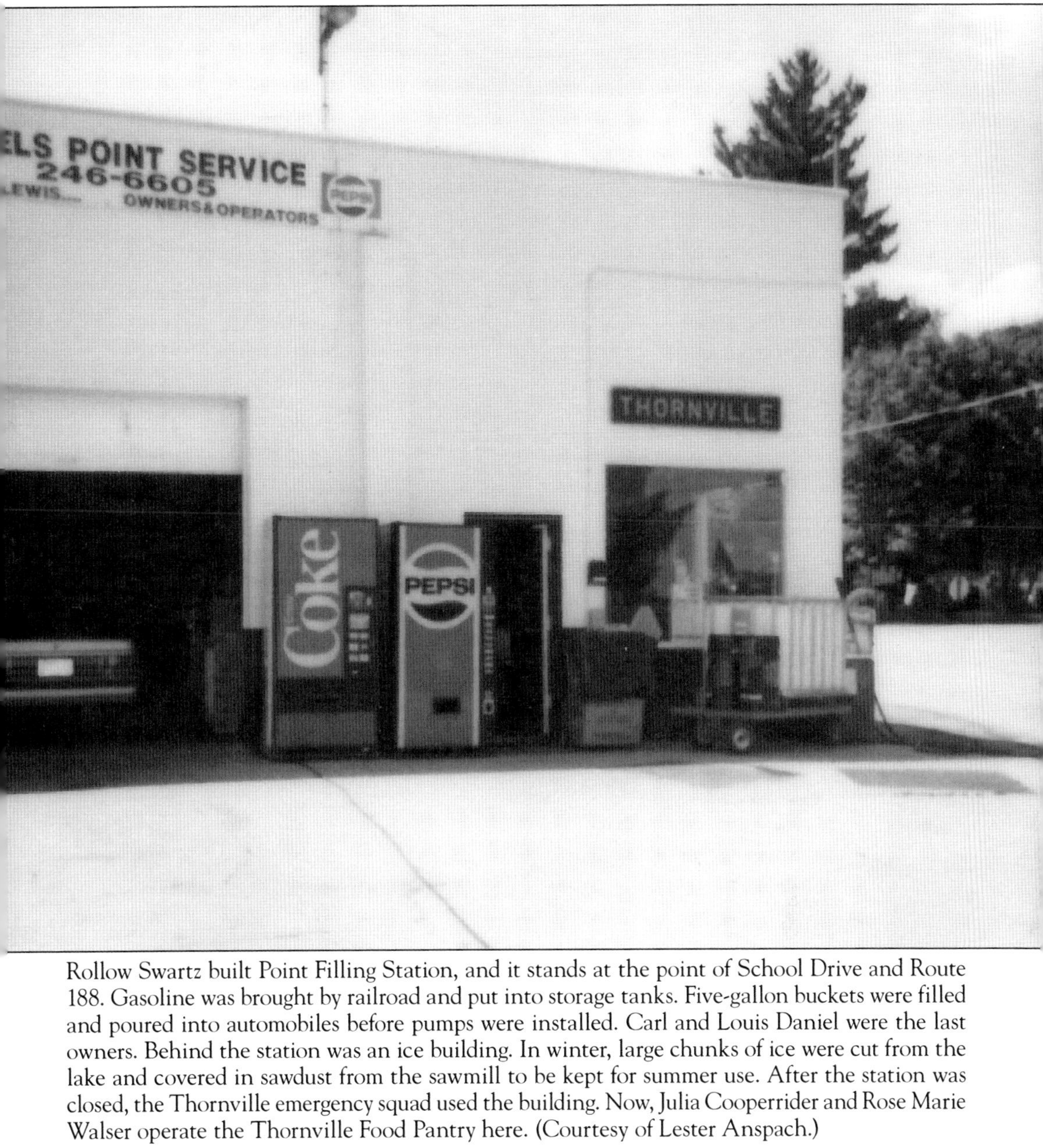

Rollow Swartz built Point Filling Station, and it stands at the point of School Drive and Route 188. Gasoline was brought by railroad and put into storage tanks. Five-gallon buckets were filled and poured into automobiles before pumps were installed. Carl and Louis Daniel were the last owners. Behind the station was an ice building. In winter, large chunks of ice were cut from the lake and covered in sawdust from the sawmill to be kept for summer use. After the station was closed, the Thornville emergency squad used the building. Now, Julia Cooperrider and Rose Marie Walser operate the Thornville Food Pantry here. (Courtesy of Lester Anspach.)

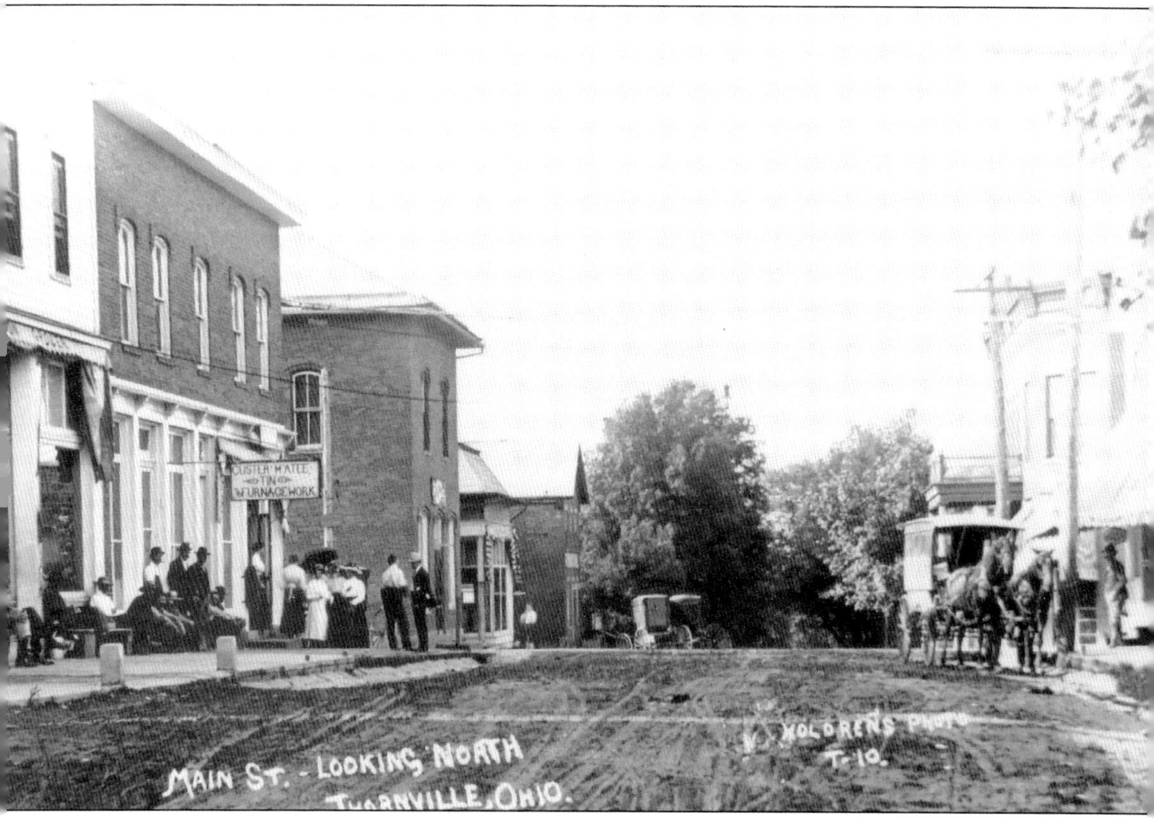

The Custer McAtee shop was on the left side of Main Street if looking north. Benches were provided for residents to sit and socialize when they came to town. Saturdays were usually busy shopping days in Thornville, as people would bring their eggs and cream to town. Other businesses included Packer and Lynn Garage, Martin Blacksmith, Donsan's Dance Hall, Bank Head Sawmill, Sidle Barber Shop, and Edmund Feed Store.

Four

Fun and Games

Residents of Thorn Township have always had Buckeye Lake as a respite after a hard workweek. Boating, fishing, and swimming have been favorite pastimes from the beginning. In the fall and winter, hunters look for deer, squirrels, and ducks. In town, people have been entertained by concerts, ice cream socials, parades, ball games, and other events.

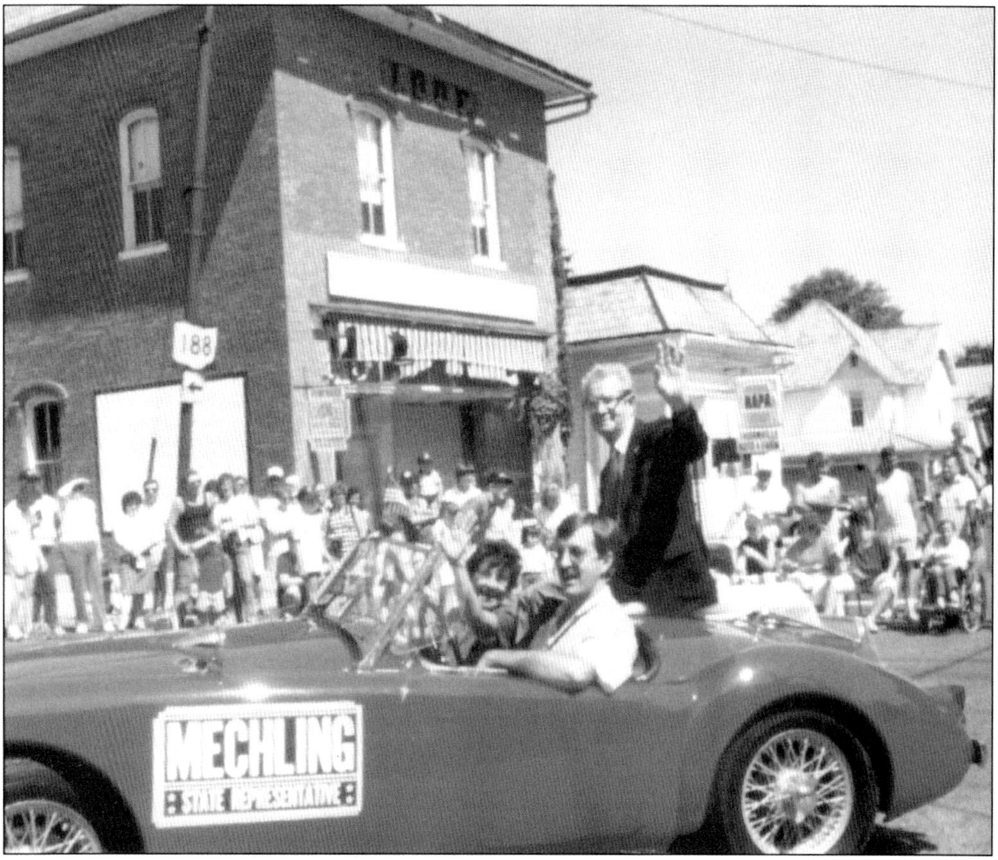

In the 1986 Independence Day parade, state representative Paul Mechling, from Glenford, waved to Thornville residents at the corner of Routes 188 and 204. (Courtesy of Ann Starr.)

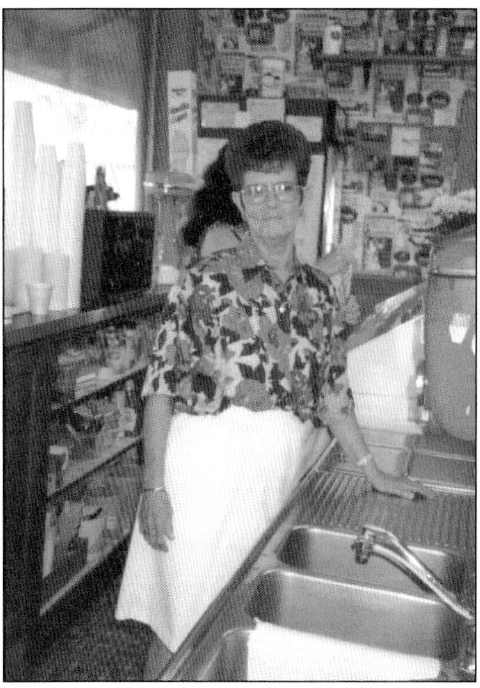

Judy and Wirt Barrera have resided in Thornville for years and have been involved with various community affairs. Judy, who worked at the drugstore for 30 years for various owners, including the Skinners and Whetstones, has been a medic for the emergency squad and a council member. She also directed the Thornville Community Aid, which provided Christmas gifts to area children, and the Fourth of July celebrations throughout the years. (Courtesy of Judy and Wirt Barrera.)

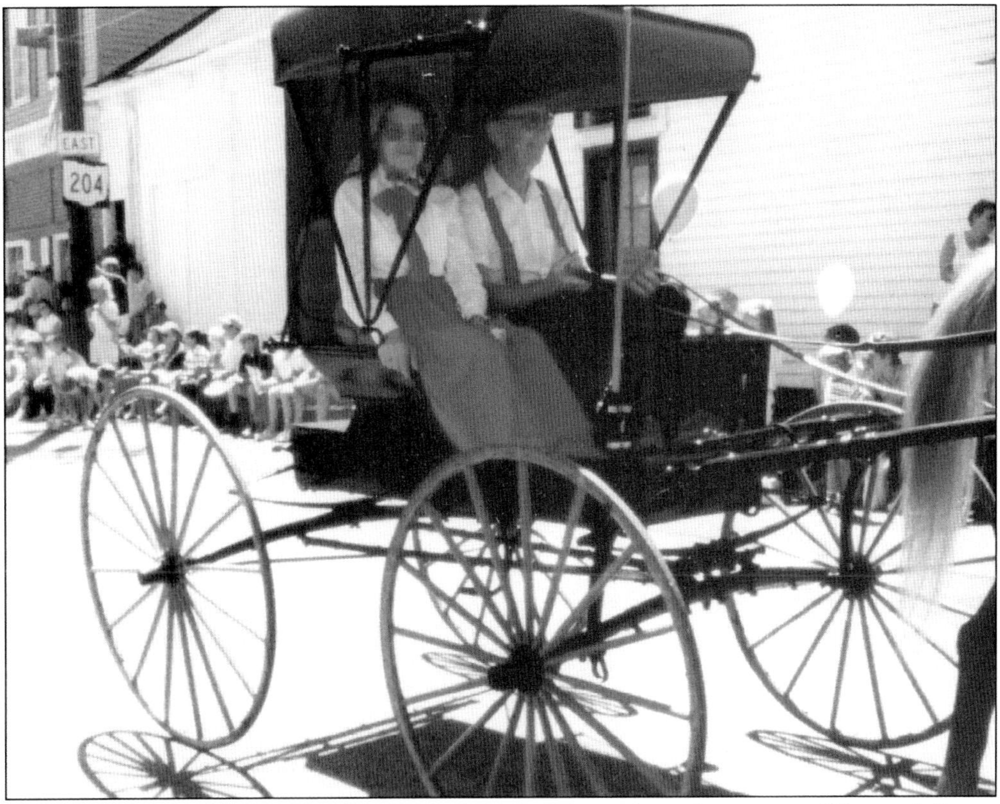

Richard and Mabel Drumm lived at 55 South Main Street, where they operated Drumm's Buggy Shop. Richard was a veteran of World War II. They enjoyed riding in one of their buggies in the area parades. (Courtesy of Ann Starr.)

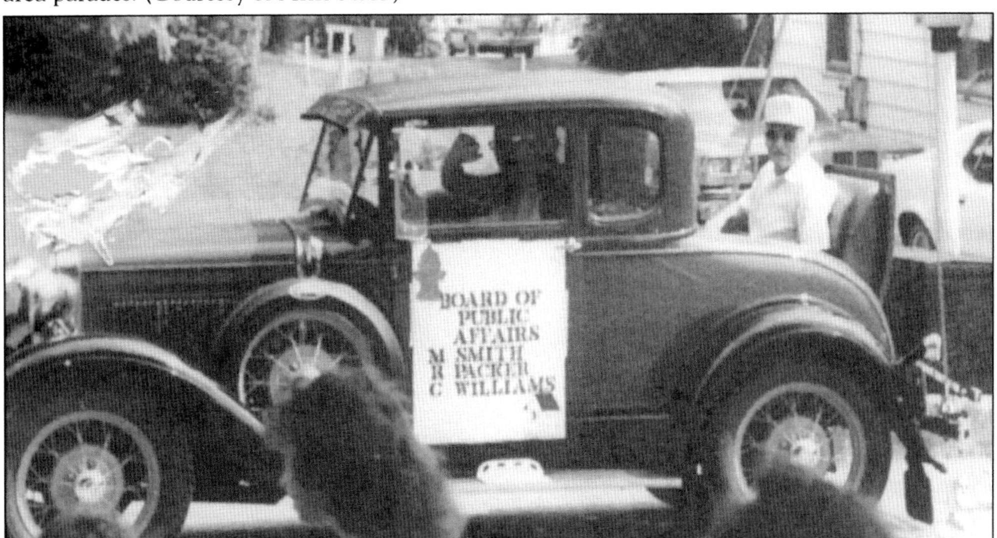

Charlie Williams (passenger seat), Bob Packer (driving), and Maurise Smith, who served on the Thornville Board of Public Affairs, are pictured participating in one of the parades. (Courtesy of Charles Williams.)

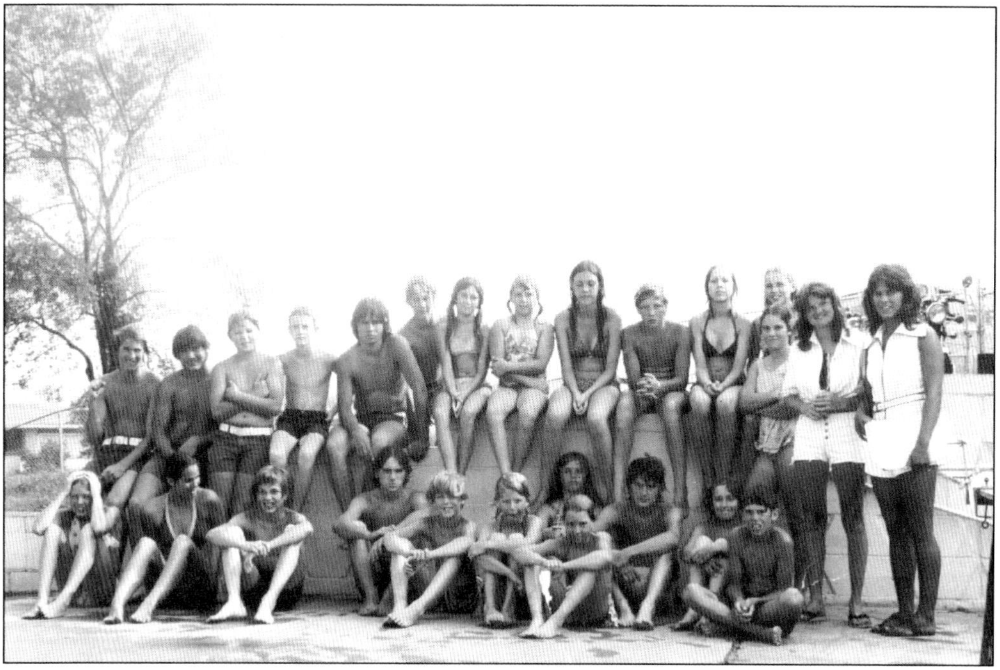

In 1974, Luann Cooperrider (second from right) and Jamie Braig (far right) formed the first swim team in Thornville. Luann is now the Perry County probate juvenile judge, and Jamie operates the Buckeye Lake Historical Society. (Courtesy of Luann Cooperrider.)

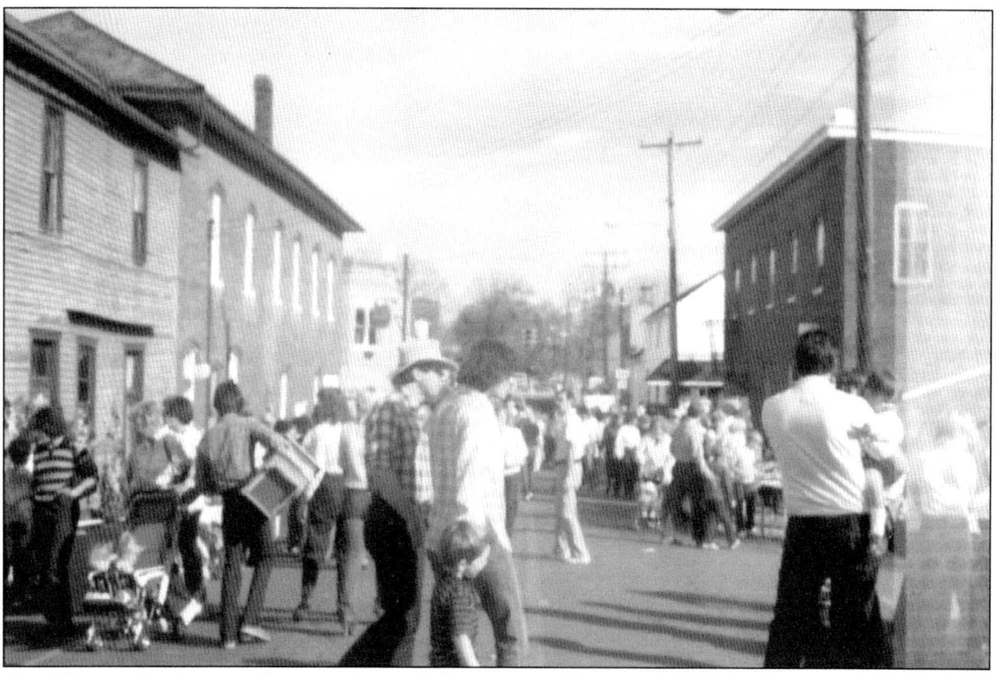

The Thornville Country Fair is still one of the most popular tourist draws in Perry County. Hosted by the Lions Club, vendors from all over the state come to Thornville and set up shop the third weekend in October. (Courtesy of Thelma Crader.)

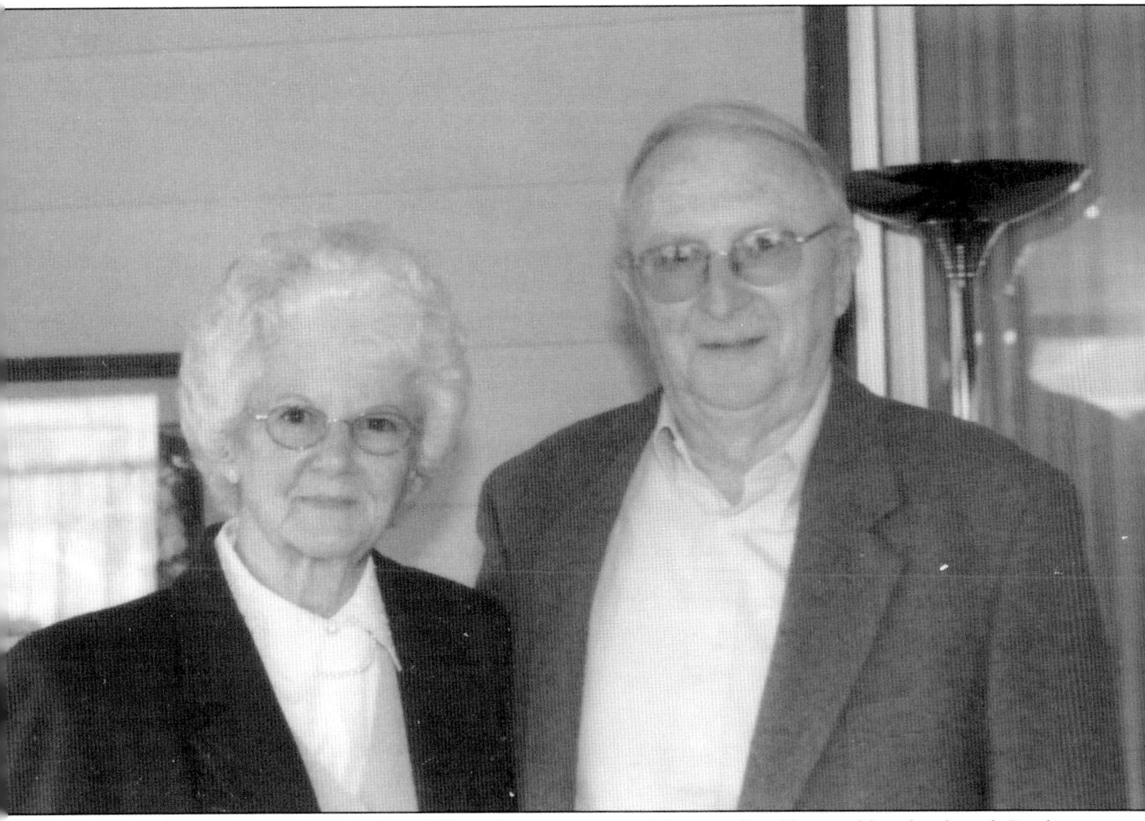

Barb Packer used to work in the old hotel restaurant in Thornville. She and her husband, Dick, who worked for the Shelly Company, have made significant contributions to the community throughout the years. (Courtesy of Barb Packer.)

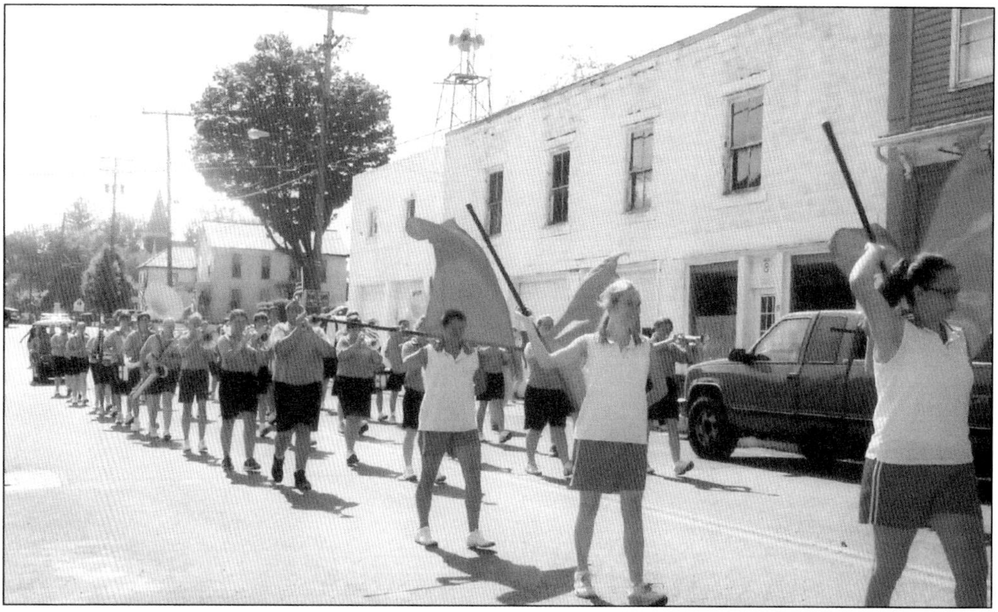

School bands provide parade music, as well as concerts, throughout the year. The Sheridan High School band leads the way in the 2011 Memorial Day parade in Thornville.

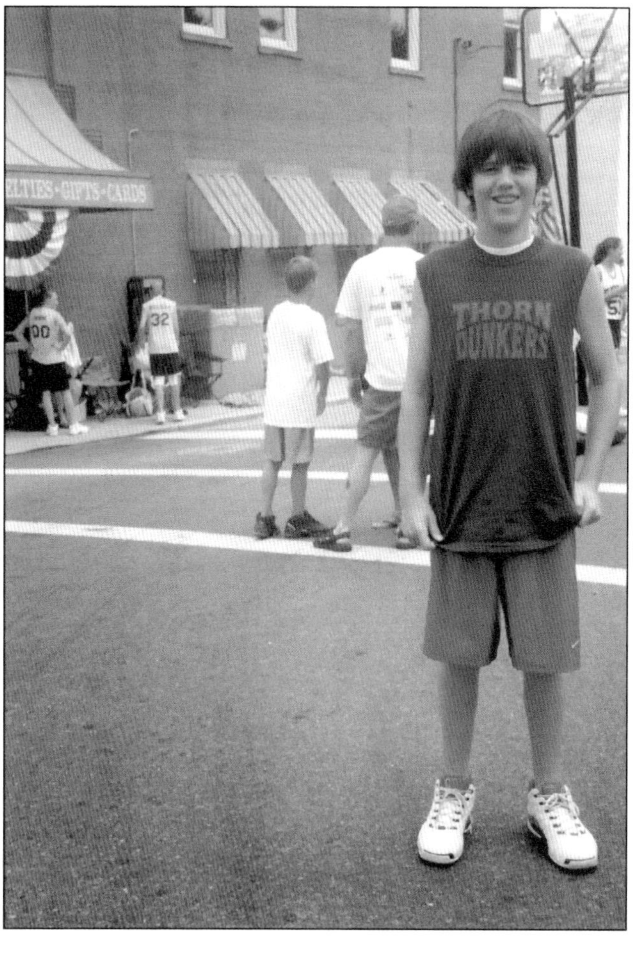

The Thorn Dunker basketball tournament is a popular event for area players on July Fourth weekend. Brian Crader, a 1998 Sheridan High School graduate, is now a junior on the Marietta College basketball team.

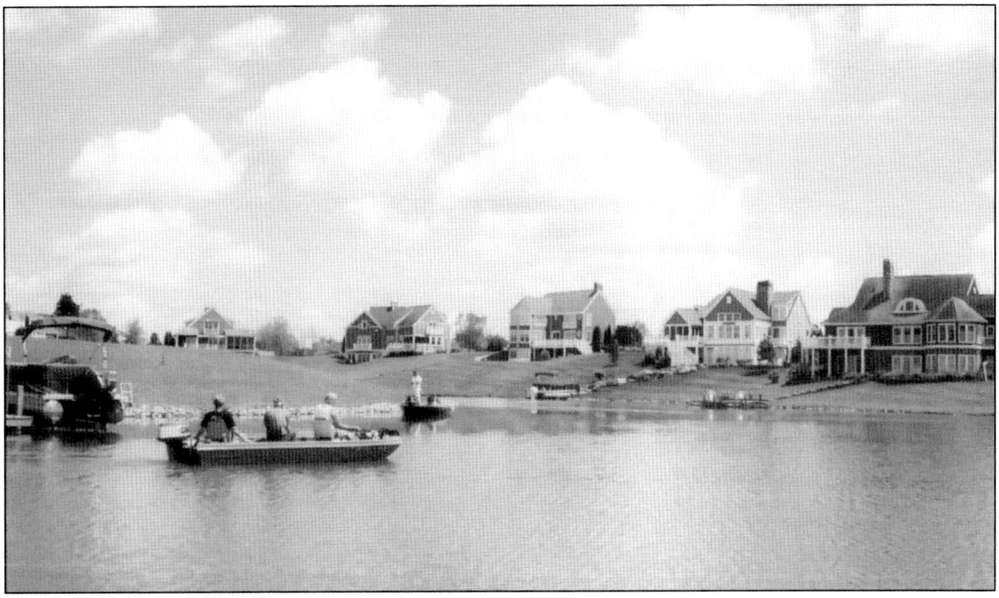

Many area residents enjoy fishing on Buckeye Lake. Bass, stripers, catfish, and bluegill are caught from pontoons, bass boats, and from the shore. Club tournaments, such as those of the Cranberry Marsh Bass Club, are often held on Buckeye Lake.

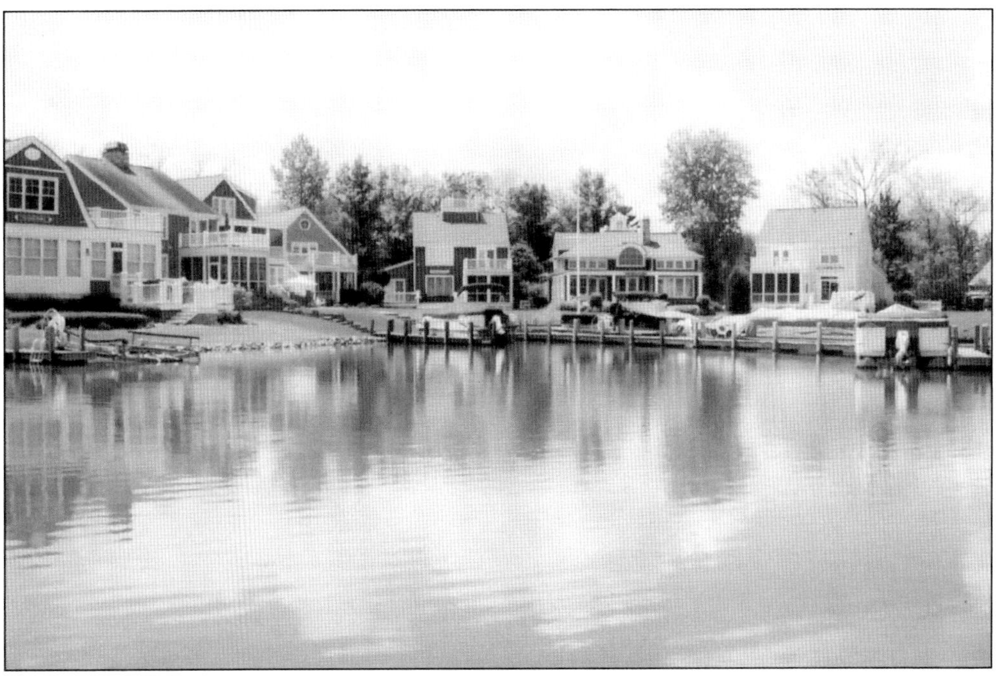

Boating has always been a favorite pastime for area residents. Because many Thorn Township residents live on the south shore of the lake, boat repair shops and restaurants have bolstered the area's economy.

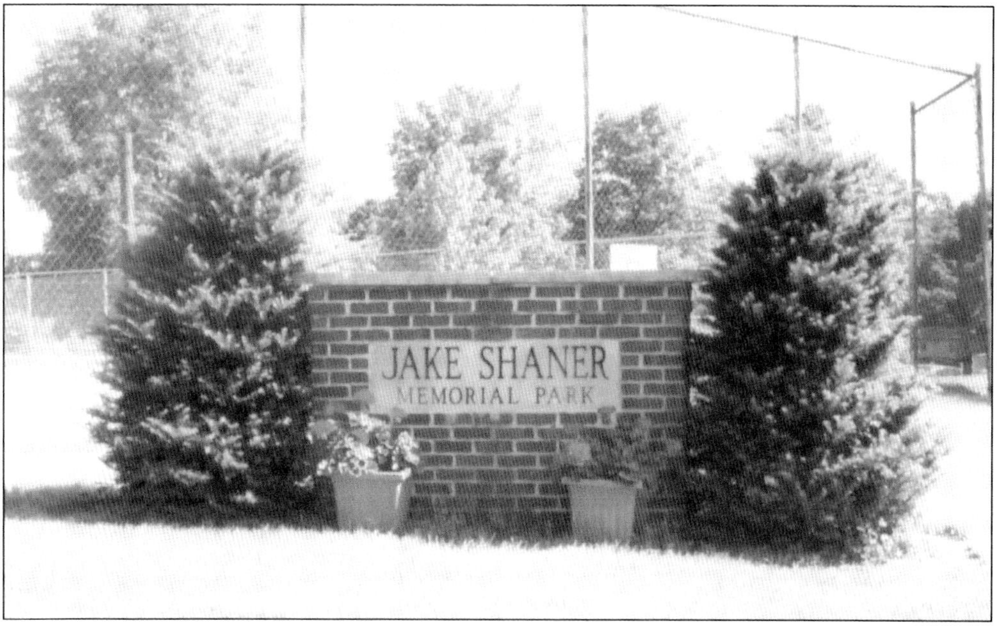

In 1953, the Lions Club undertook the task of making an area in Thornville for gatherings. Dr. Harry L. Hite willed a part of his estate to fund a park. C.V. Clum donated five acres of land, a baseball field was added, and a shelter house was built in 1957. The park was named Jake Shaner Memorial Park after a park employee who lost his life while working there.

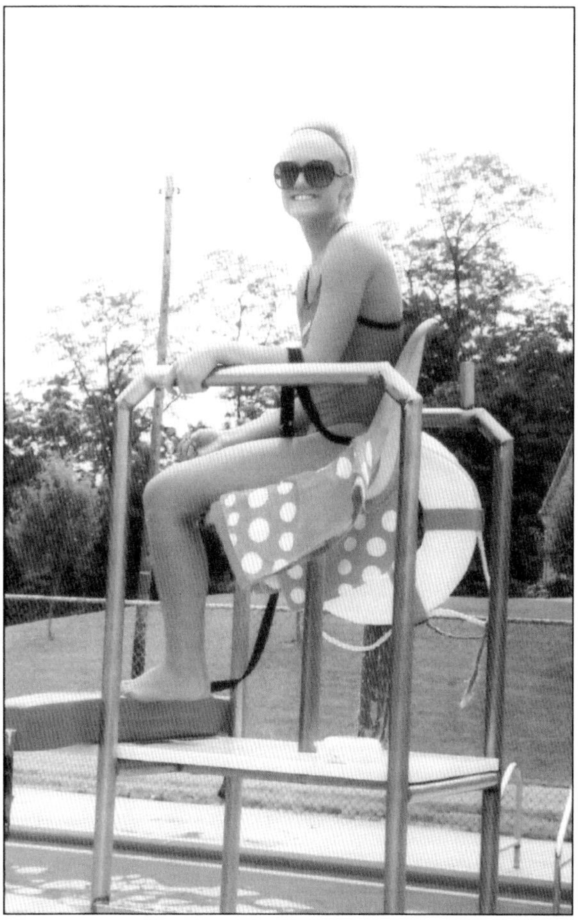

Mackenzie McCartney watches over swimmers at the Thornville pool during the summer of 2011.

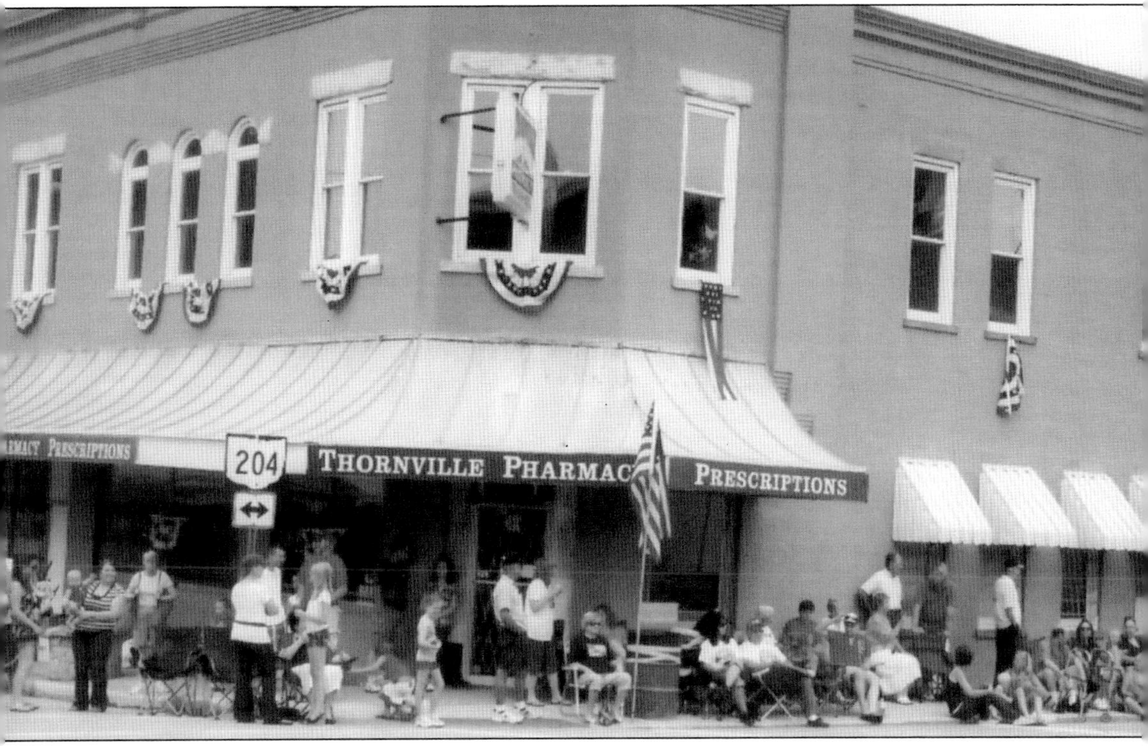

Here, Thornville Pharmacy is decorated in red, white, and blue bunting, and township residents are waiting for the Fourth of July parade to pass. John Ulmer served as emcee for the event in 2011.

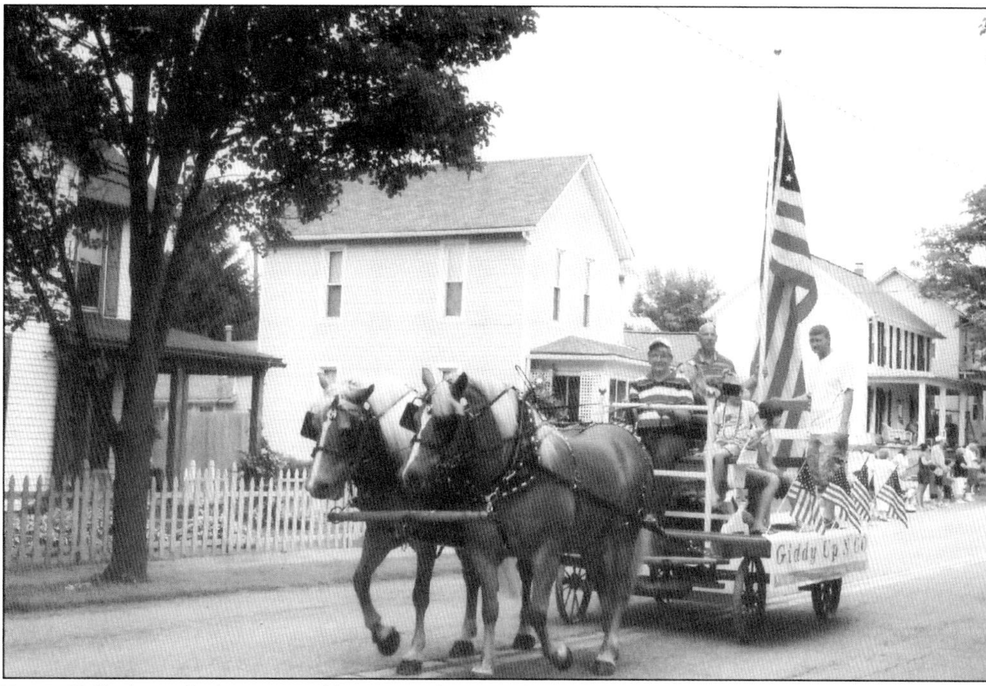

Roger Hillis brought his team of horses to the parade, and riding in the wagon were Rita Crossan, 100-year-old Nora Sulzer, Susie Saffell, and Brenda Standeford.

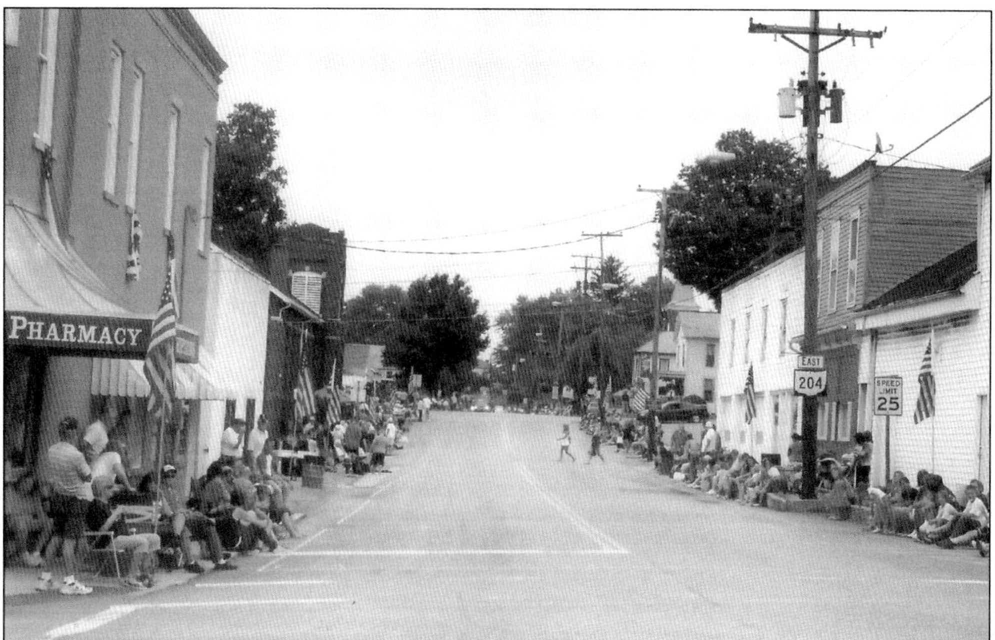

Spectators line Columbus Street to see the 2011 Fourth of July parade. On the right, one can see the former fire department, and on the left is the Methodist church.

Five

Two Hundred Years of Faces

One might notice that various last names found in these pages are the same. Although many residents have moved from the area during the recent past, many families have stayed here, with their children and grandchildren remaining in the township as well. Many farms that were started in the 1800s are still passed on to the next generation of family members.

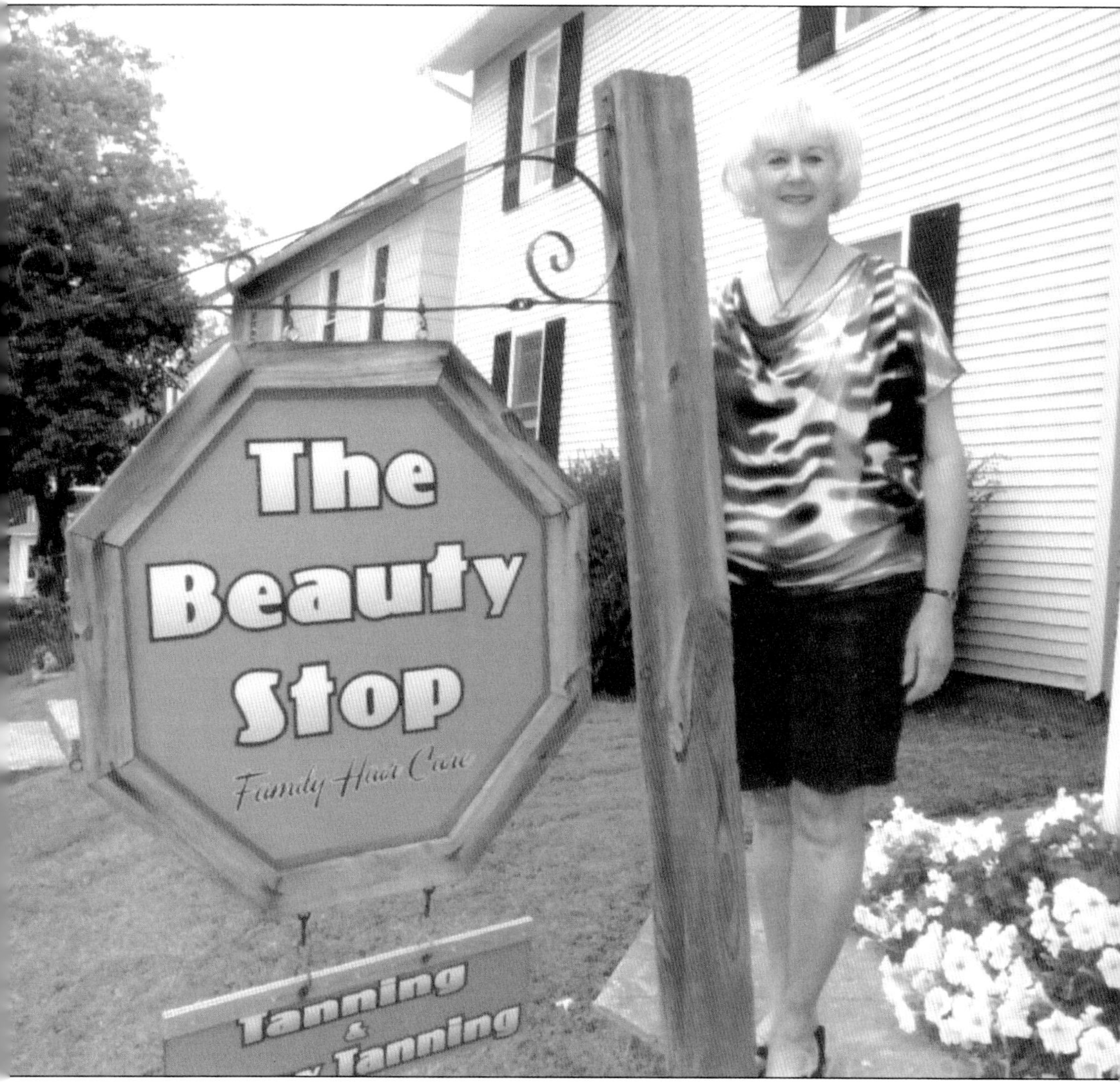

The Beauty Stop at 11 South Main Street is the oldest established business in Thornville. Rebecca "Becky" White Krumlauf purchased the shop in 1973. Born in 1949 to James and Ruth Courson White, Becky and her son Kevin are members of the Buckeye Lake Chamber of Commerce, which is working to make the Thornville region a better place to live.

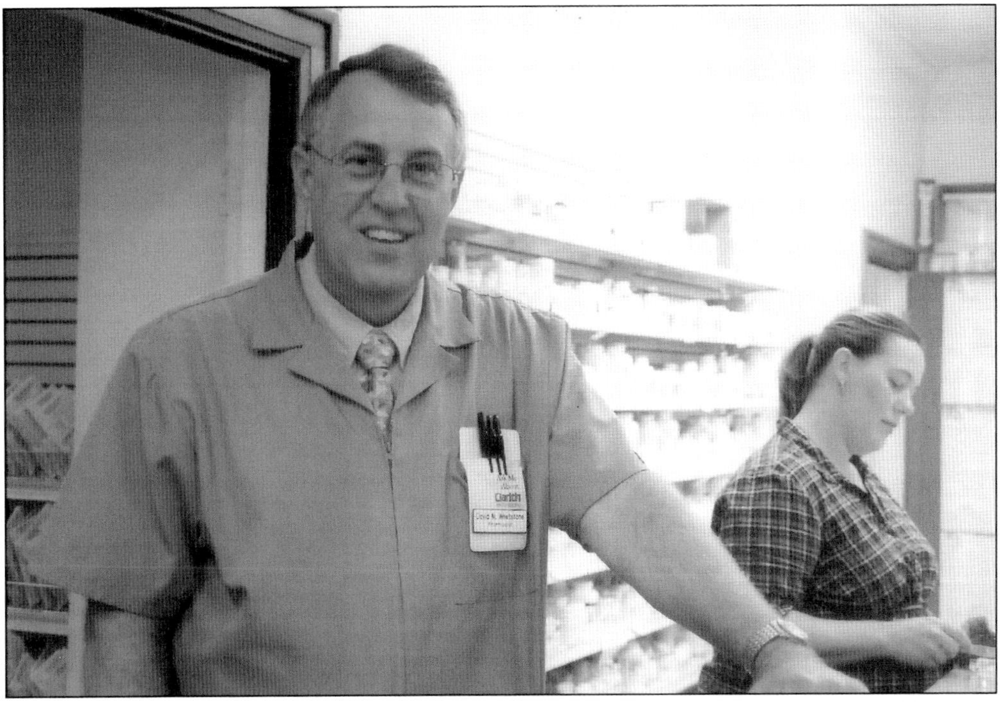

David Whetstone is the only pharmacist in Thorn Township. He and his wife, Linda, own Thornville Pharmacy at the intersection of Routs 204 and 188. (Courtesy of Lena K. Bowman.)

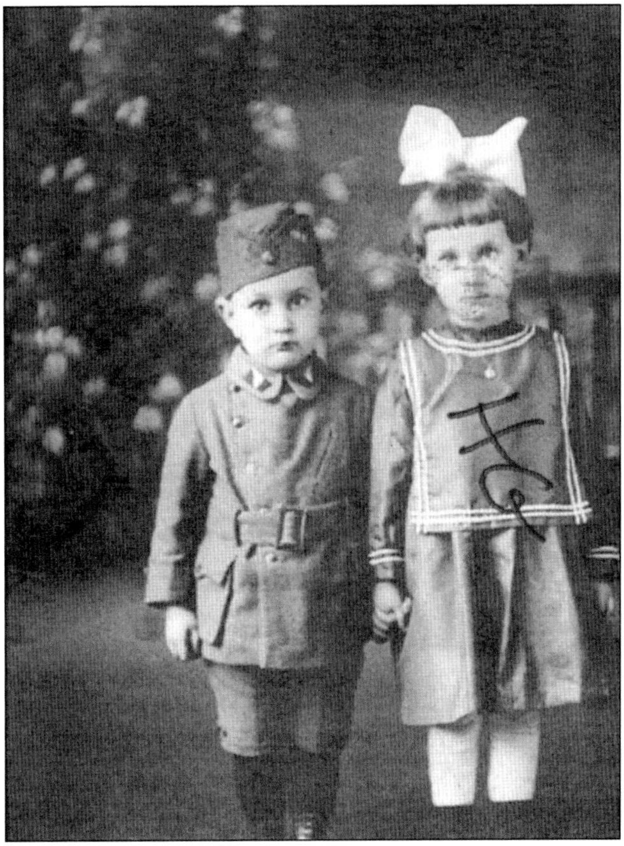

George and Edna Mechling grew up in Thornville; George taught at Thornville School and, later, was superintendent of Millersport schools. (Courtesy of Helen George.)

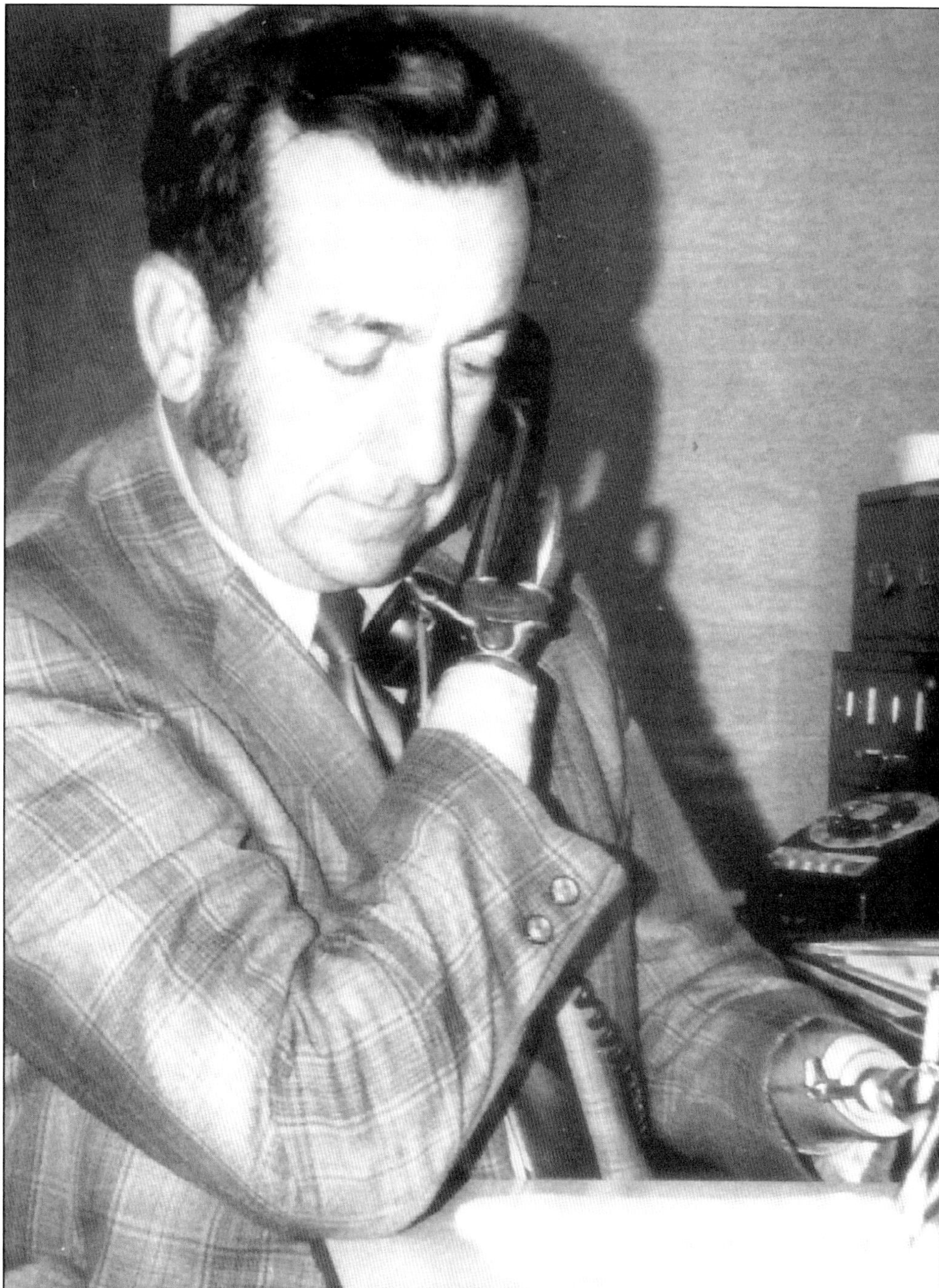

Charlie Boring was a well-known Thornville businessman, as well as a farmer. Through the years, he was a mail carrier and a funeral director. In 1950, he and wife Jean purchased the mortuary on South Main Street, which they operated until 1985, when they sold it to Larry Sheridan. In 1957, while working at the farm, Charlie lost both hands, but with the aid of prostheses, he was able to continue his activities, including the farm, Lions Club, the Masons, and the fire department. In 2001, he received an award for overcoming extreme physical adversity.

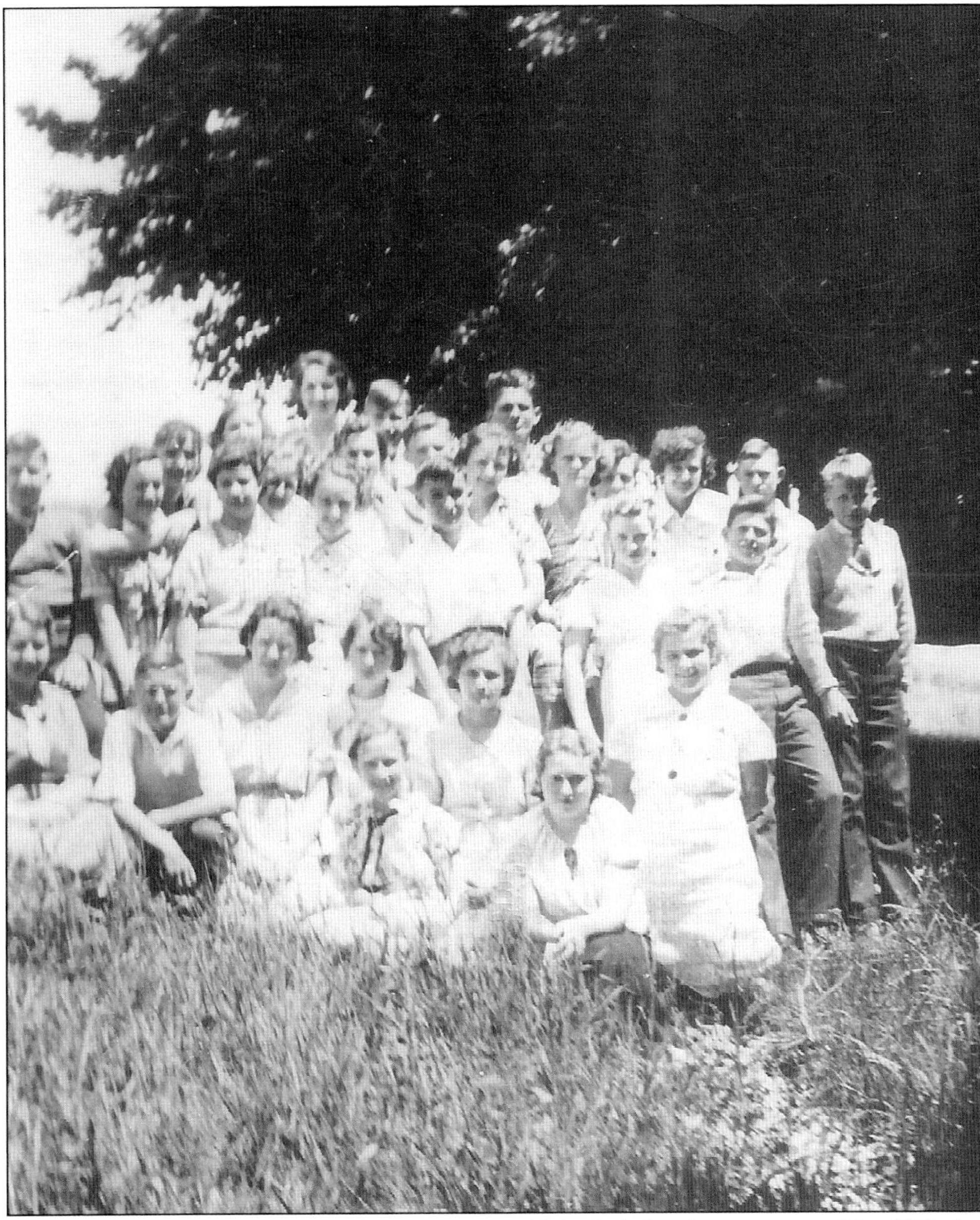

Thornville freshmen got together for a picnic in 1935. Included in this picture are Harold Taylor, Winogene Foster, Imogene Fisher, Mary Swinehart, Marjorie Frame, Esther Cooperrider, Helen Long, Raymond Cooperrider, Rita Harlan, Lewis Courson, Helen Taylor, Catherine Miller, Ed Hurd, Jaineta Fisher, and Paul Packer. (Courtesy of Helen George.)

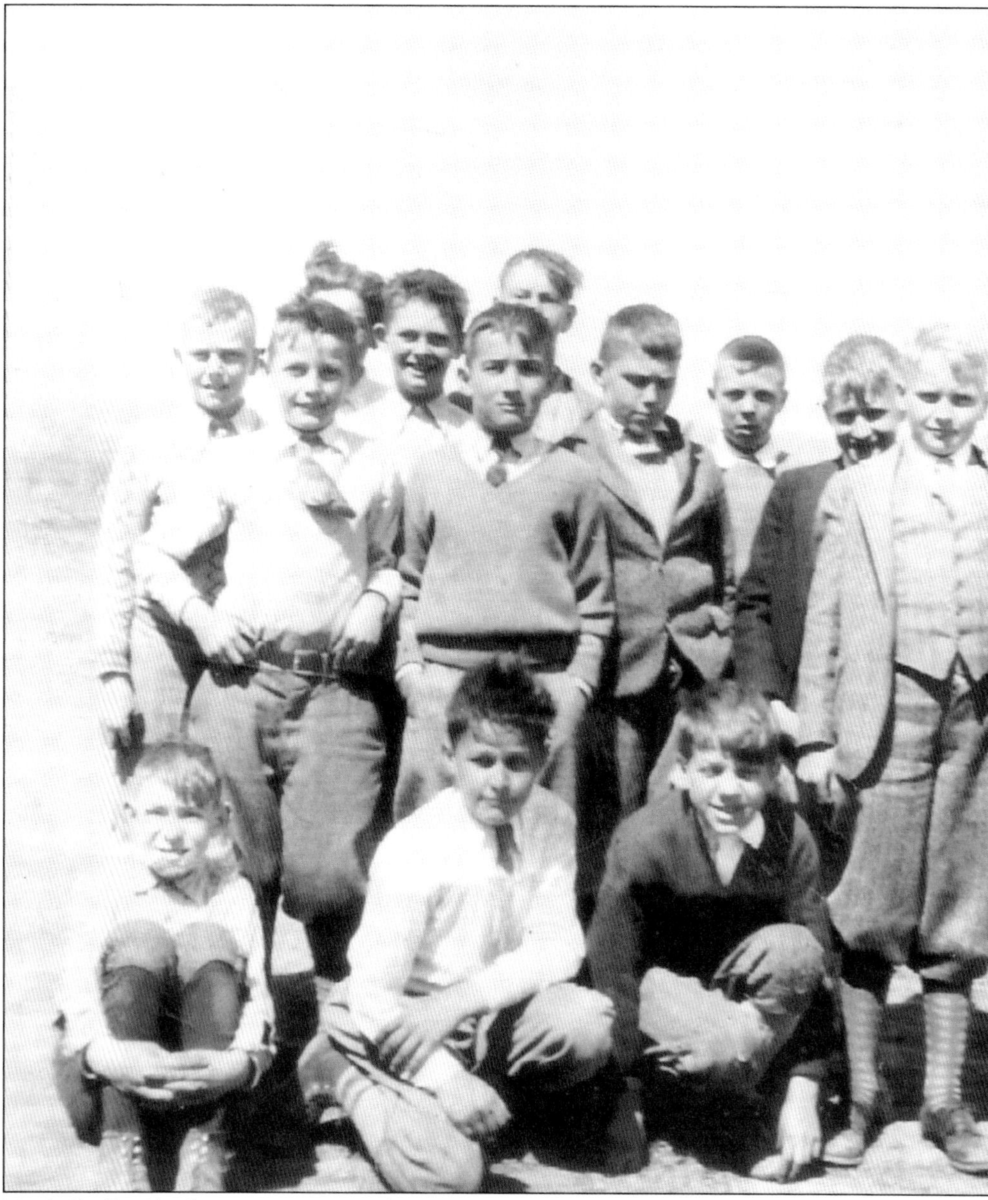

Noah Shelly, Charles Cooper, Jesse Whetington, George Eppley, Lewis Courson, Joe Foster, Robert Snider, Raymond Shell, Charles Packer, Harold Taylor, Raymond Cooperrider, and Paul Packer are some of the sixth-grade students shown here in 1931. (Courtesy of Helen George.)

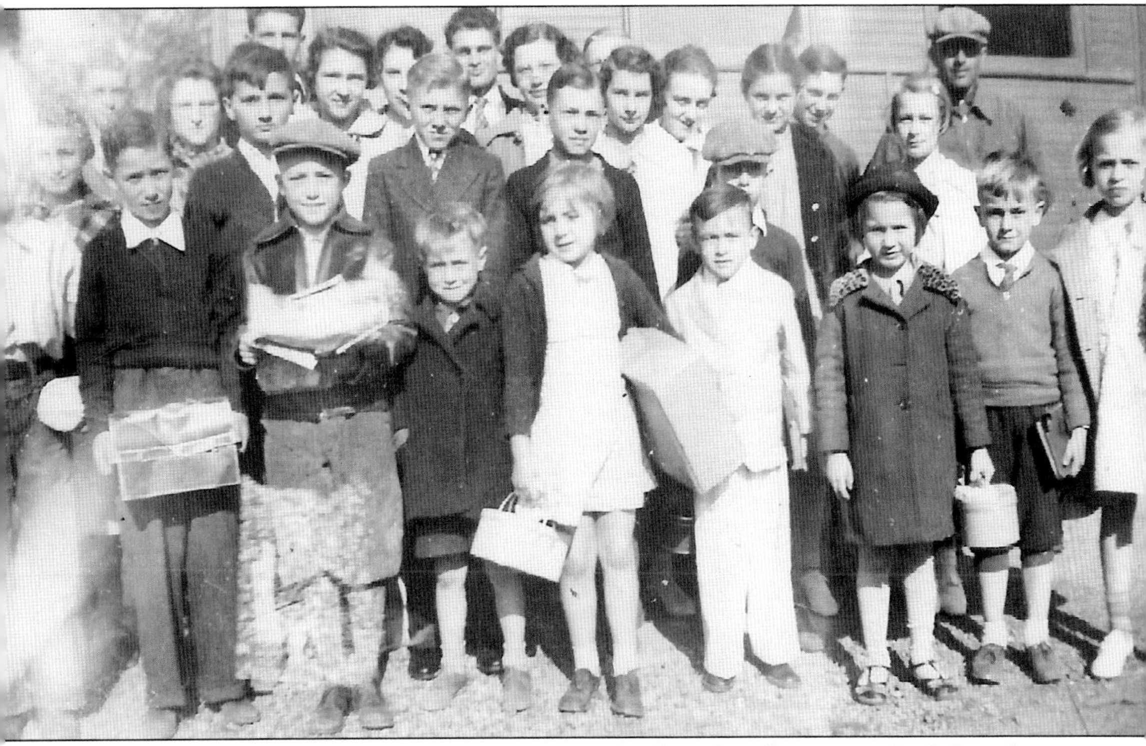

A few of the students seen in this image are Bob Hurd, Ed Hard, Dallas George, Ruth Swinehart, Betty Alspach, Dorothy King, Helen Long, Homer Leckrone, Vivian George, Vernon Hanby, Betty Kennedy, Harry King, Max Yost, Bill Mayer, and Charles George. (Courtesy of Helen George.)

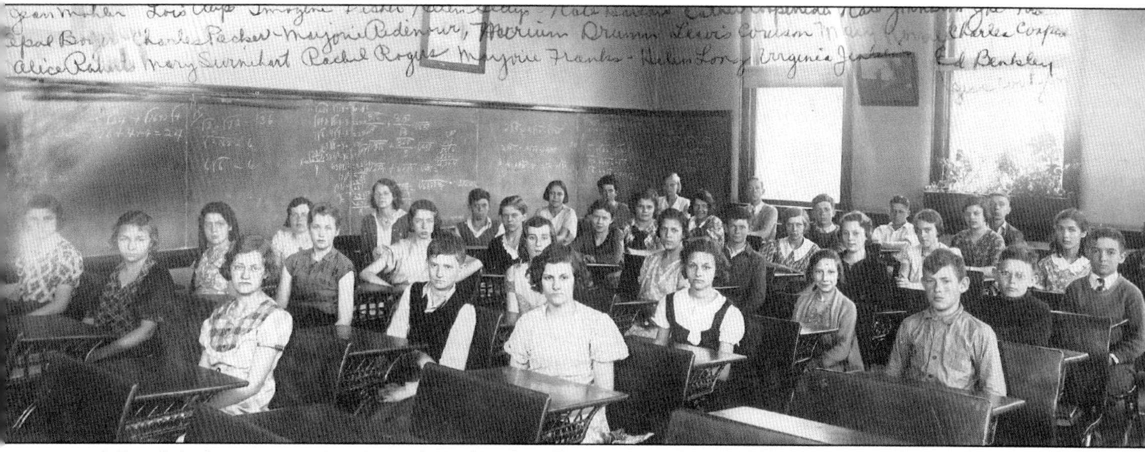

School desks were made of wood, with inkwells and pencil holders on the top. Usually, they were all the same size, regardless of a student's girth. Teachers used blackboards instead of computers and projection screens. (Courtesy of Helen George.)

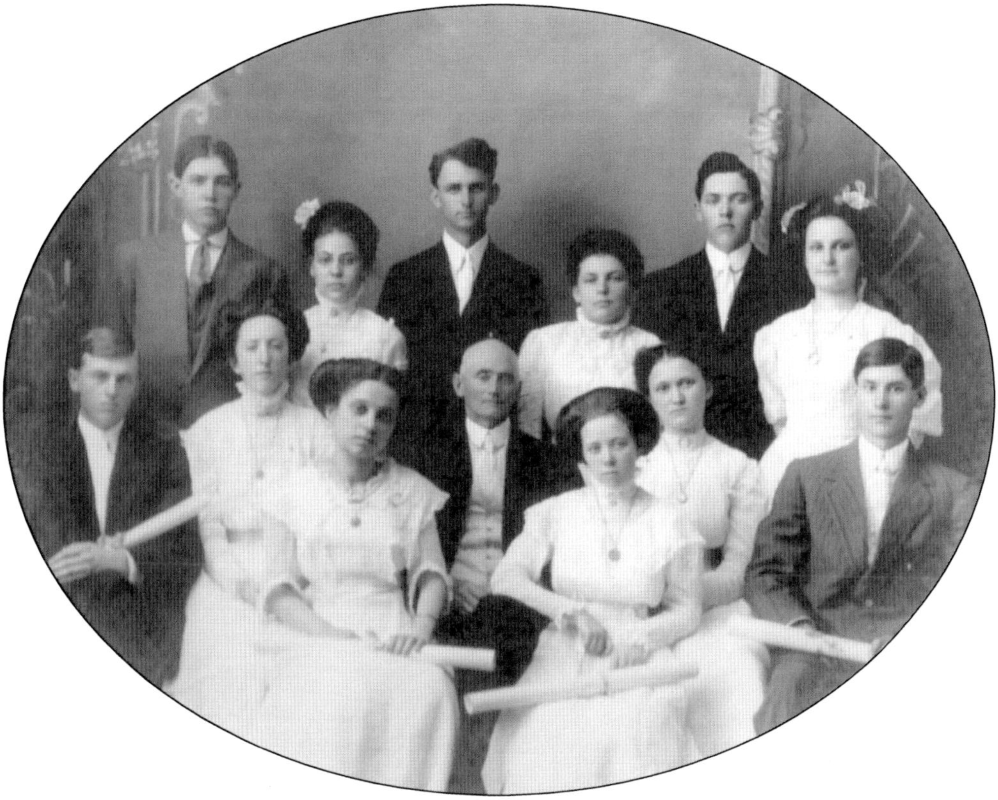

This is the graduating class of Thornville High School in 1909. Members shown here (order unknown) are J.C. Bowman, Effie Fisher Drumm, Carrie Warron Bier, C.L. Williams (superintendent), Bessie Batton Crist, Attie Stevens Anspach, Homer Shelly, Leo A. Caryer, Noel R. Zollinger, Maurice Helser, Lula Shiplett Hinshaw, Grace Neel Cooperrider, and Edna Pannebecker Hite. (Courtesy of Lester Anspach.)

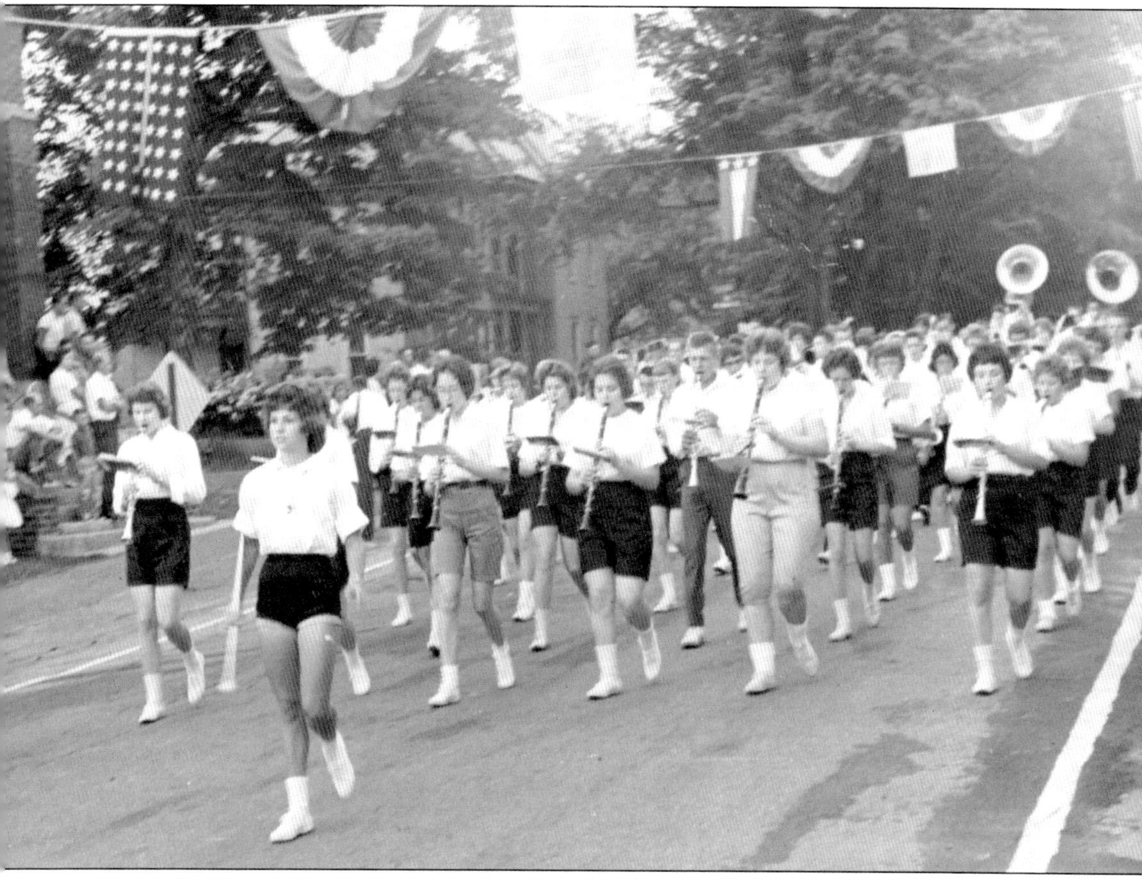

During the Thornville sesquicentennial in 1961, the Sheridan High School band marched through the village. (Courtesy of Lester Anspach.)

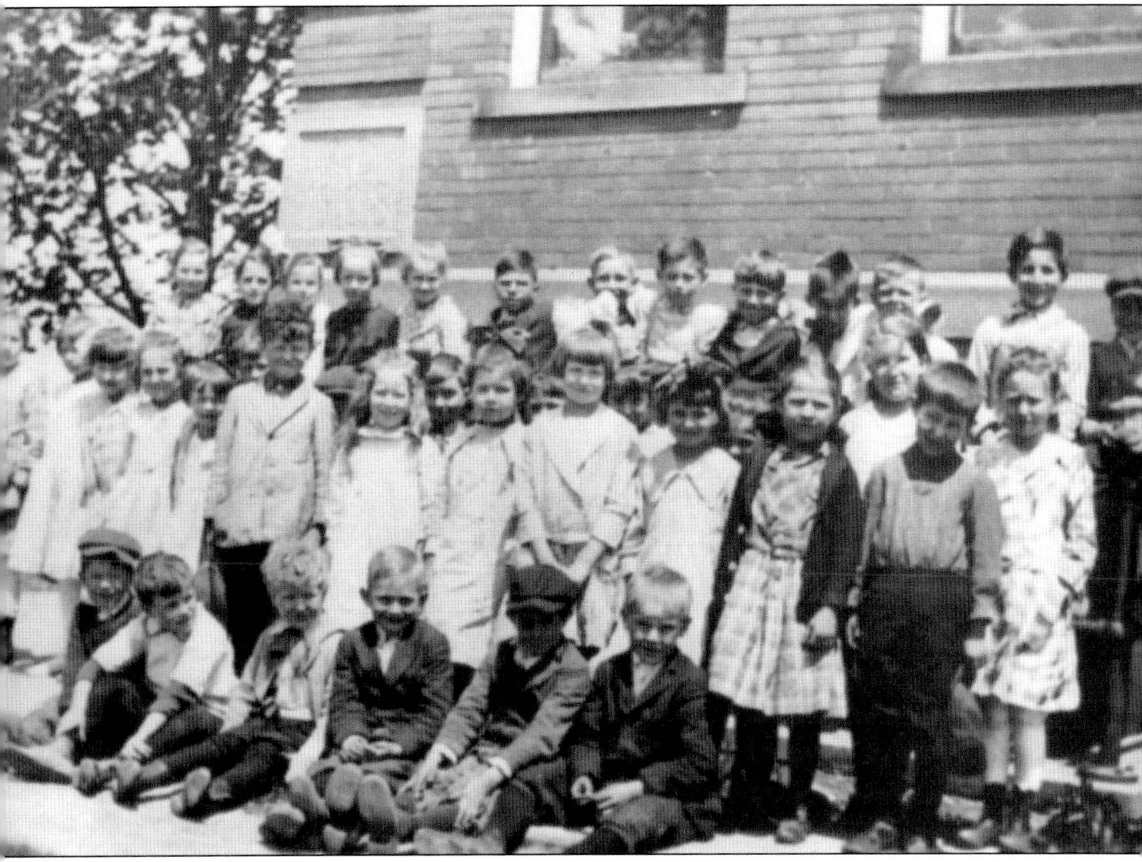

Waiting for school to begin at the old Thornville School were Marvin Long, Mary Packer, Ed Helser, Mary Letherman, Vera Herendeen, and Wayne Clum, among other students. These children were graduates of 1929, 1930, and 1931. (Courtesy of Helen George.)

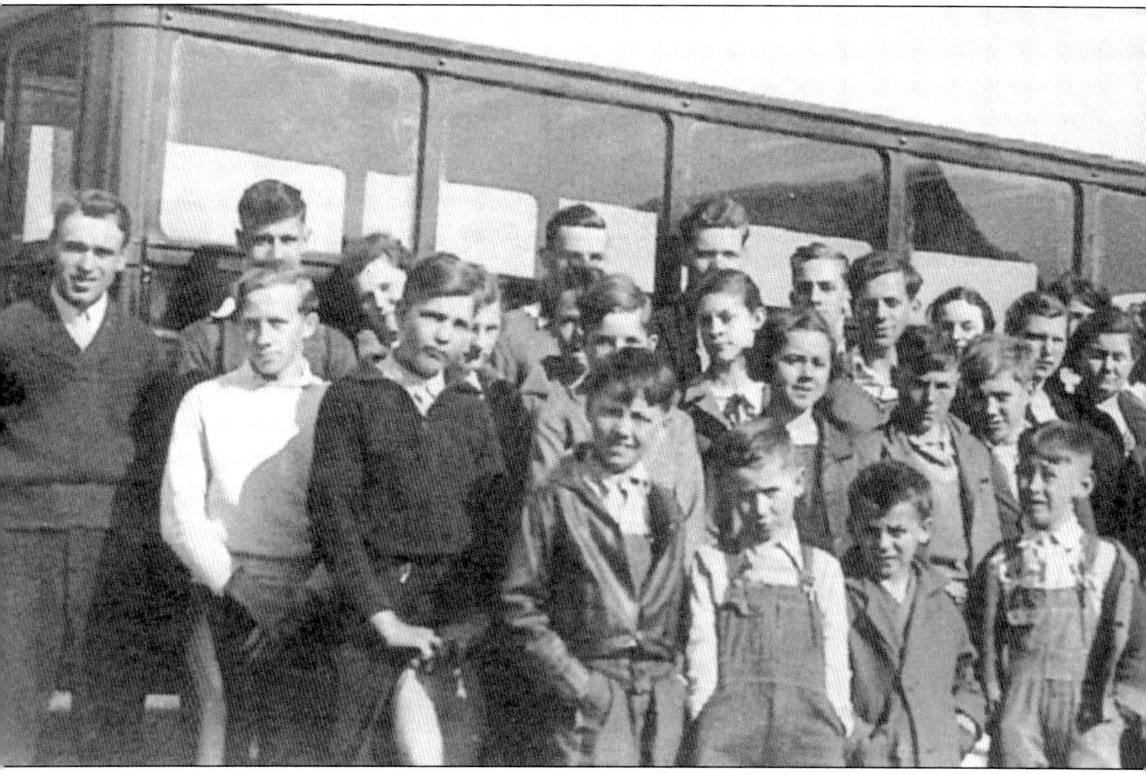

Miller's school bus transported many area students to school. This 1936 photograph includes Bob King, Helen Boyer, Carl Rhea, Frank Rousculp, Jane Cooperrider, Harry King, Jesse Whetington, Verna Hanby, and Jim Rhea. (Courtesy of Helen George.)

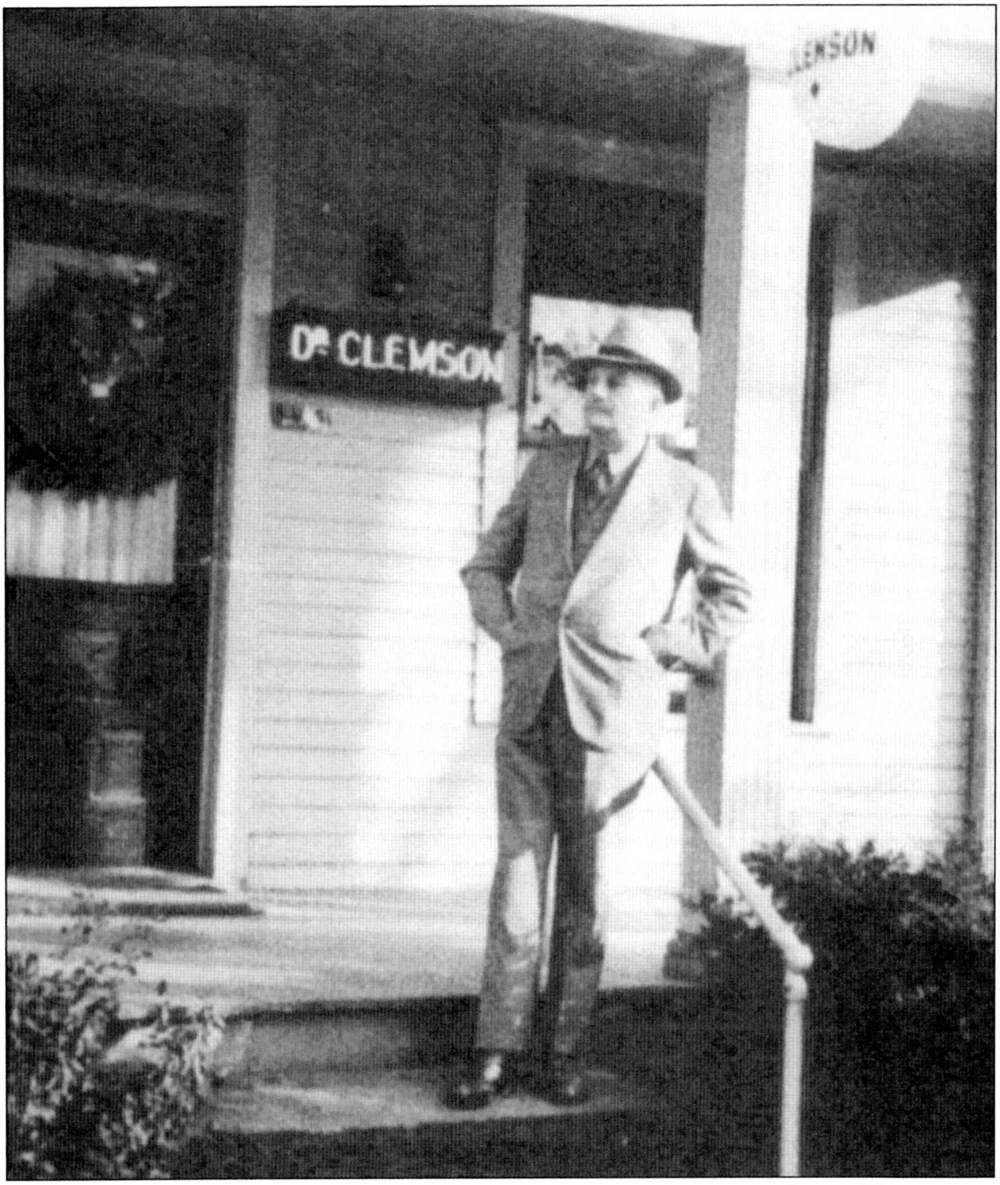

Dr. Frank R. Clemson graduated from Starling Medical School in 1898 and moved his practice from Glenford to 36 South Main Street in Thornville. He served in World War I and maintained horses to pull buggies or sleighs over the muddy roads to see his patients through the 1920s. He charged $5 to deliver a baby. (Courtesy of Thelma Crader.)

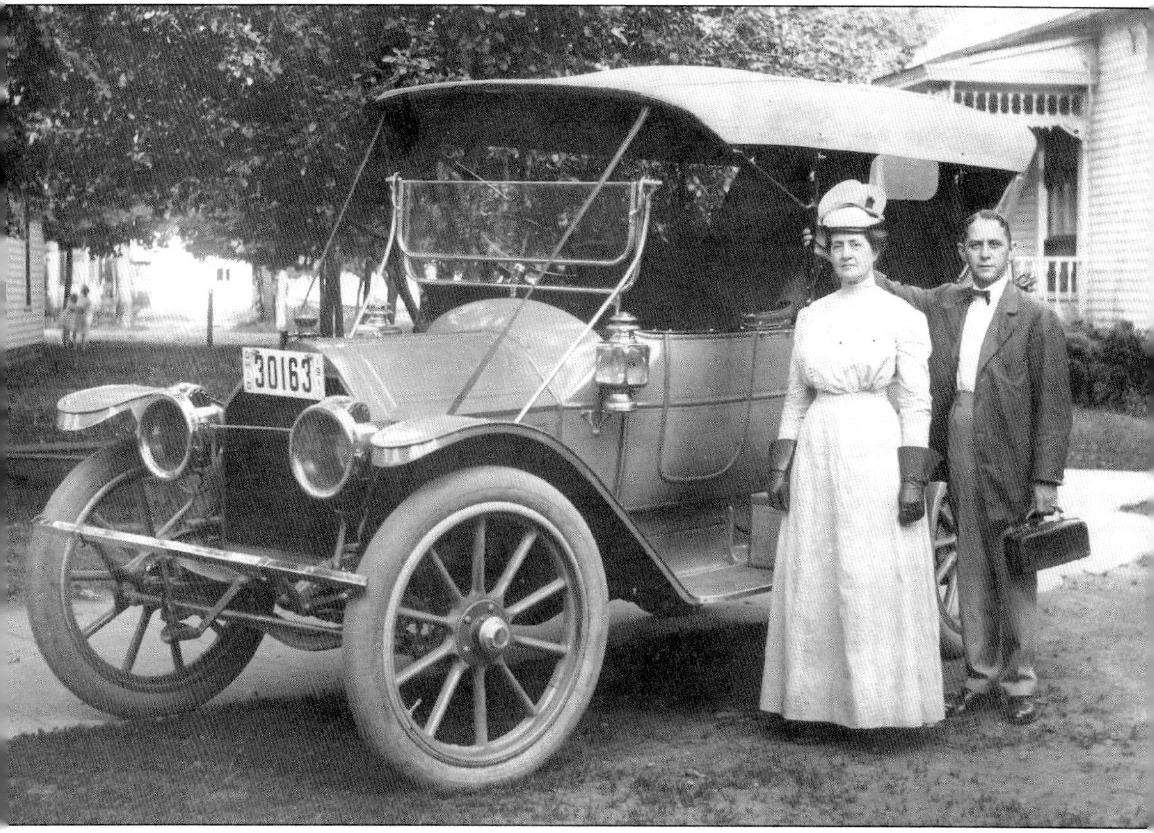

Dr. Omie Joe Letherman and his wife, Emma, stand beside their Cadillac, one of the first automobiles in Perry County. Dr. Letherman graduated from Starling Medical School in 1903 and set up practice in the Odd Fellows building. He served in World War I, was a member of the American Legion, and attended to the community for 37 years. (Courtesy of Helen George.)

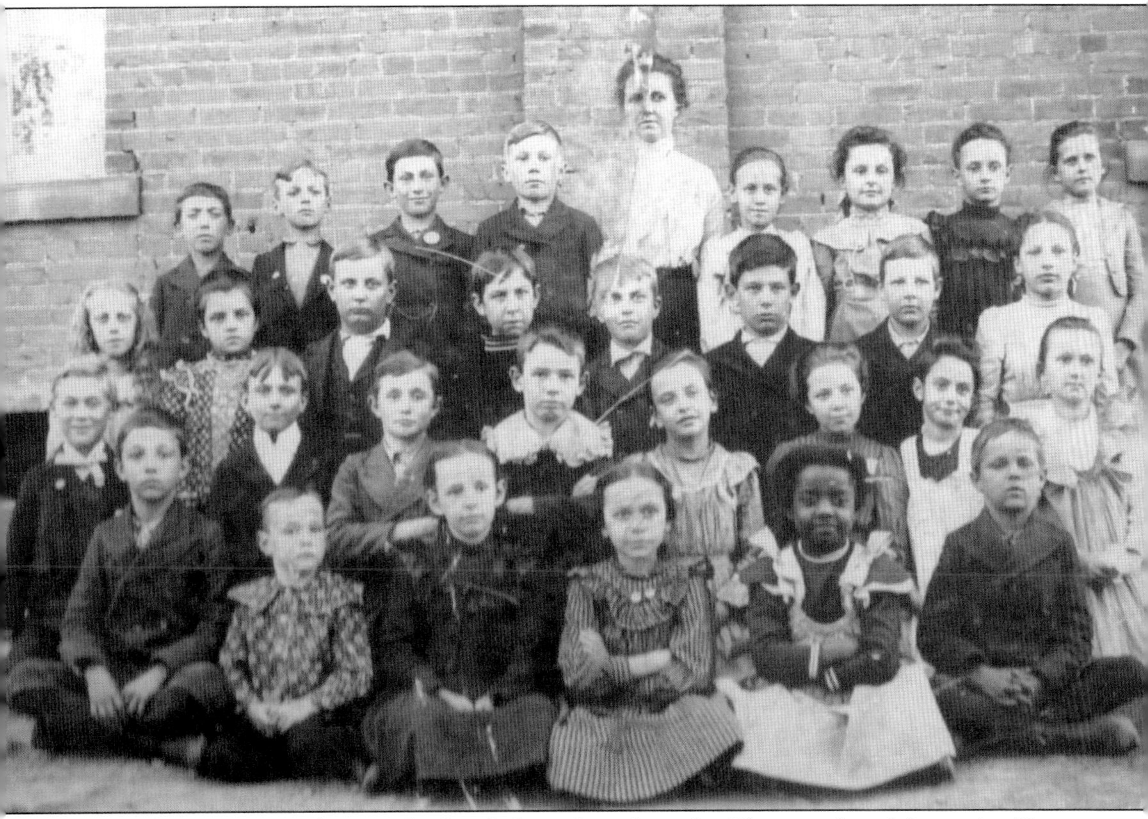

Pictured in 1902 are students in the fourth through sixth grades. They are, from left to right, (first row) Ray Gutelieus, William Yost, Alice Yost, Burdena Lynn, Norma Purl, and Lester Gutelieus; (second row) Bronson Durant, Raymond Lawyer, Russell Kisler, Clarence Kindle, Beryl Pugh, Bessie Battan, Edith Soliday, and Attie Stevens; (third row) Cla Burkett, Mary Trovinger, Homer Beagle, Hayden Risler, Bob Clemson, Harry Kindle, Richard Martin, and Bessie Clum; (fourth row) Elvin Tabler, Albert Grubb, Allen Chalfant, Mark Miller, Jeanette Stevens (teacher), Ethel Gordon, Edna Pannabecker, Jessie Yost, and Vivian Hunt. (Courtesy of Charles Williams.)

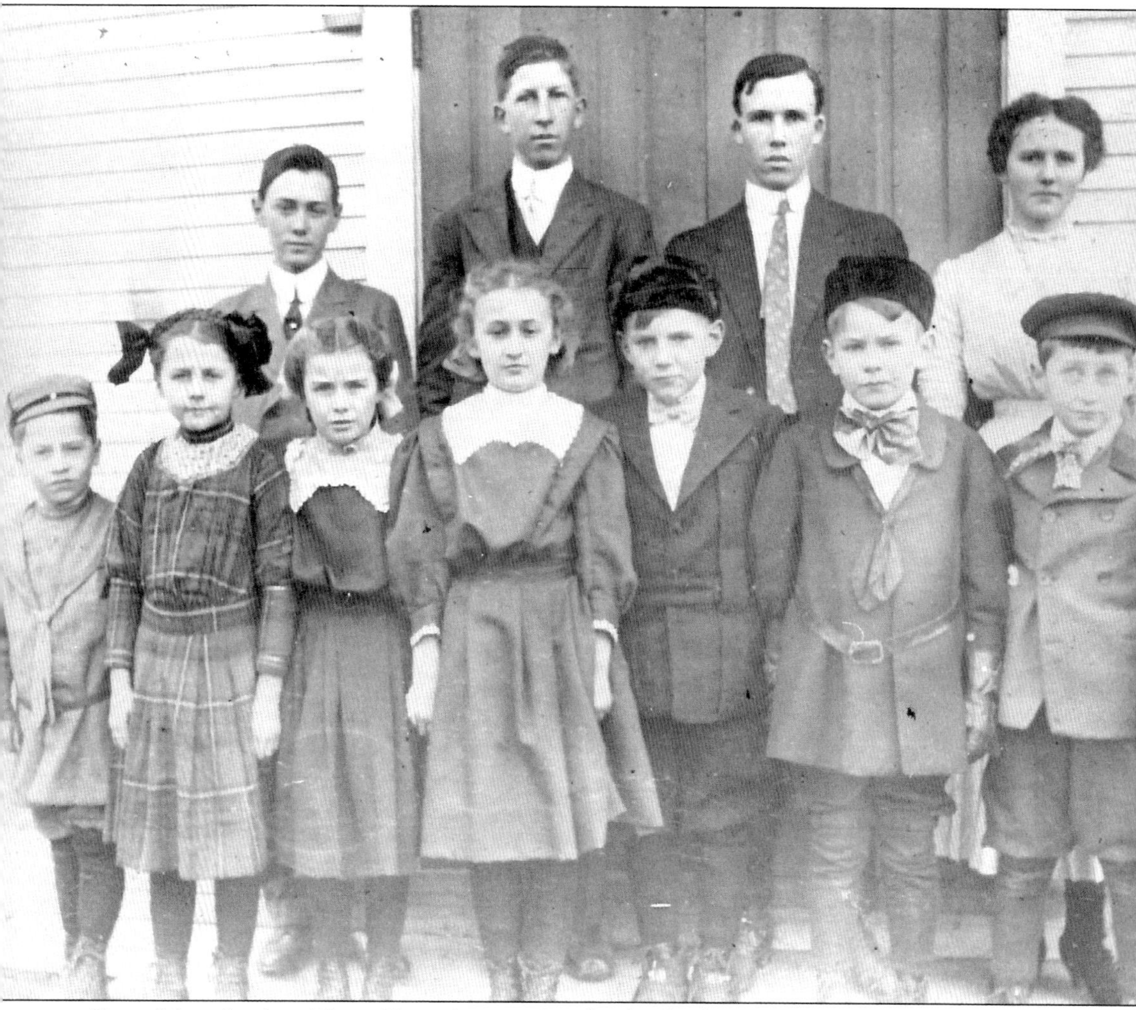

One of the schools in Thorn Township was Good School. These students attended there in 1912. Those pictured, in no specific order, are Ora Warner, Walter McClintock, Hazel Dupler, Harold Helser, Addie Miller, Dessie Starkey, Dessie Helser, Ralph Winegardner, Roe Helser, and Hudon Miller. Their instructor was Roy King. (Courtesy of Helen George.)

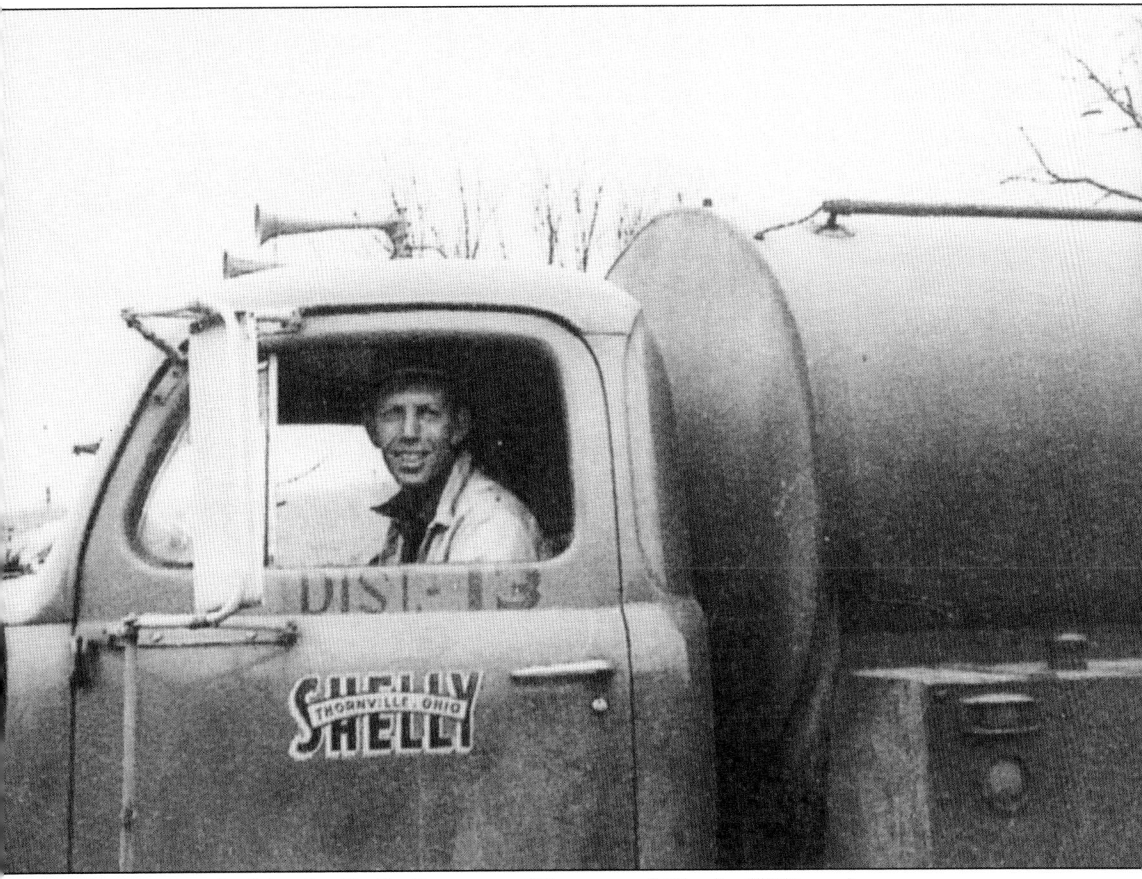

Al Deaver worked for the Shelly Company. (Courtesy of Charles Williams.)

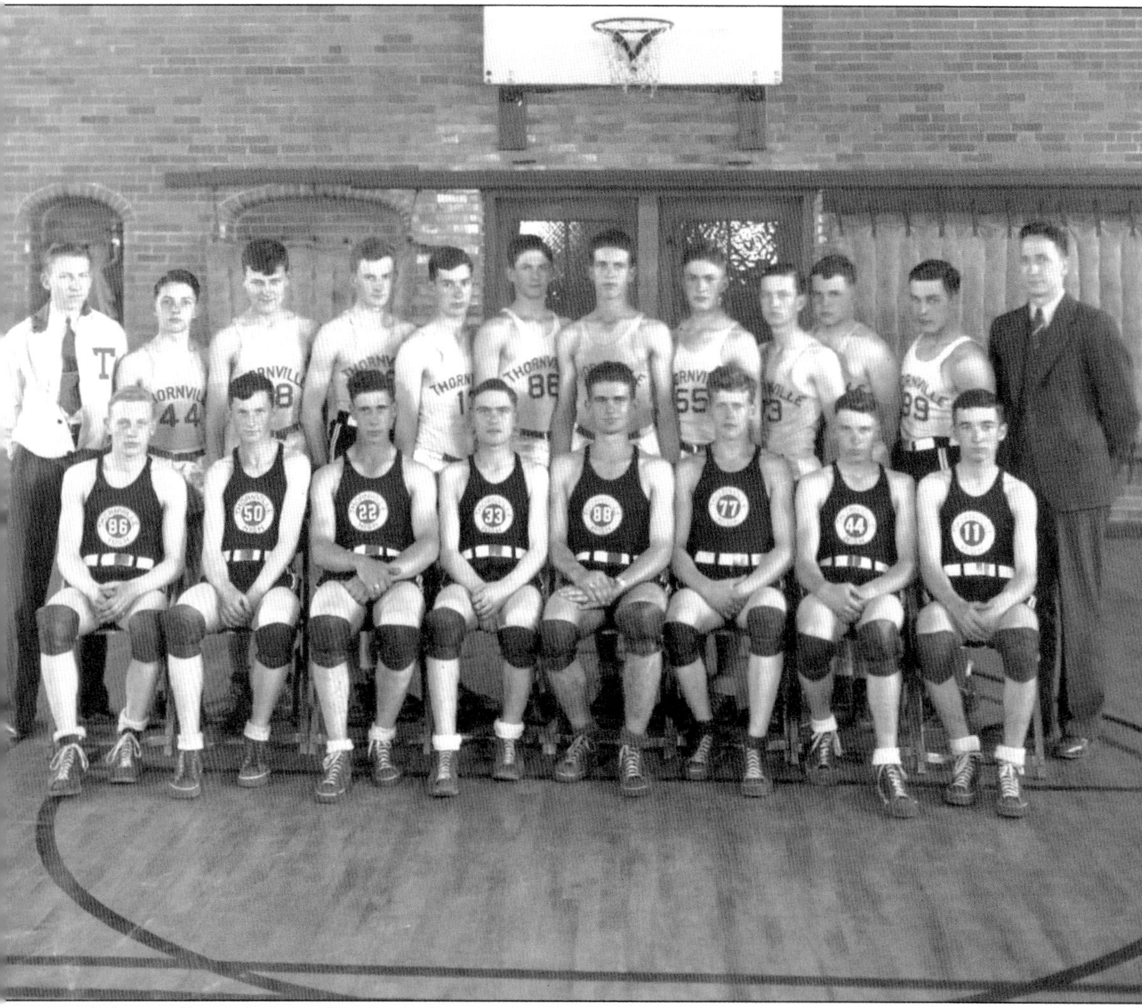

Thornville High School basketball team members are, from left to right, (first row) Maynard Peters, Wayne Parr, Robert Kind, Charles Edmund, Edwin Hurd, Lewis Anspach, Eugene Mohler, and Ray Cooperrider; (second row) Luther Lyle (manager), Joseph Murphy, Richard Brandon, Charles Packer, Wendle Shelly, Lewis Courson, Robert Hurd, Ralph Clum, Paul Cooper, William Yost, Charles Cooper, and coach Clayton Hackman. (Courtesy of Helen George.)

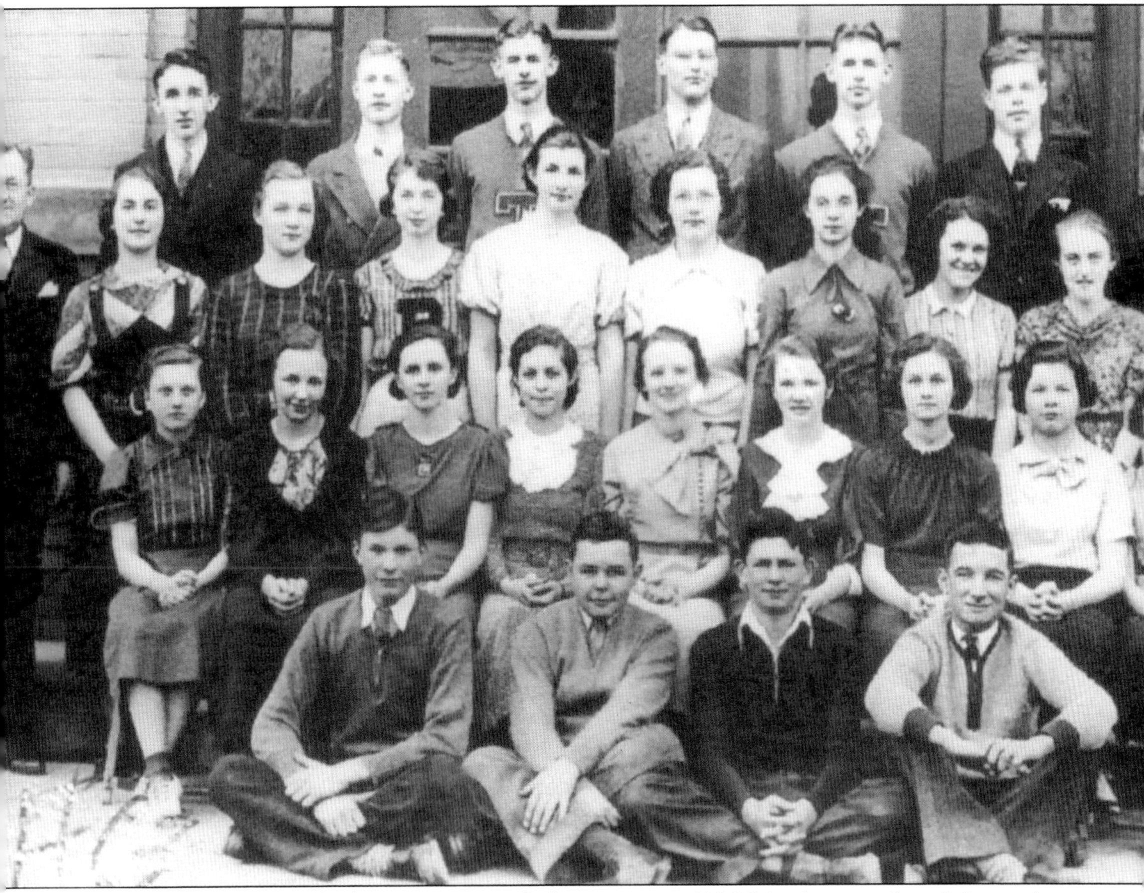

Thornville High School had a competitive scholastic team in 1936. Members are, from left to right, (first row) Ralph Clum, Billy Yost, Lewis Courson, and Raymond Cooperrider; (second row) Margaret Harpester, Jean Mohler, Eunice Watkins, Pauline Grubb, Betty Foster, Dorothy Cooperrider, Mary Swinehart, Betsy Langhans, and Melba Snider; (third row) Mr. Kagay, Margaret Helser, Vera Cooperrider, Imogene Fisher, Thelma Cooperrider, Winogene Foster, Francis DeRolph, Helen Mohler, Helen Long, and Kathryn Murphy; (fourth row) Huxley Fisher, Floyd Clum, Charles Bope, William Hite, Frank Bope, Frank Rousculp, and Gale Hanby. (Courtesy of Helen George.)

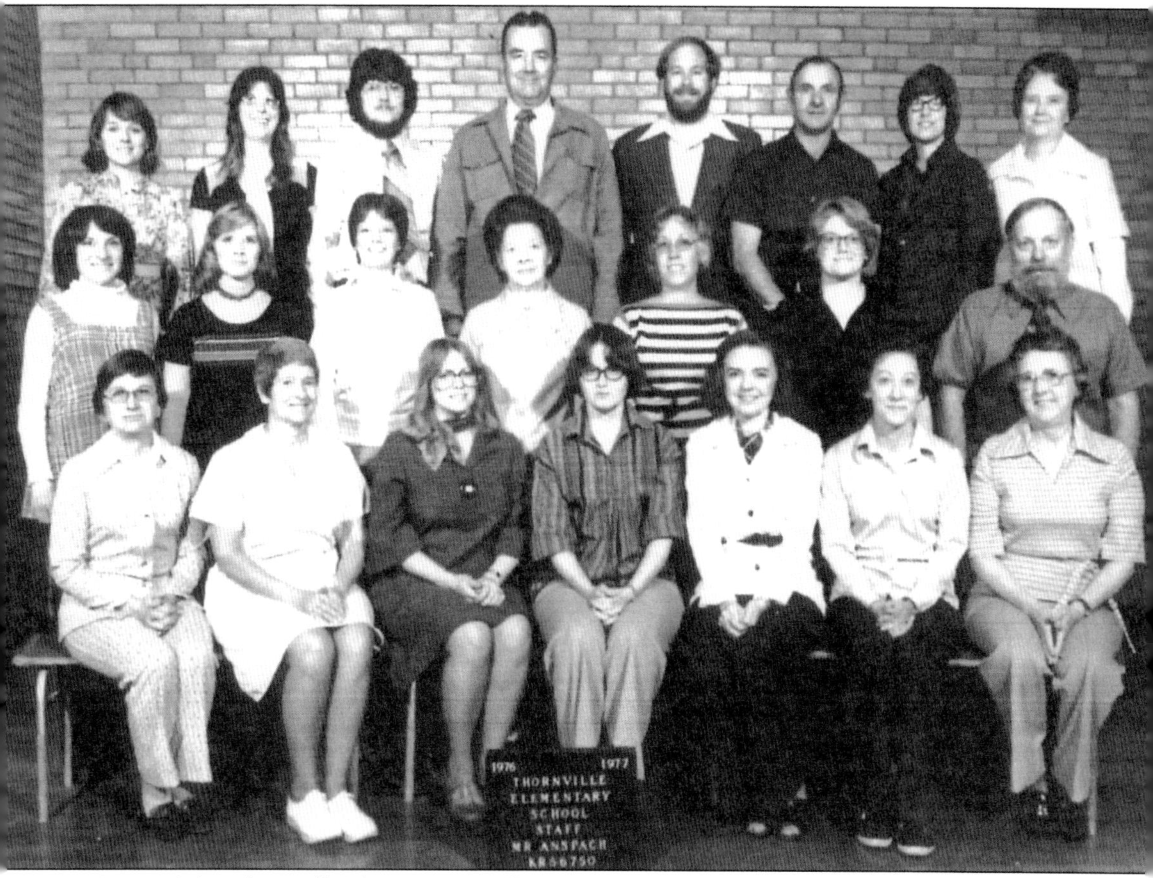

Some of the Thornville Elementary staff members in 1974 included Margaret Grabau, Marilyn Fehrman, Christine Trimmer, Margo Crow, Joanne Hoover, Glorene Gordon, Sarah Wolfe, Judy Bowers, Roma Swinehart, Virginia Pletcher, Alpha Black, Tomi Clum, Ann Starr, Bernard Palmier, Louie Cooperrider, John Paxton, and Nick Anspach.

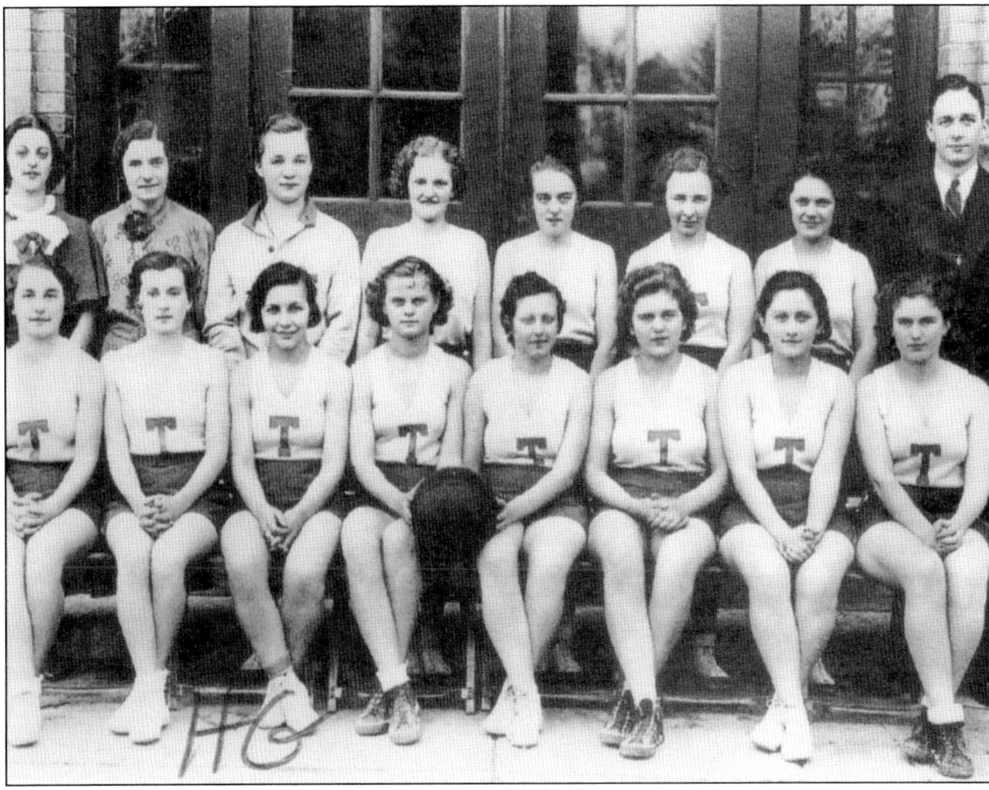

Members of the Thornville High School girls' basketball team of 1935 included, from left to right, (first row) Margaret Helser, Marjorie Ridenour, Jane Cooperrider, Juanita Fisher, Fern Grubb, Helen Gettys, Eileen Hanby, Louise Gettys; (second row) Pauline Clark (manager), Miss Love (advisor), Vera Cooperrider, Opal Boyer, Helen Long, Jean Mohler, Helen Mohler, and Coach Hackman. (Courtesy of Helen George.)

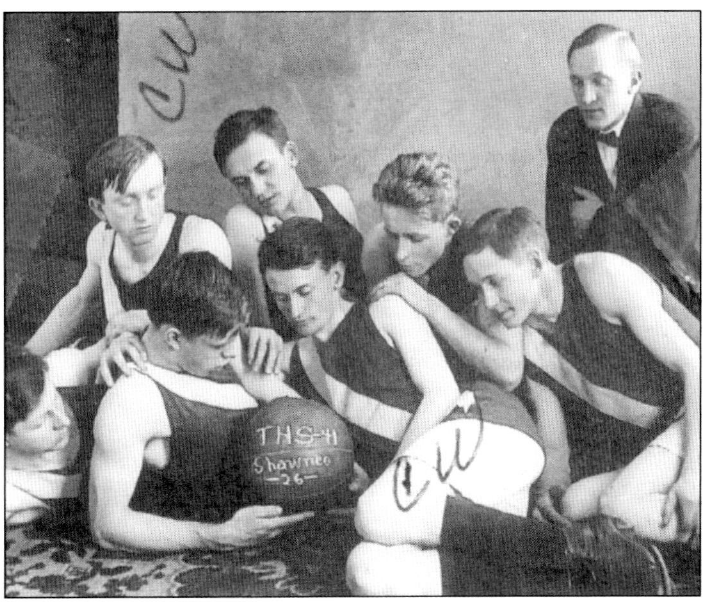

Thornville High School's first boys' basketball team had to play its games in the old town hall; the players were (in no particular order) John Yost, Elden Fisher, Fred Edmund, Lloyd Clum, Ensel Franks, Ralph Alspach, and Guy Williams. Their coach was J.A. Wagner, and they had beaten Shawnee 41-11. (Courtesy of Charles Williams.)

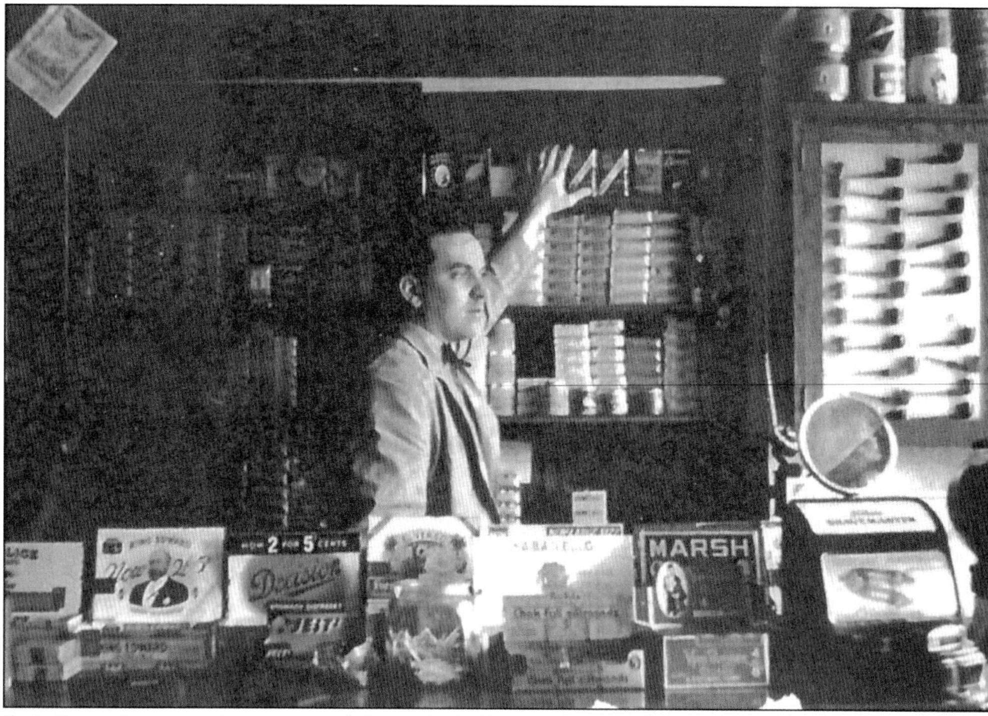

Bob Spangler was the owner of Spangler's Drugstore in Thornville. Notice the cigars on the counter. (Courtesy of Thelma Crader.)

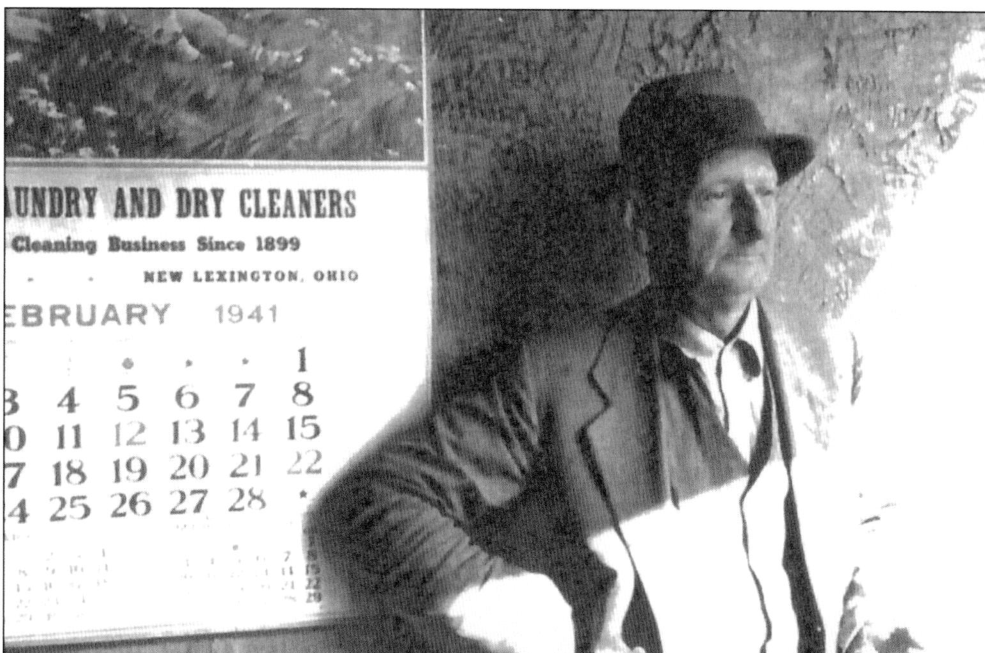

Orlo "Scant" Faller was both a game warden and mail carrier. According to the calendar behind him, this photograph was taken in February 1941—Pearl Harbor would be attacked in December of that year. (Courtesy of Thelma Crader.)

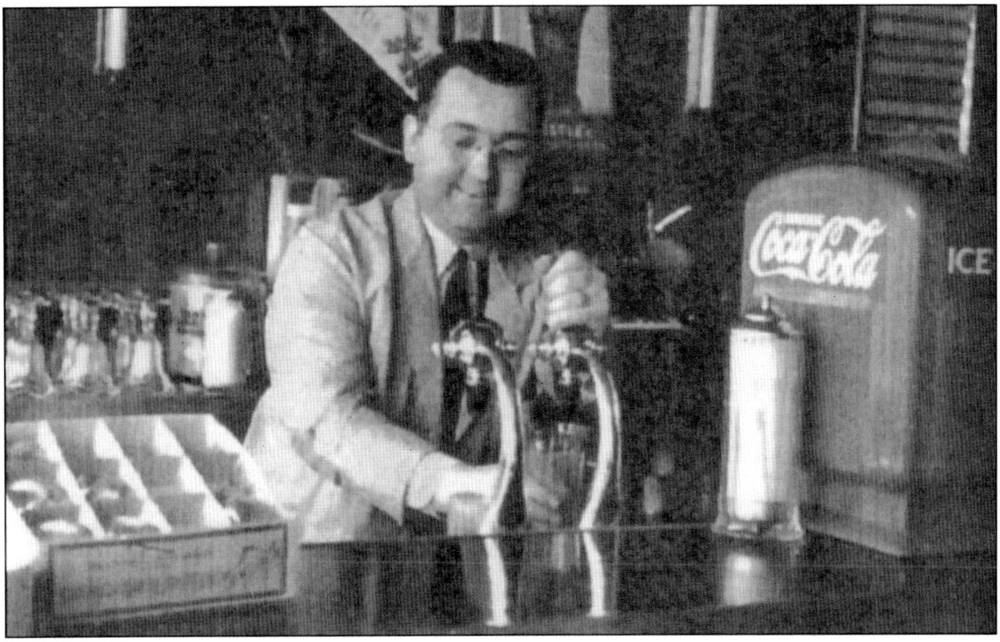

Charles Lamb served as a soda jerk, drugstore clerk, and mail carrier. His father, Harry, and Hugh Eckenrode owned the Lamb and Neel General Store in Thornville. Harry was also a road contractor and was responsible for building Route 40 between Jacksontown and Hebron. (Courtesy of Thelma Crader.)

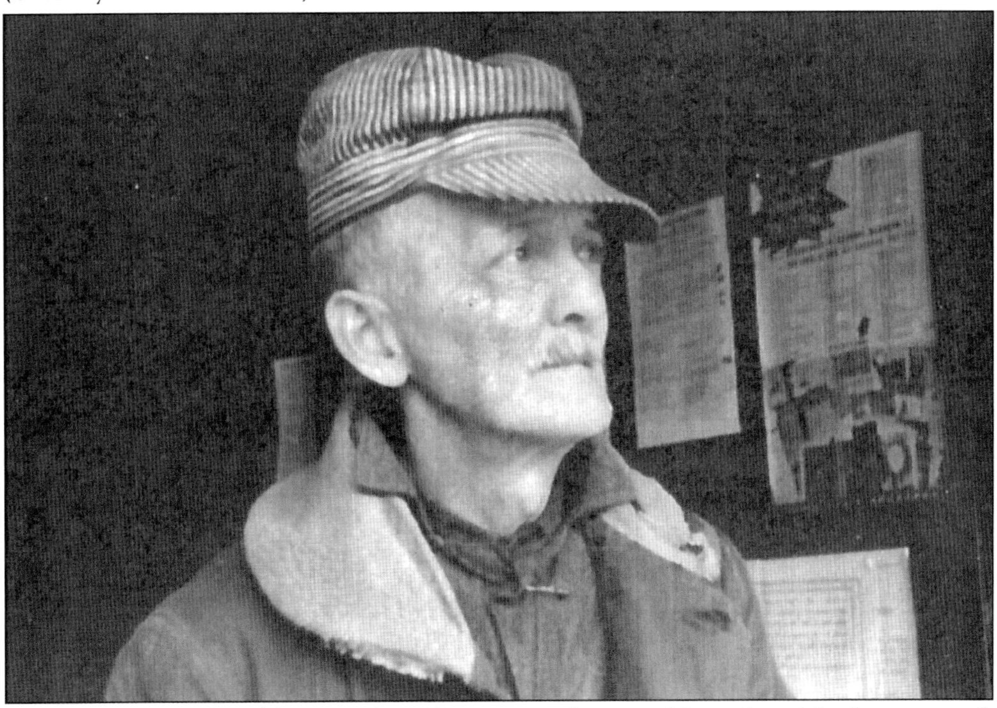
Orval Mechling graduated from Northern University in pharmacy. He purchased the drugstore, took one course in optometry, sold the drugstore, and then practiced in the village as an optometrist. He also operated a jewelry store in the village and sold schoolbooks. (Courtesy of Thelma Crader.)

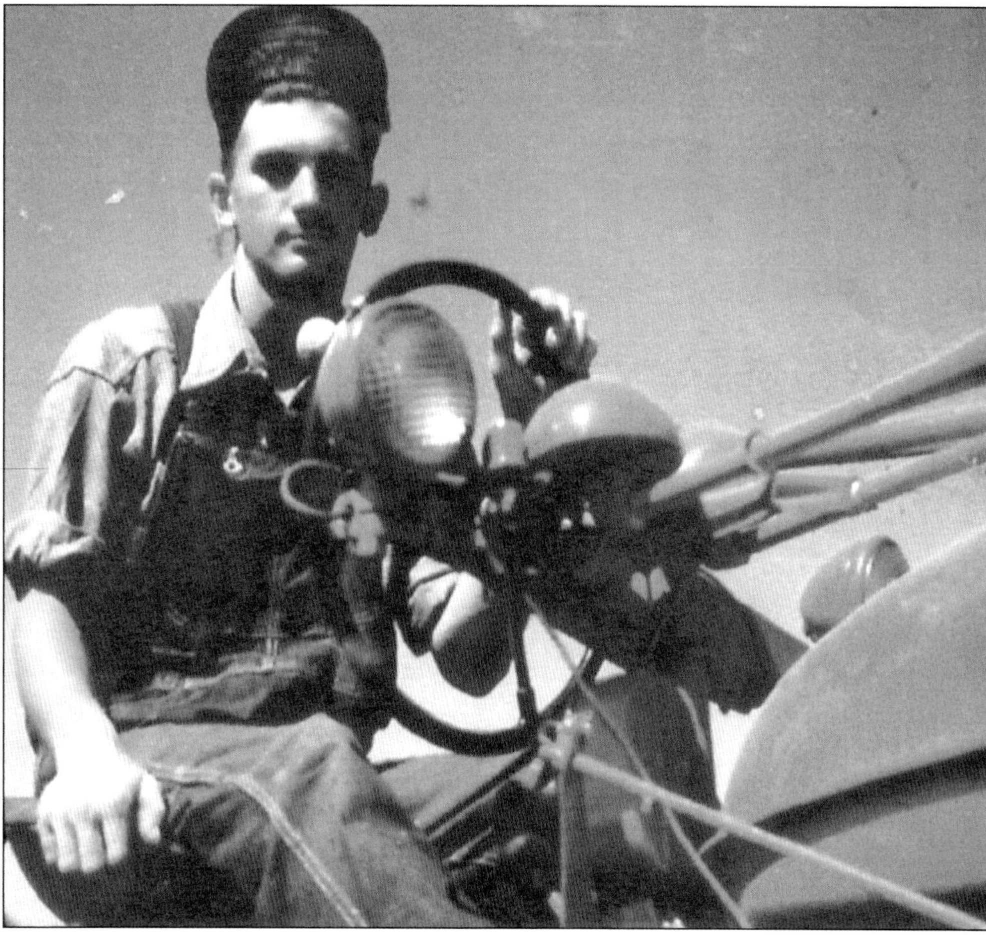

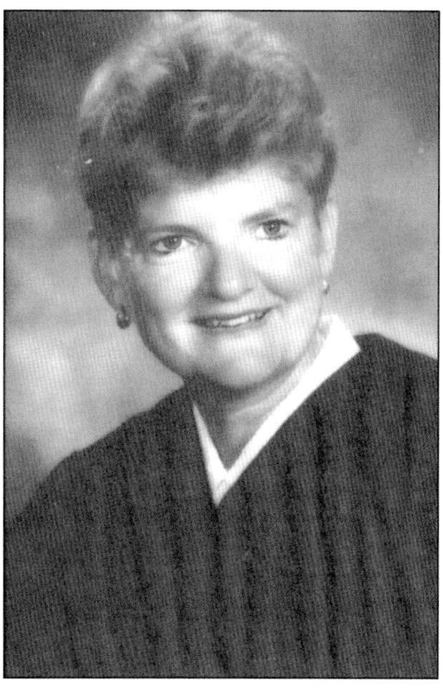

Dallas George, 1922–1969, learned the skill of welding in shop class at Thornville High School. He became a dairy farmer, and as his farm tools needed repair, he bought a welder and other tools to repair them. Soon, other neighbors began to bring him their broken tools to be welded, and George's Repair Shop opened just outside the village on Route 204. His son David and David's grandson Dallas now operate the shop. Dallas's son Jackson will hopefully run it in the future. (Courtesy of Helen George.)

Luann Cooperrider, born and raised in Thorn Township, opened a law office in Thornville in 1983. In 1991, she was elected the Perry County probate juvenile judge and still serves the county in that capacity. She and husband, John Gillogly, are the parents of son Cooper. (Courtesy of Luann Cooperrider.)

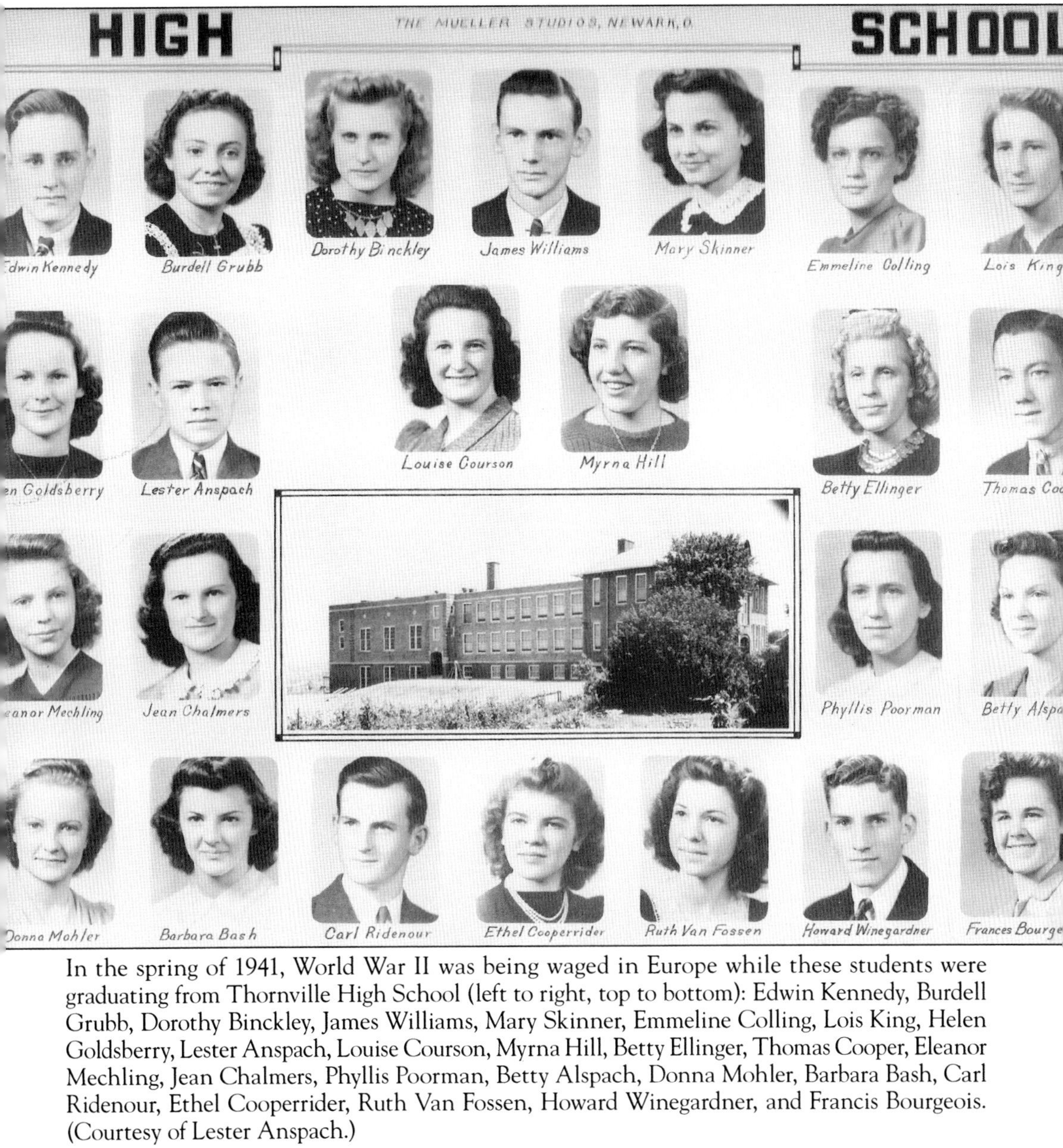

In the spring of 1941, World War II was being waged in Europe while these students were graduating from Thornville High School (left to right, top to bottom): Edwin Kennedy, Burdell Grubb, Dorothy Binckley, James Williams, Mary Skinner, Emmeline Colling, Lois King, Helen Goldsberry, Lester Anspach, Louise Courson, Myrna Hill, Betty Ellinger, Thomas Cooper, Eleanor Mechling, Jean Chalmers, Phyllis Poorman, Betty Alspach, Donna Mohler, Barbara Bash, Carl Ridenour, Ethel Cooperrider, Ruth Van Fossen, Howard Winegardner, and Francis Bourgeois. (Courtesy of Lester Anspach.)

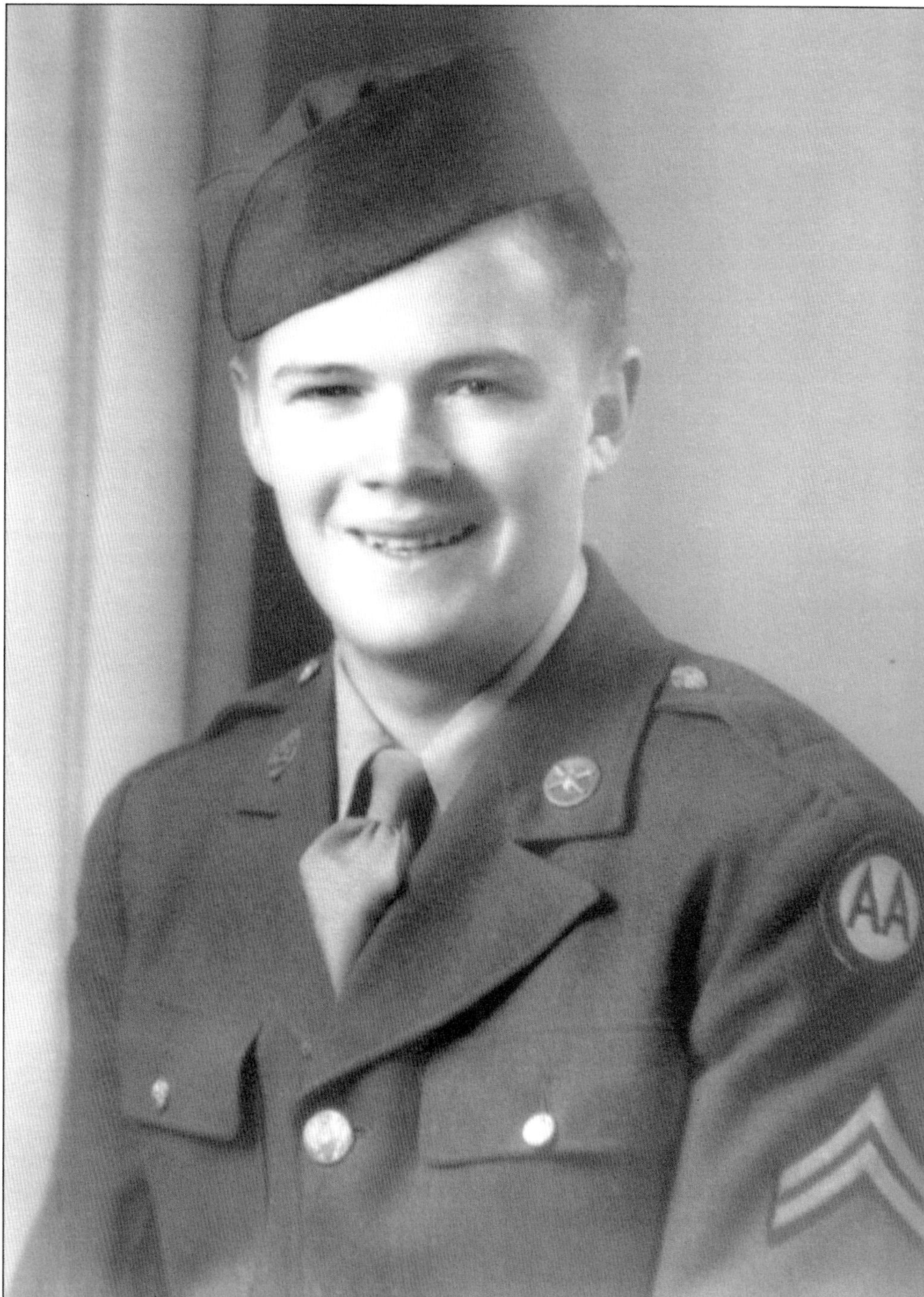

Lester Anspach graduated from Thornville High School in 1941 and served in the Army during World War II. He married Mary Foster in 1947. He worked for the Defense Supply Center in Columbus and also was a custodian at the Methodist Church and a street commissioner for many years. Lester was a local historian who loved his hometown and was very involved in civic, church, and Lions Club activities. (Courtesy of Lester Anspach.)

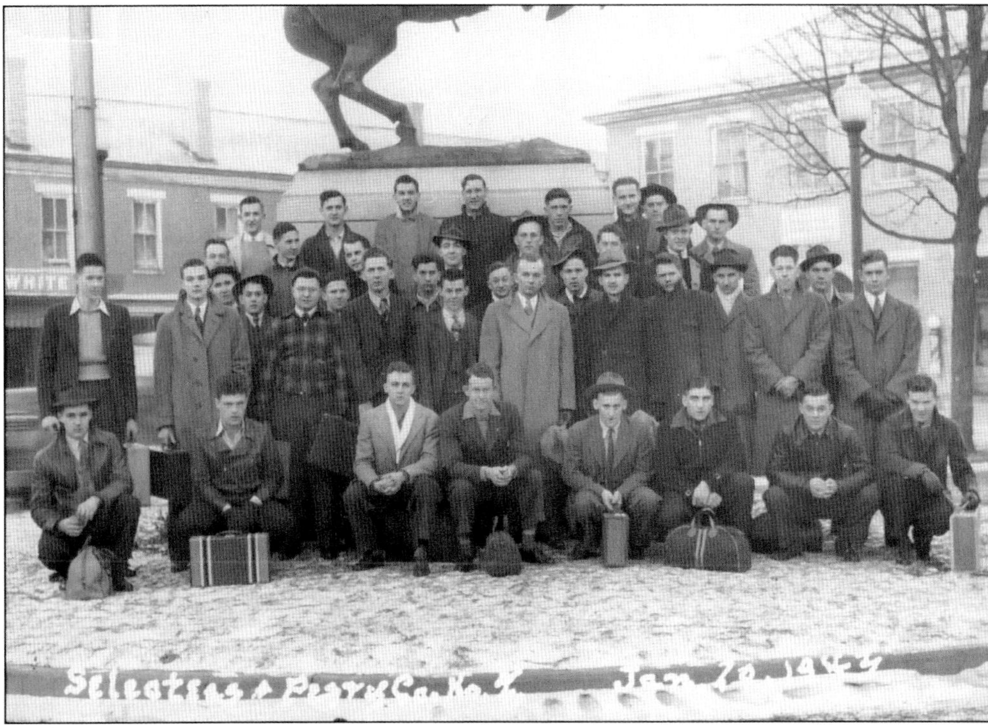

In 1943, prior to going off to war, young men from all over Perry County gathered in Somerset beneath the statue of Civil War general Phillip Sheridan. Most had just graduated from high school, and several were from Thorn Township, including Lester Anspach and Charles Williams. (Courtesy of Lester Anspach.)

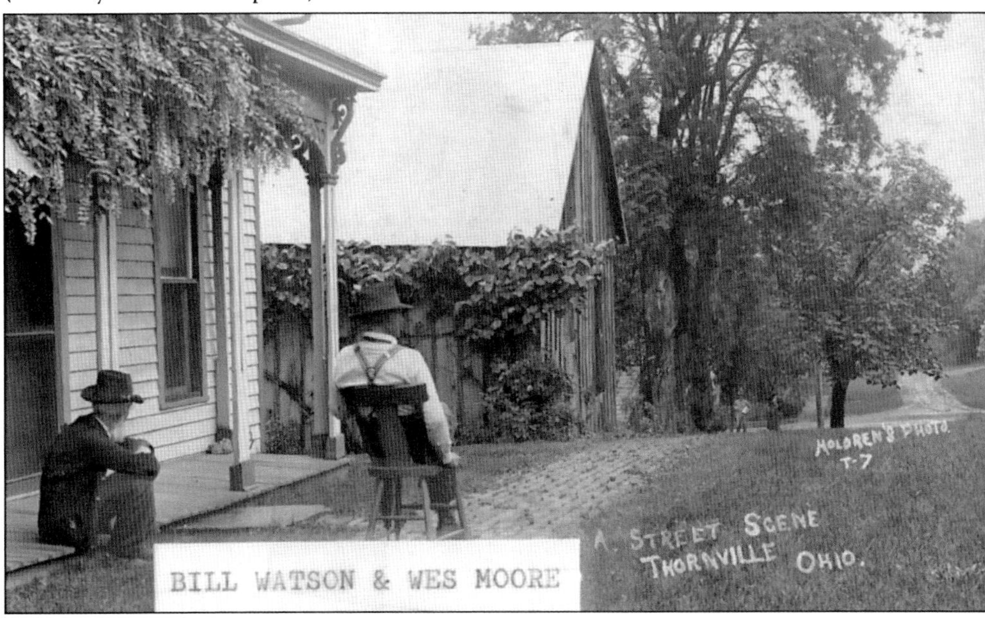

There are times when villagers just like to spend an afternoon enjoying the sunshine and good company. As Bill Watson (left) and Wes Moore visit, the wisteria blooms cascade over the house.

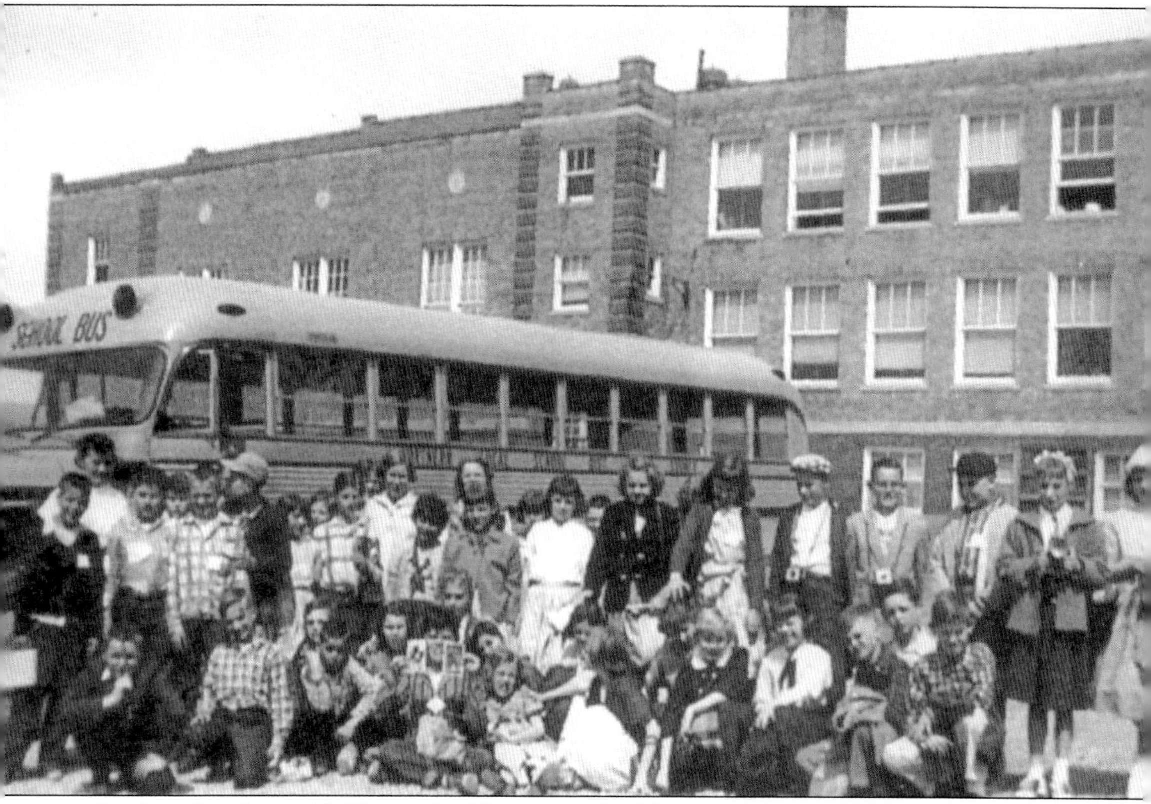

At the side of the old Thornville Elementary building is a group of fifth graders in 1958. Inventions that year included microchips, computer modems, and remote controls. (Courtesy of Charles Williams.)

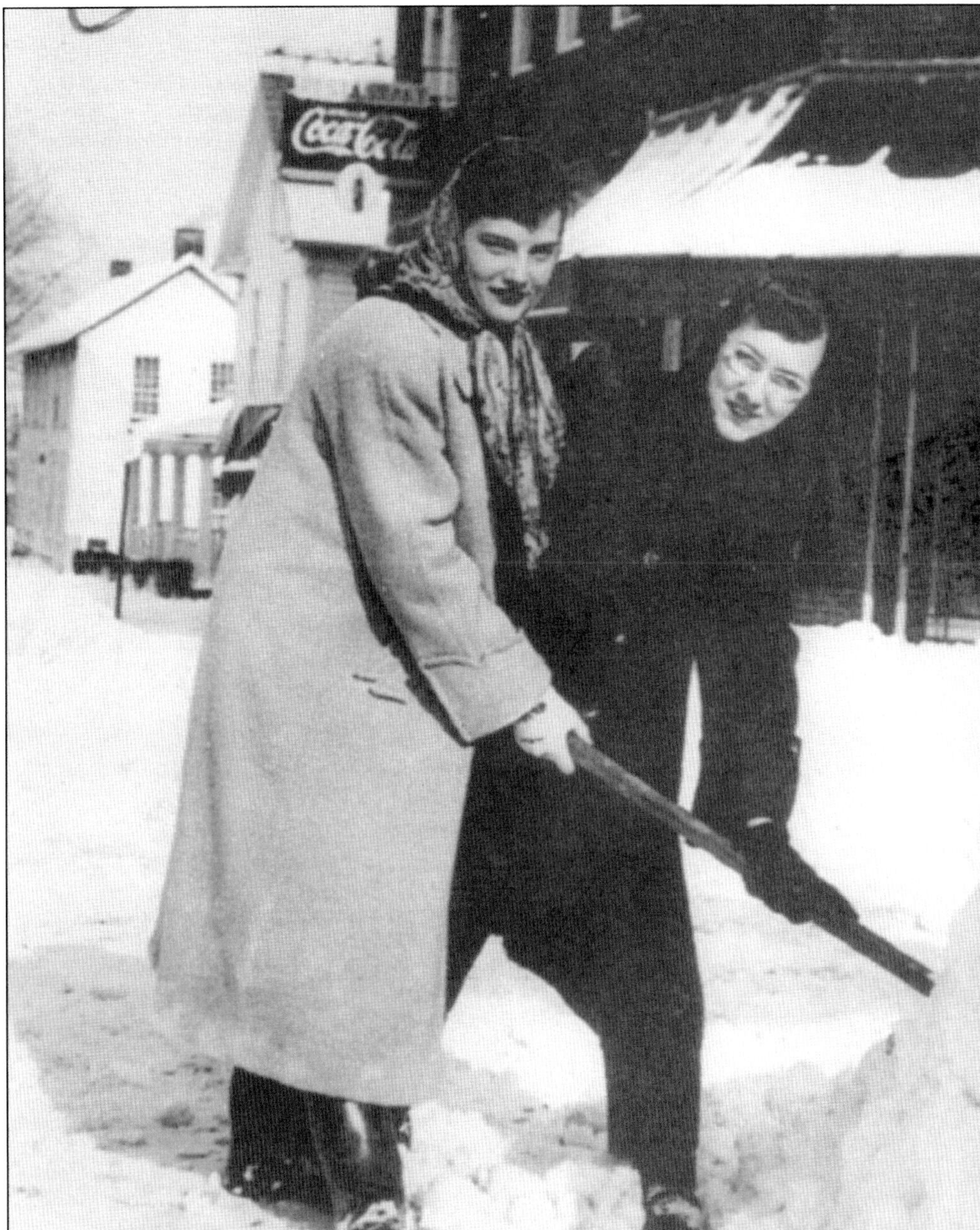

In 1950, snow blanketed Ohio, and Thornville got its share. The Martin and Chase girls were helping to shovel the snow in front of the bank building after the blizzard. (Courtesy of Charles Williams.)

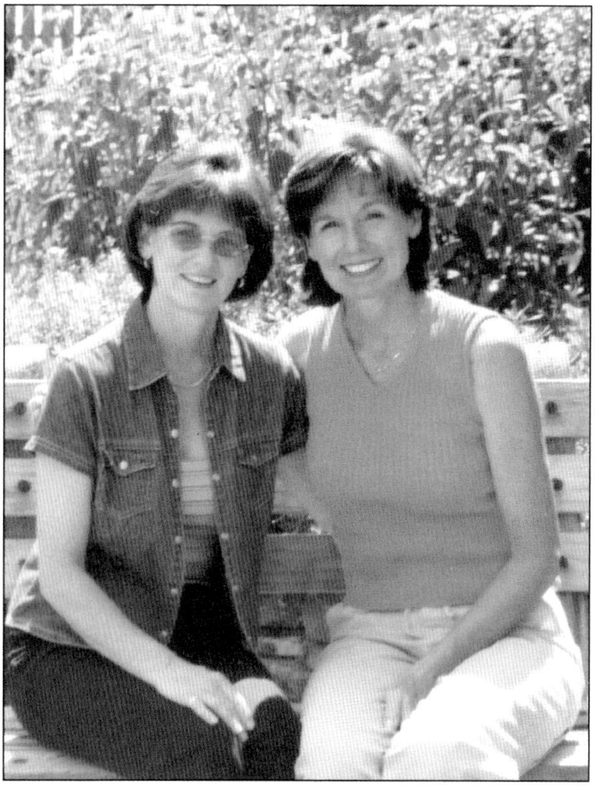

Shirley Packer (left) and Patty Ridenour have served the village of Thornville by keeping the downtown planters filled with colorful flowers. (Courtesy of Shirley Packer.)

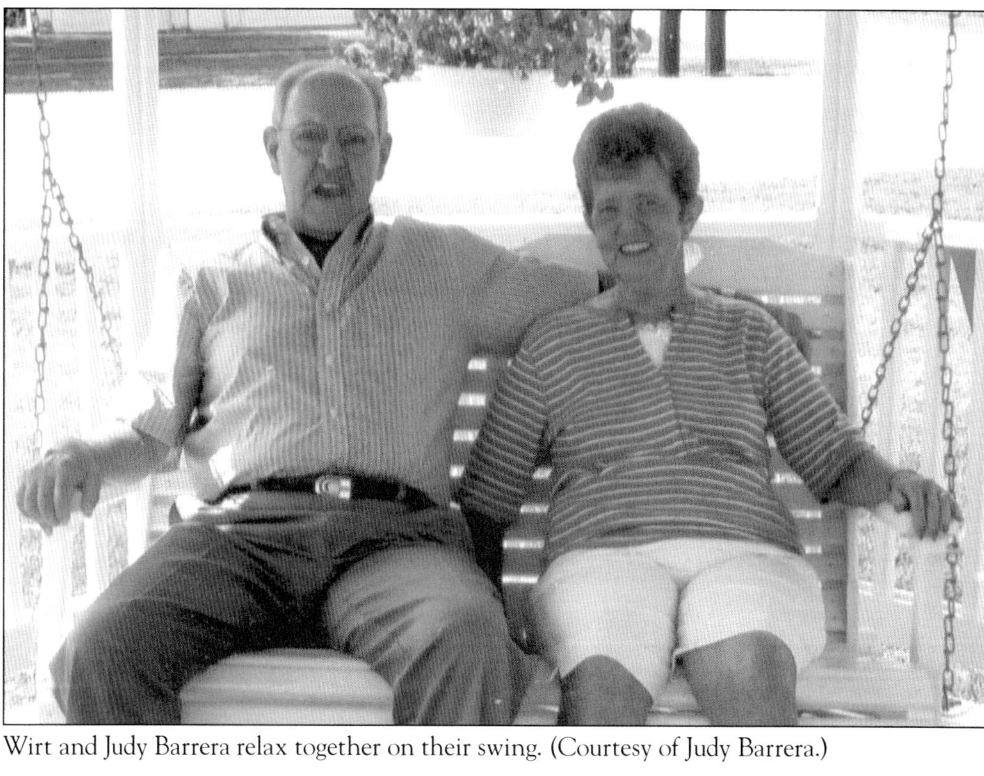

Wirt and Judy Barrera relax together on their swing. (Courtesy of Judy Barrera.)

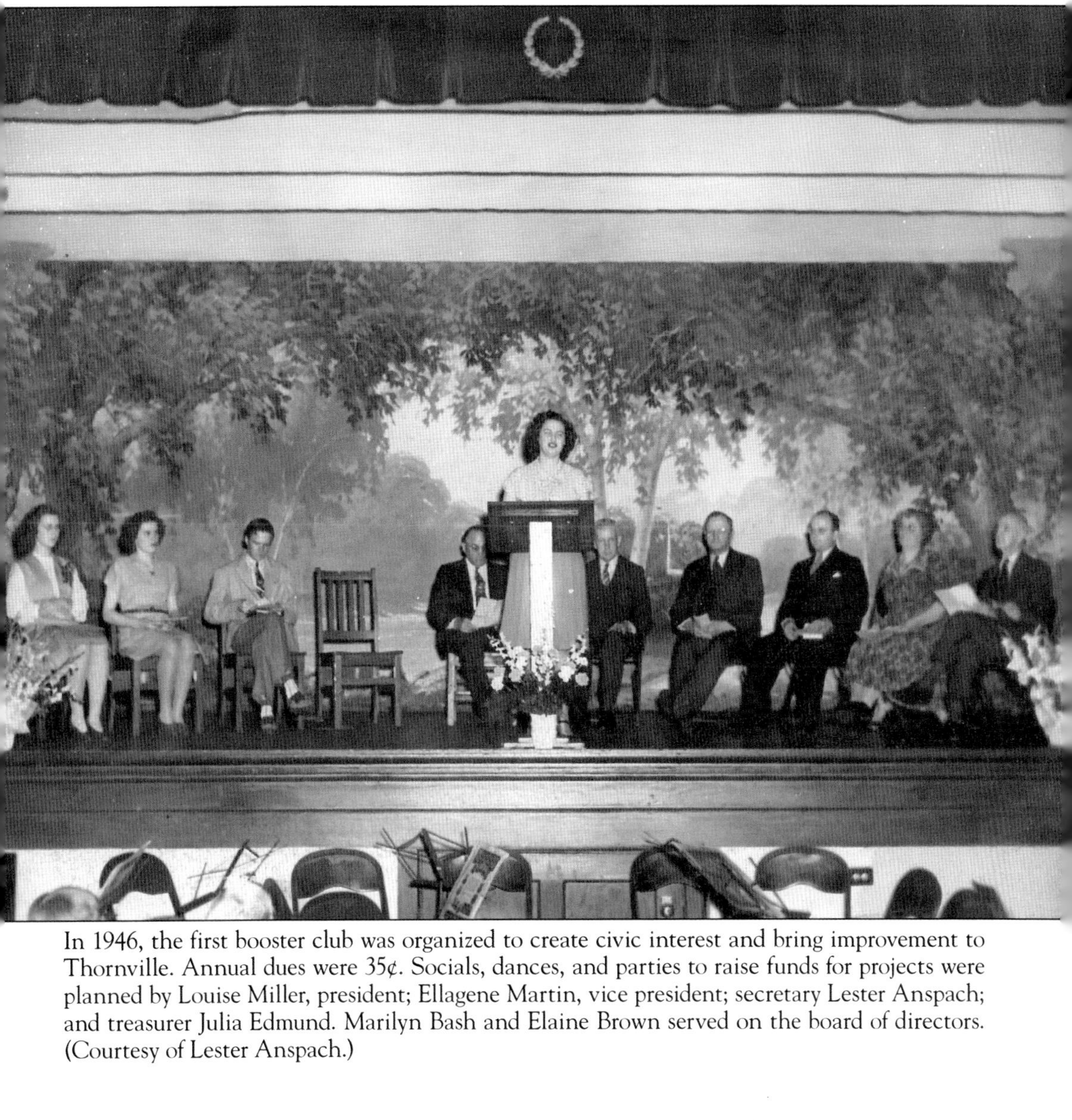

In 1946, the first booster club was organized to create civic interest and bring improvement to Thornville. Annual dues were 35¢. Socials, dances, and parties to raise funds for projects were planned by Louise Miller, president; Ellagene Martin, vice president; secretary Lester Anspach; and treasurer Julia Edmund. Marilyn Bash and Elaine Brown served on the board of directors. (Courtesy of Lester Anspach.)

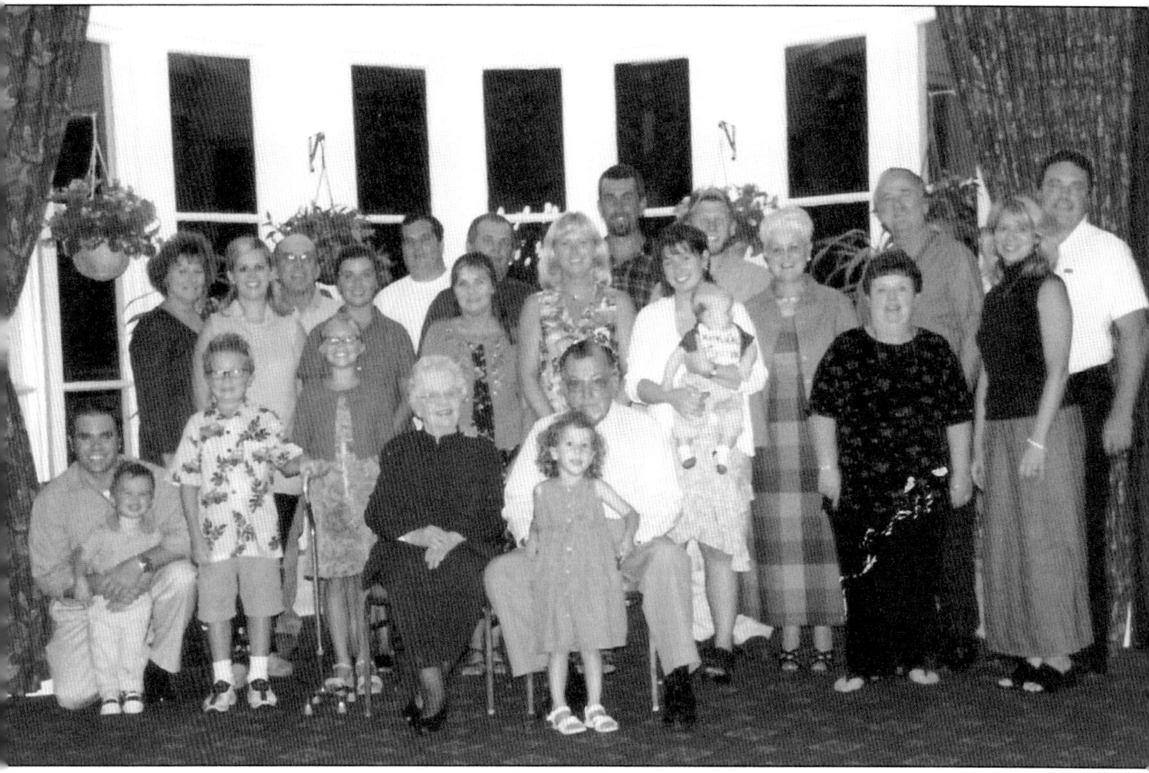

Charlie and Jean Fisher Boring were married at the Grace Lutheran Church in 1942; in 2002, they and their five children—Charlene, Robert, Richard, David, and Fred, who all live near Thornville—gathered to celebrate their 60th wedding anniversary. Jean served the community as a teacher, and both Charlie and Jean were very active in the Lions Club. (Courtesy of Charlene Roberts.)

Thornville mayor George Stevens retired in 1962 and, at 89 years of age, was the oldest mayor serving in Ohio at that time. Harry Cooper replaced him. W.A. Hite Jr. was the solicitor, and the councilmen included Lester Anspach, James Callahan, Evan Clark, Elmer Epply, and Maurice Walser. (Courtesy of Lester Anspach.)

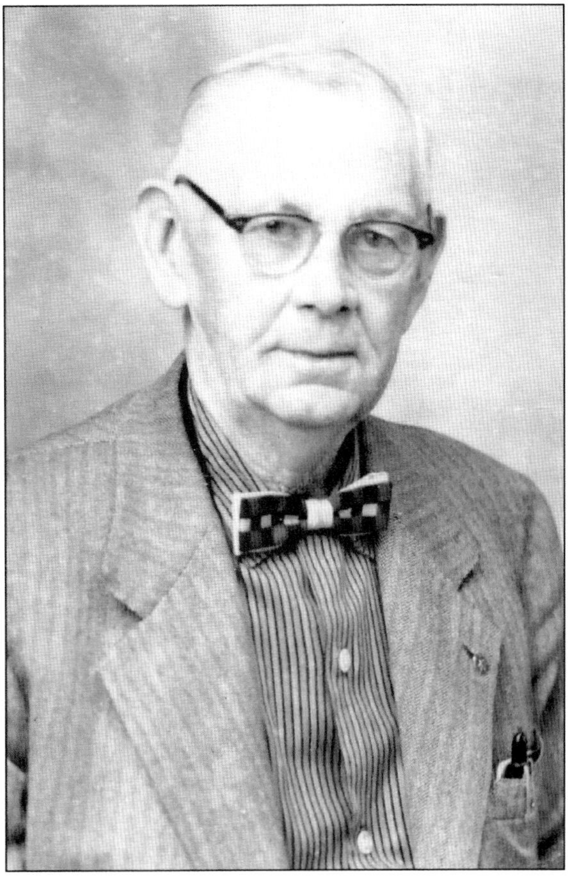

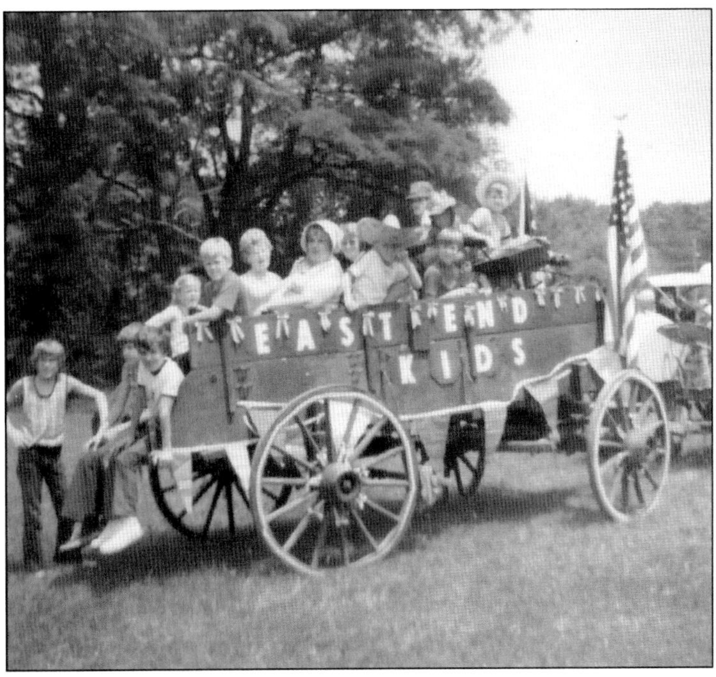

A group of East End kids ride in one of the many Thornville parades.

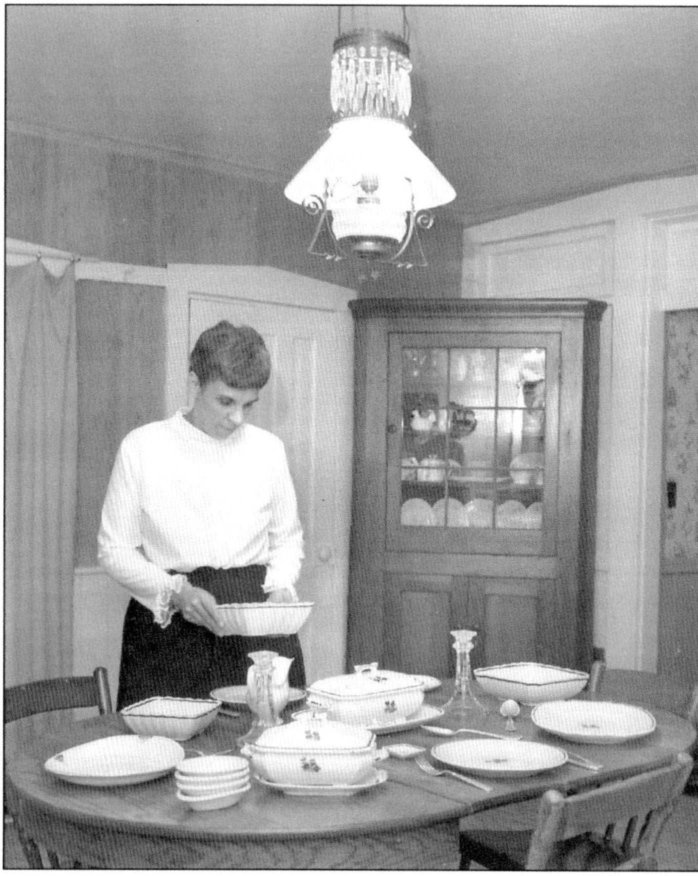

In 1969, Mary Anspach was preparing for the Thornville Tour of Homes. Mary and Lester have two daughters, Ruth and Vickey. (Courtesy of Lester Anspach.)

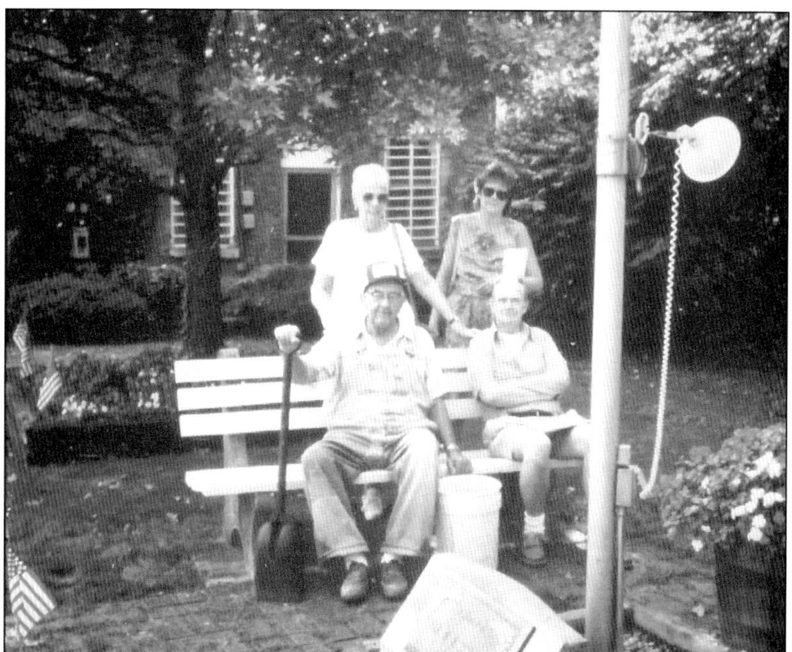

Lester and Mary Anspach (left) visit Veteran's Park in the summer of 1991 with their daughter Ruth Palmer and her husband Russel Palmer. Mary passed away in the fall of 2011. (Courtesy of Lester Anspach.)

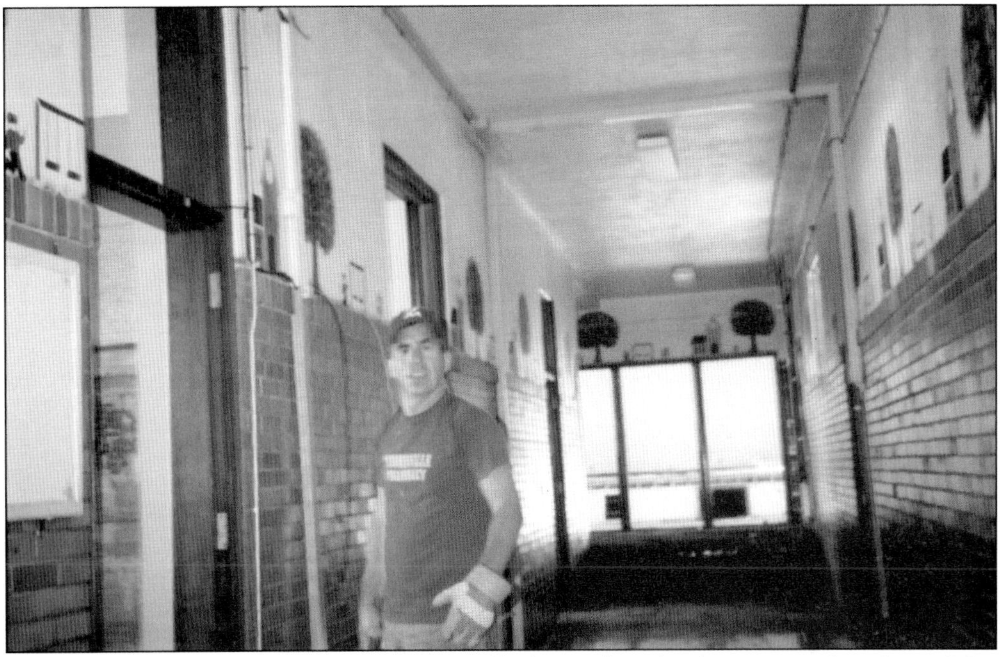

John Ulmer is standing in the hallway of the old Thornville School prior to its demolition. John retired as the Perry County extension agent and now serves as president of the Perry County Chamber of Commerce. He and his wife, Barb, who is a teacher in the Northern Local Schools, have always taken part in civic activities. (Courtesy of Helen George.)

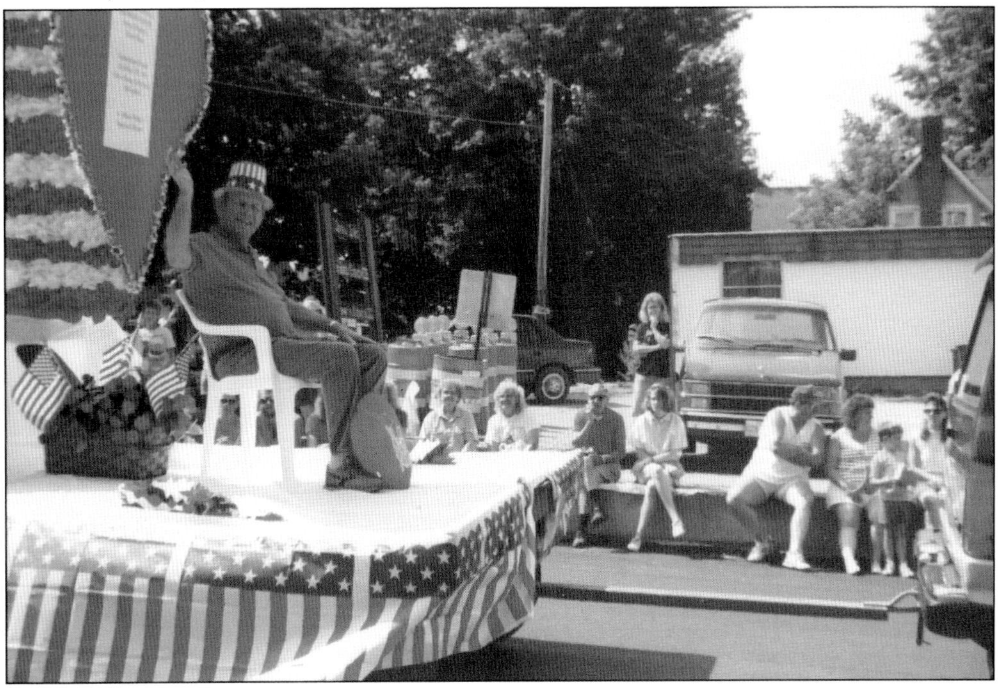

George Foster, Perry County's first heart transplant patient, was the Grand Marshal at the Thornville Fourth of July parade in 1992. His wife, Connie, has been a volunteer in the community, serving the library, school, and the Clothes Closet. (Courtesy of Connie Foster.)

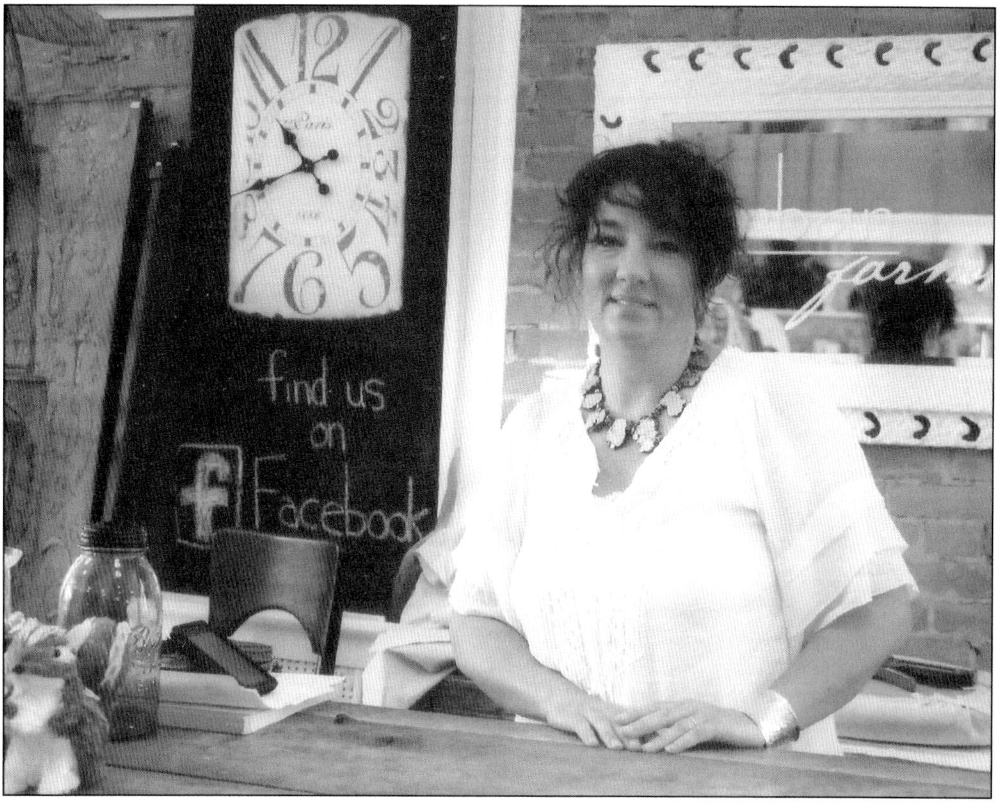

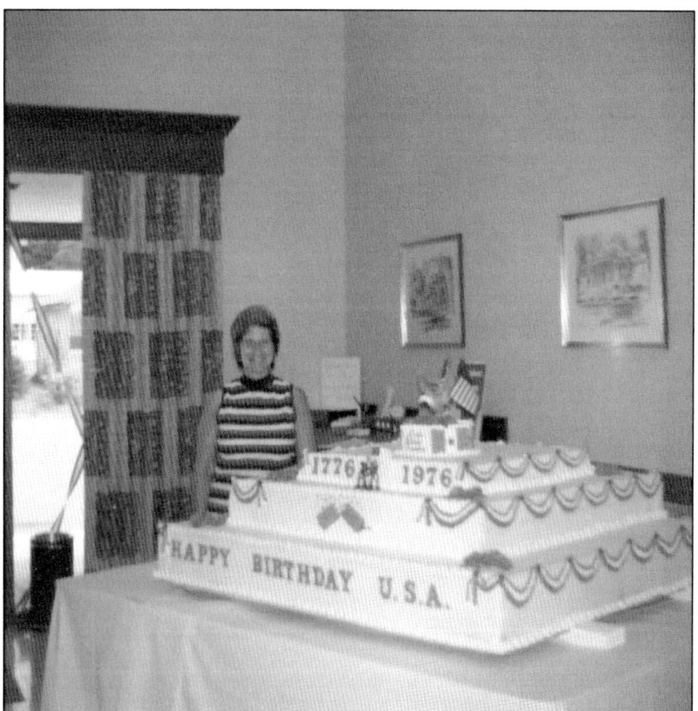

Lisa Maughmer has operated the Urban Farmhouse in the Odd Fellows building for six years. She advertises eclectic, iconic, and simple goods for the home and garden. (Courtesy of Lena K. Bowman.)

Ann Starr stands ready to cut the cake to celebrate America's birthday in 1976. Ann and husband George raised three children in Thornville. She worked in the kitchen at Thornville Elementary for years and is a great cook, according to former students. (Courtesy of Ann Starr.)

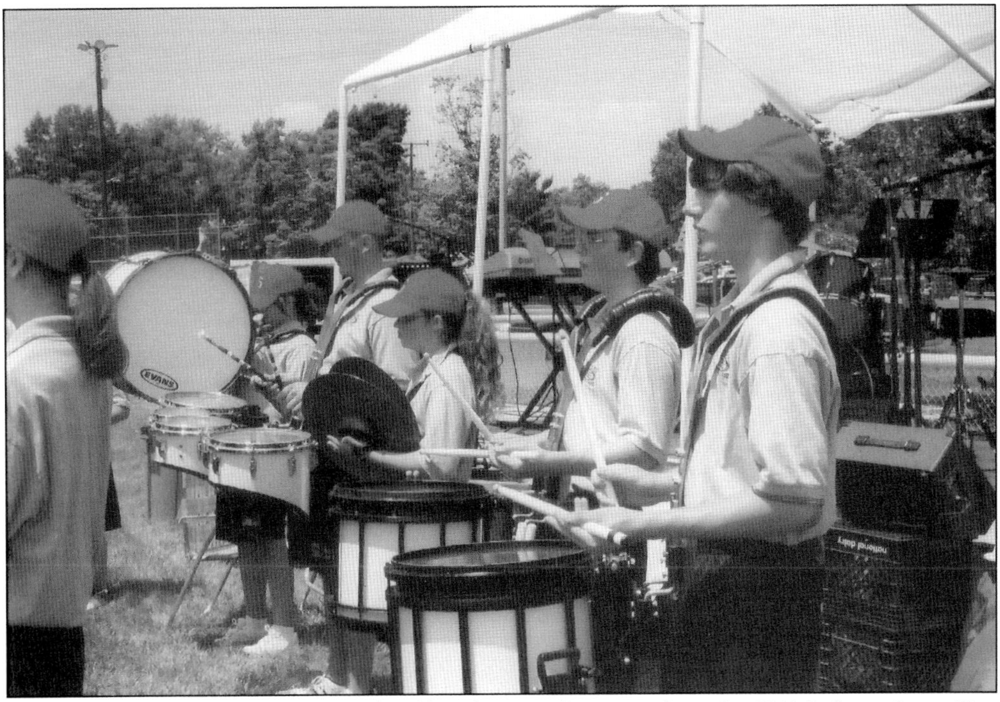

Drummers in the Sheridan High School band are ready to march in the 2011 Independence Day celebration in Thornville.

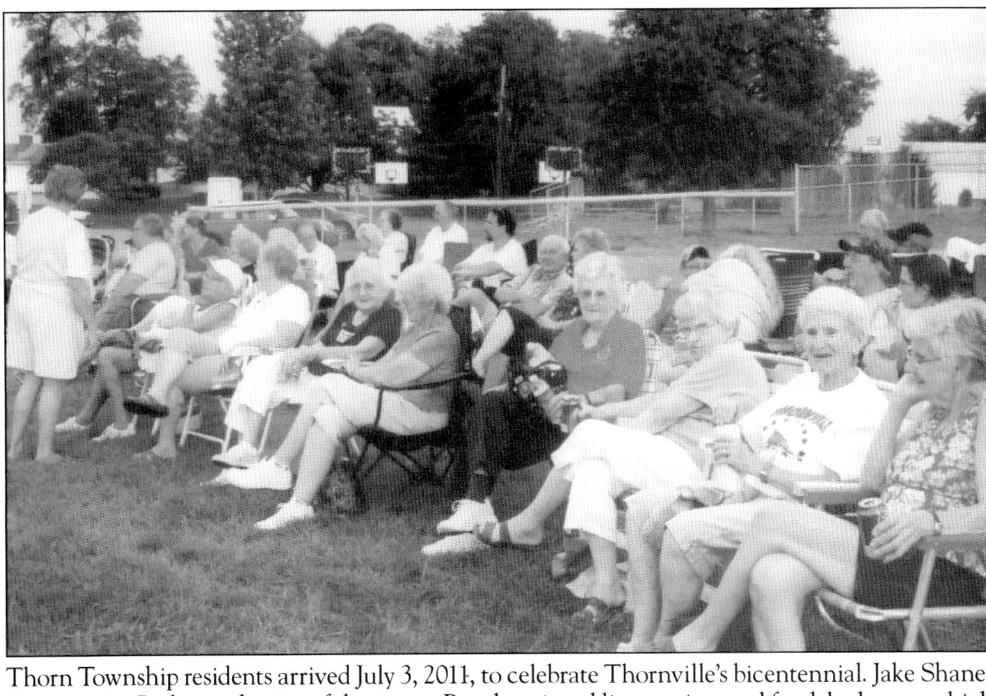

Thorn Township residents arrived July 3, 2011, to celebrate Thornville's bicentennial. Jake Shaner Community Park was the site of the event. People enjoyed live music; good food; bed races, which had also been held at the 1961 sesquicentennial celebration; and a historical slide show narrated by Luann Cooperrider at dusk.

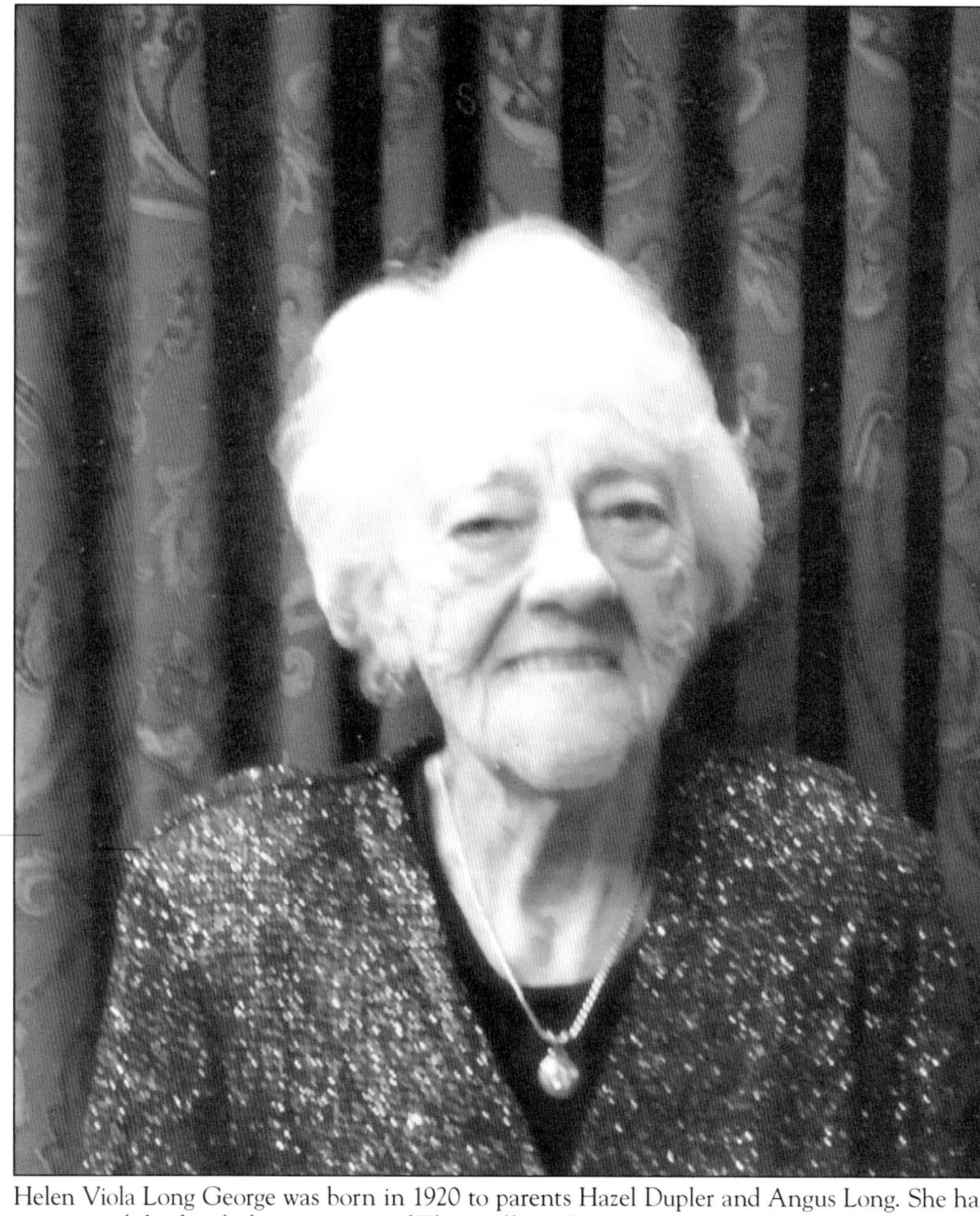

Helen Viola Long George was born in 1920 to parents Hazel Dupler and Angus Long. She has maintained the family farm just west of Thornville on Route 204 and is still actively involved in George's Repair Shop with son David. Her daughter Jane Kennedy has been employed by PNC Bank since 1968. Having resided in Thorn Township for all of her 92 years, Helen is one of the area's most prolific local historians. (Courtesy of Helen George.)

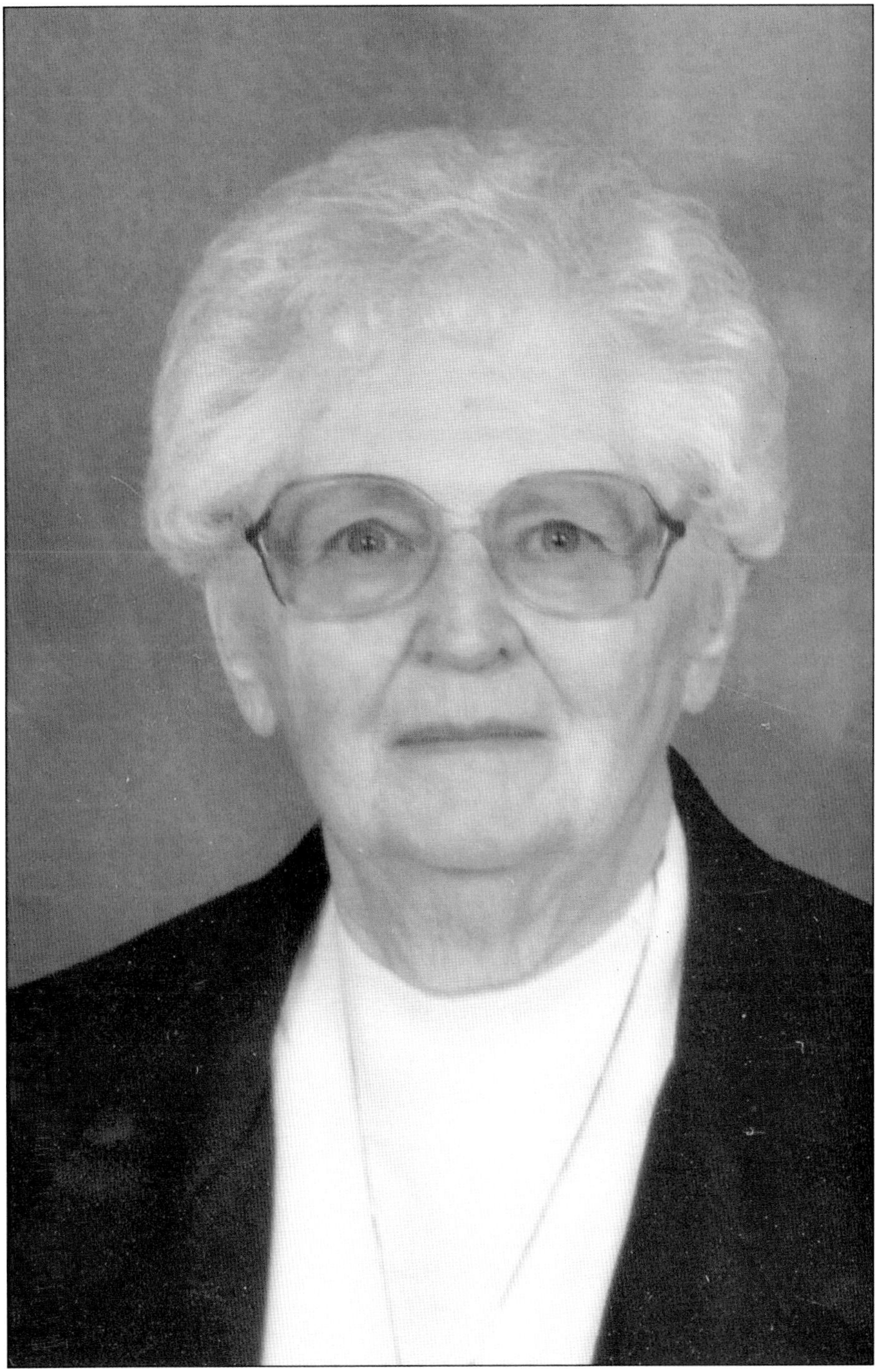

Ruth Courson White was born August 6, 1924, near Thornville. Her parents were Carl and Estelle Edmund Courson. Ruth married James "Perk" White, and they had seven children: Linda, Mike, Becky, Bill, Kaye, Nancy, and Lea. Ruth has always been civic-minded and involved in Grace Lutheran Church. She helped to organize the Girl Scouts and, having lived in Thorn Township all her life, is also one of the area's most knowledgeable historians. (Courtesy of Becky Krumlauf.)

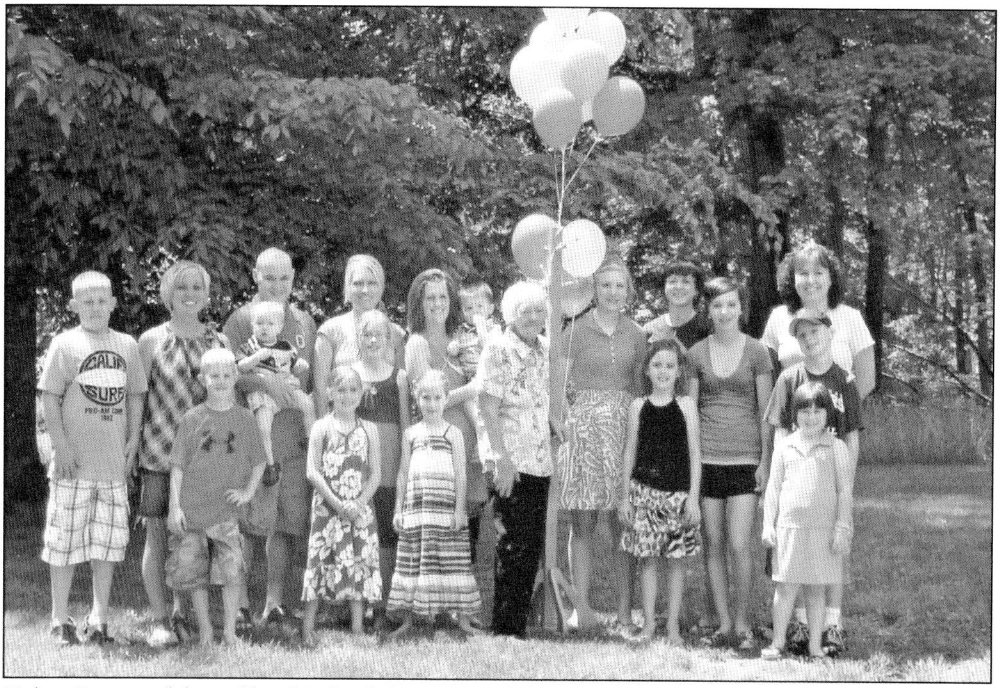

Helen George celebrated her 91st birthday surrounded by her grandchildren and great-grandchildren in 2011 at a surprise party in her honor. (Courtesy of Helen George.)

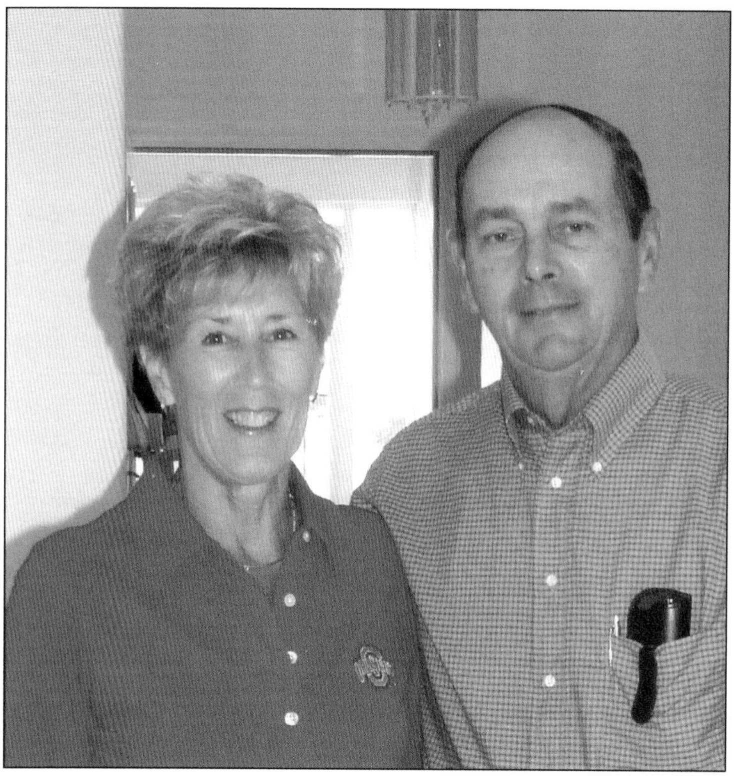

Bonnie and Gene Goldsberry, owners of Terra Health and the Athletic Zone, have also made significant contributions to the region. Gene is a former Shelly employee, and Bonnie has served as an emergency medical technician for the fire department. (Courtesy of Bonnie Goldsberry.)

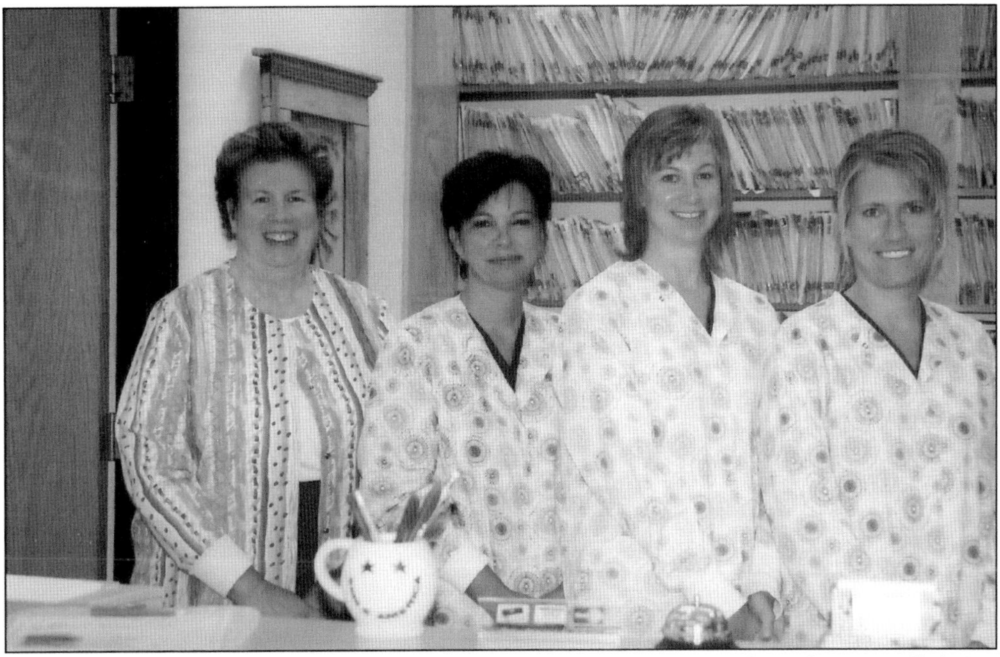

From left to right are Dr. Joy Stovcik, Julie McGlaughlin, Vickie Erwin, and Mindy McCandlish. Dr. Stovcik (or Dr. Joy, as she is affectionately called) opened her dentist office in Thornville in 1975 after graduating from Ohio State University Dental College and is the only dentist in Thorn Township. Her office is on South Main Street and located where Dr. Clemson's house once stood.

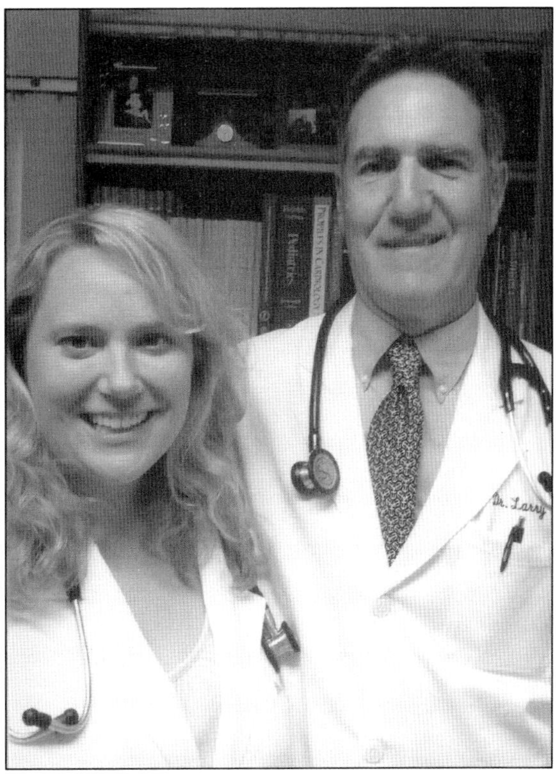

The only physicians serving Thorn Township are Dr. Larry Cowan and Dr. Shelby Raiser. Dr. Cowan has been taking care of area residents since 1984, when Mayor Oscar England asked him to leave his practice in New Lexington. Polly Walker was his first nurse. Dr. Cowan has been the team doctor for the Sheridan High School football players. Dr. Raiser joined the Thornville Family Medical Center in 2005 after graduating from Lake Erie College of Osteopathic Medicine and serving an internship and residency at Doctors Hospital in Columbus. (Courtesy of Thornville Medical Center.)

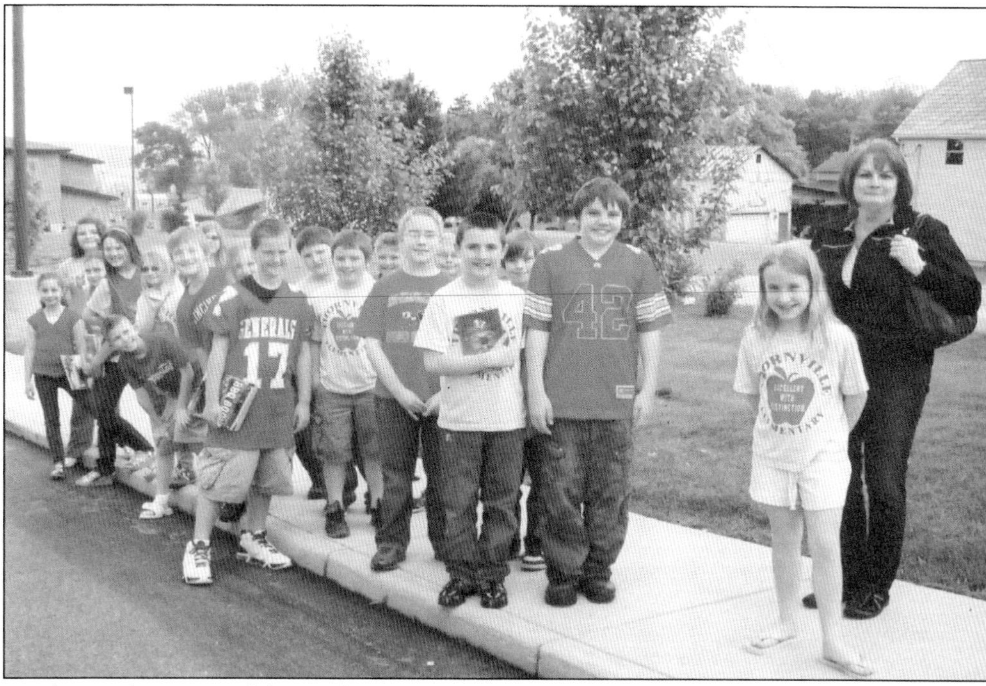

Teacher Linda Davis took her students to visit the public library during the 2011 school year. Some of the students to accompany her were Dakota Schevuront, Chance King, Jarod Ison, Austin Walker, Collin Hill, and Sammy Lockman. (Courtesy of Lena K. Bowman.)

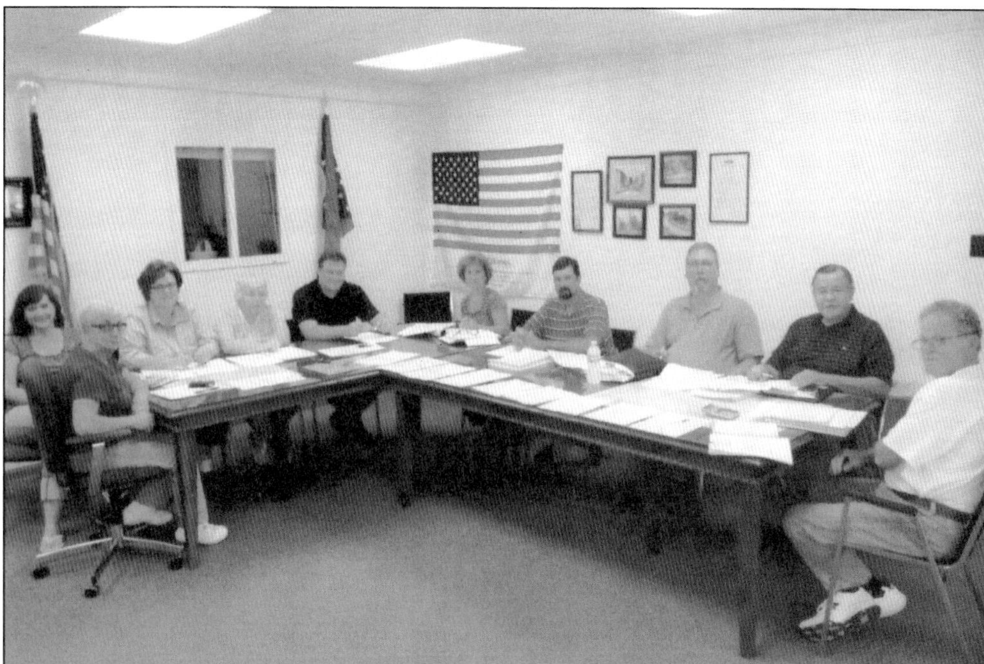

The 2011 members of Thornville's village government are, from left to right, Sandy Davis, Melissa Tremblay, Mayor Beth Patrick, Lynn Snider, Brian Dunlap, Dana Patrick, Dale Brussee, Ron Dittoe, Terry Lynn, and Ron Koehler. (Courtesy of Beth Patrick.)

Six

SCHOOLS

The first school was established in 1806 when a Lutheran minister taught the children of early settlers in a log hut that stood on the present site of the Zion Church of Christ's cemetery on Highpoint Road. Prior to 1855, the Ohio General Assembly passed an act that provided for schools in each township. There were originally 11 schools within Thorn Township. They included Vorhees, Thornville, Swamp, Prairie, Eight Square, Good, Fisher, Rosebud or Bruno, Frog Pond, Thornport, and County Line. Of these, only three remain on their original sites: Thornville, Thornport, and Bruno.

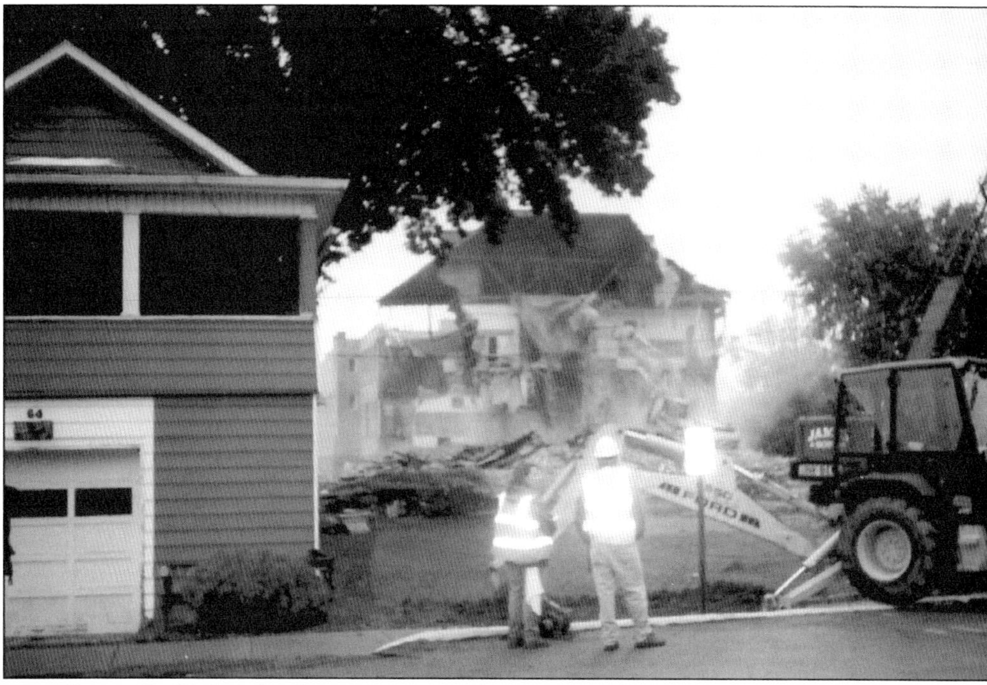

The Thornville High School comes to an end in 1960, with the last class having graduated in May. (Courtesy of Judy Cupp.)

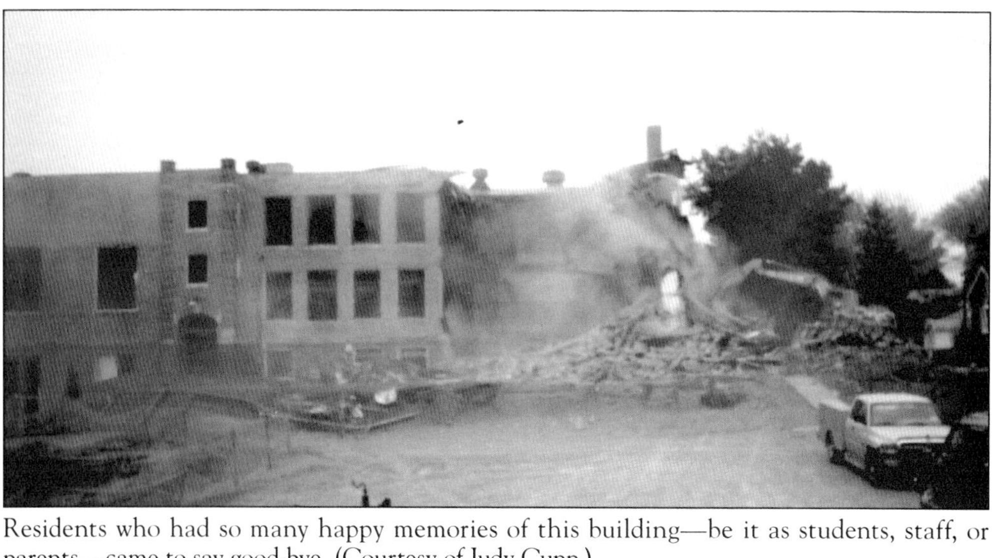

Residents who had so many happy memories of this building—be it as students, staff, or parents—came to say good-bye. (Courtesy of Judy Cupp.)

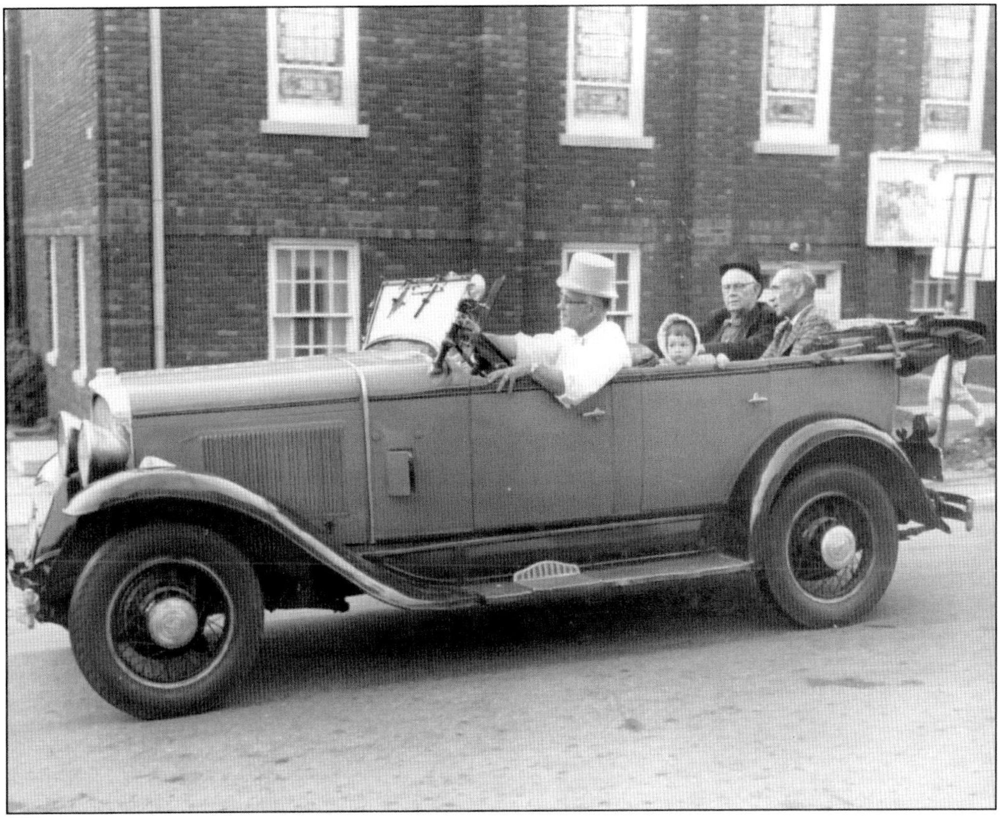

The parade marshal leads the sesquicentennial parade in 1961.

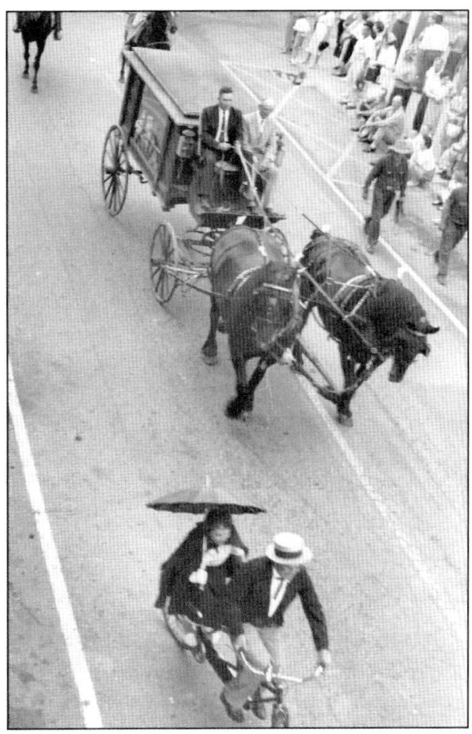

A team of horses draws a wagon through the village streets in 1961 as area residents celebrate the village's 150th birthday.

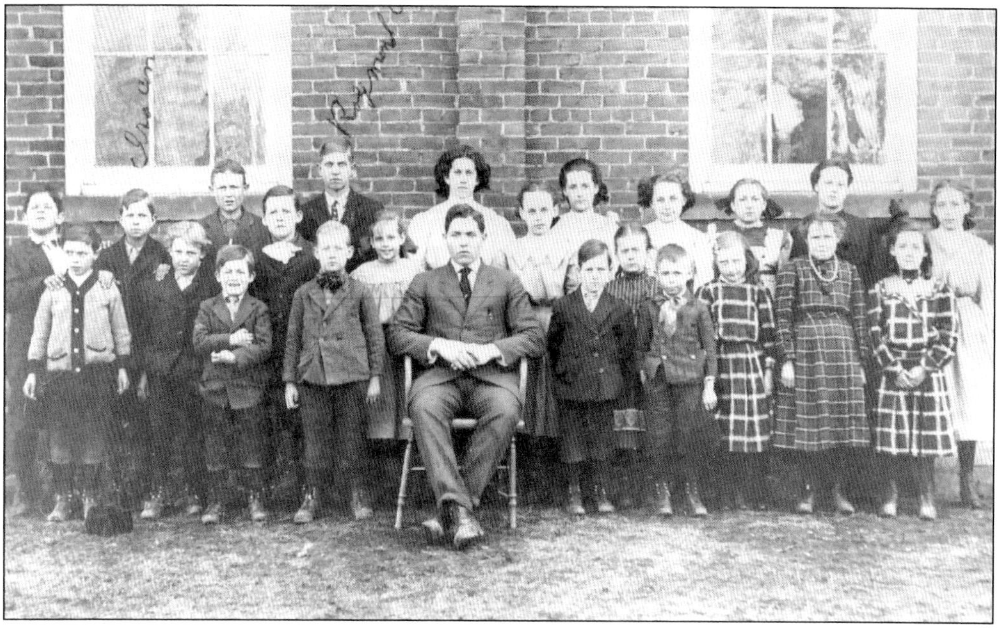

The Vorhees School was west of Thornville, about half a mile south of Route 204. The original brick building burned in February 1914 and was replaced by a frame building located closer to the corner of Routes 204 and 37. The Vorhees School was last attended in 1926. (Courtesy of Helen George.)

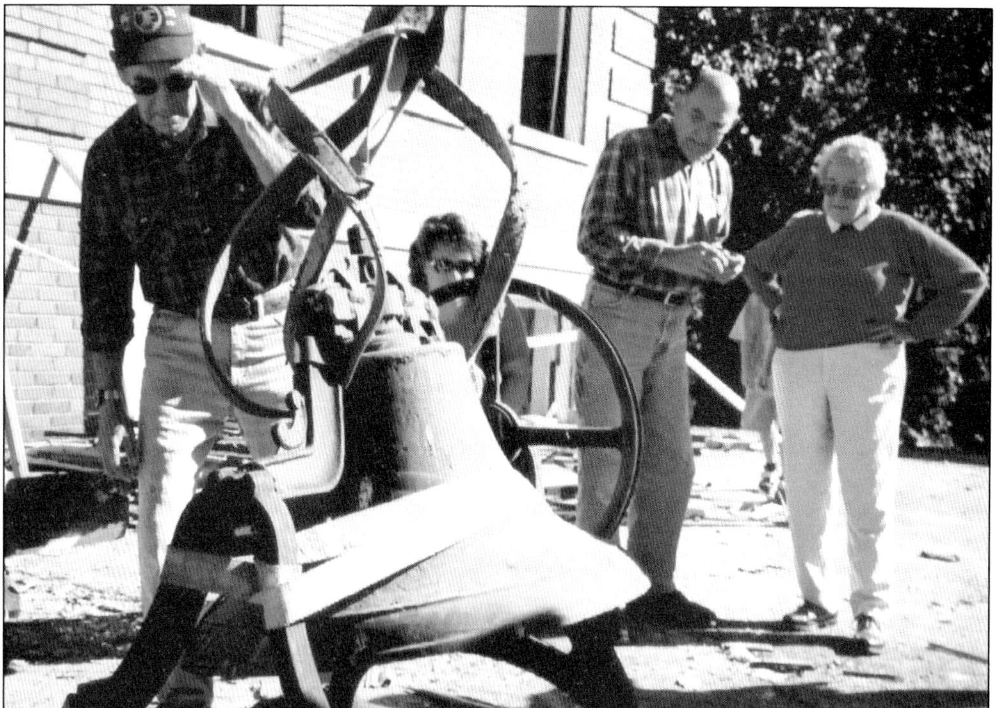

The school bell, which used to be outside Thornville High School, now greets visitors to Thornville Elementary at the Columbus Street entrance. (Courtesy of Helen George.)

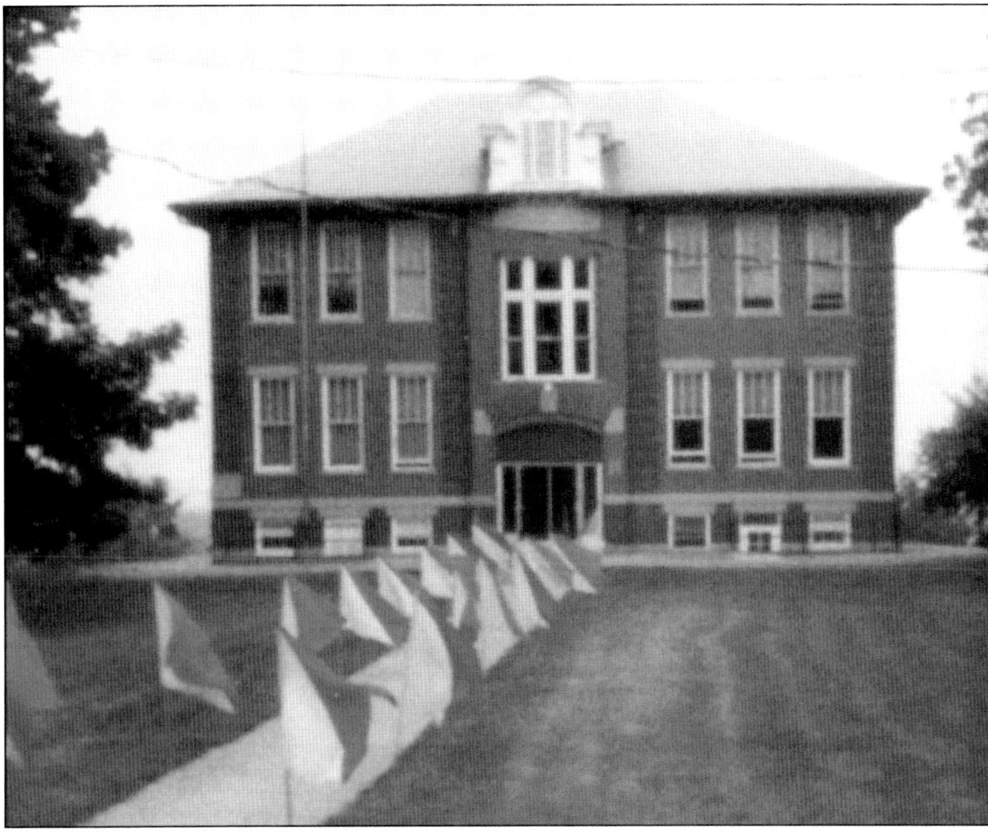

Thornville High School sat in front of the current elementary school on Columbus Street. The last class graduated in 1960. (Courtesy of Lester Anspach.)

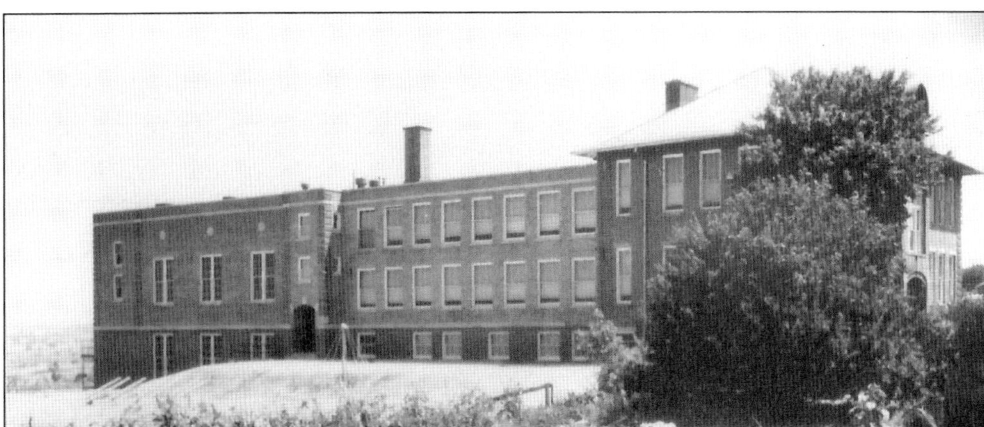

The expansion in 1928 added rooms for home economics and agriculture, a gymnasium with shower facilities, a stage and auditorium, and much-needed restrooms. (Courtesy of Lester Anspach.)

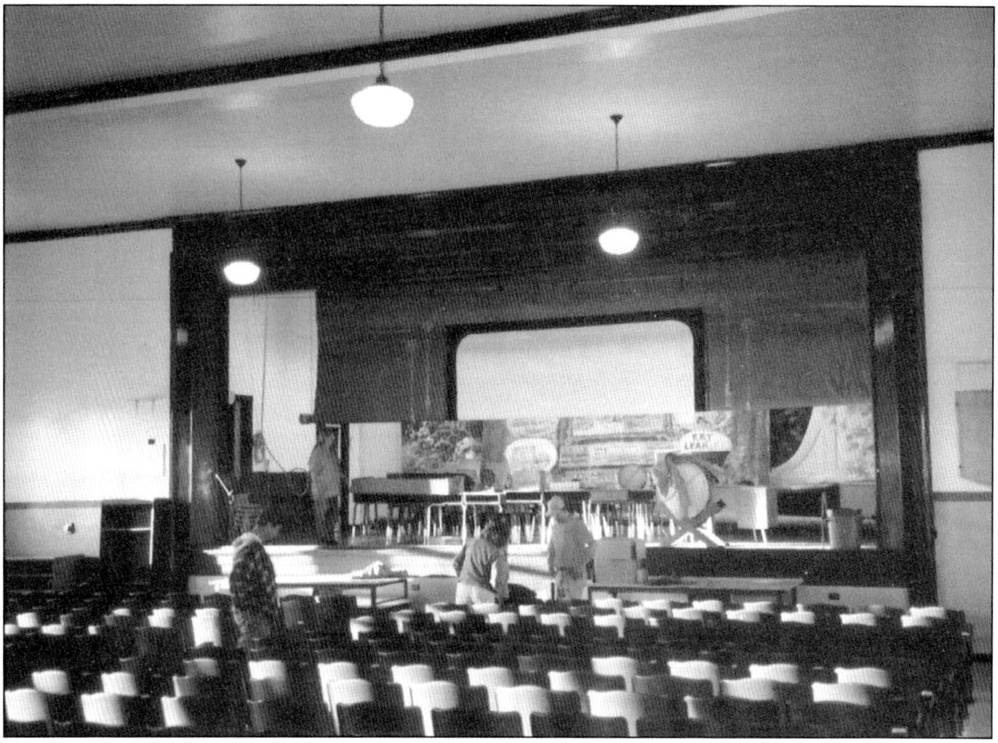

The stage and auditorium in the old Thornville school were used for community and school events. In 1935, Harpster & Zollinger, the local Ford dealer, invited residents to watch "Free Talking Pictures" in the auditorium. *Rhapsody in Steel*, *Ford and a Century of Progress*, and a scene from an upcoming world's fair film were shown. (Courtesy of Thelma Crader.)

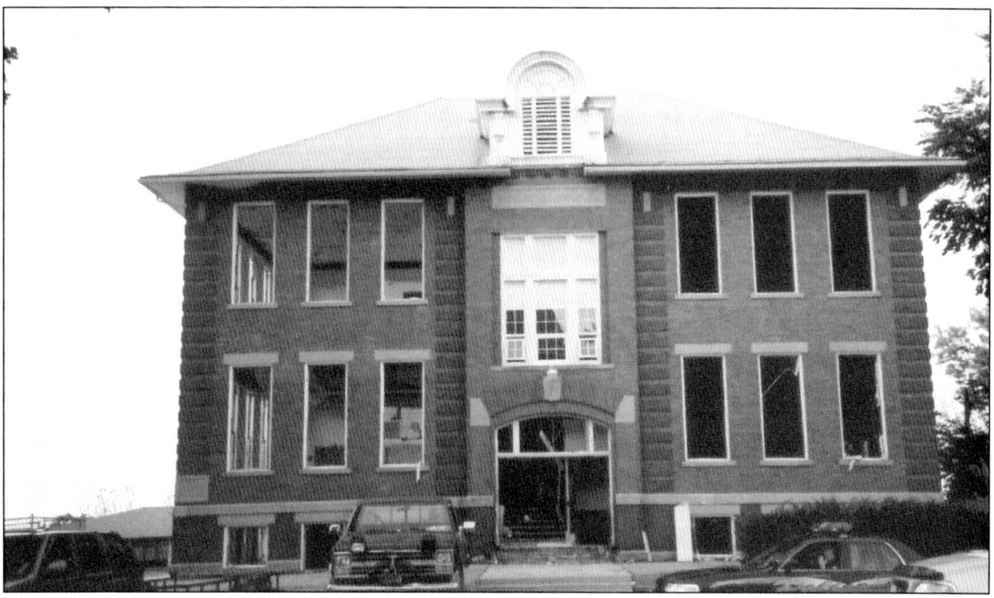

In 1960, this was the last day the old Thornville School would stand along Columbus Street. The windows and doors had already been removed for demolition. In the fall, elementary students would enter a brand-new building. (Courtesy of Helen George.)

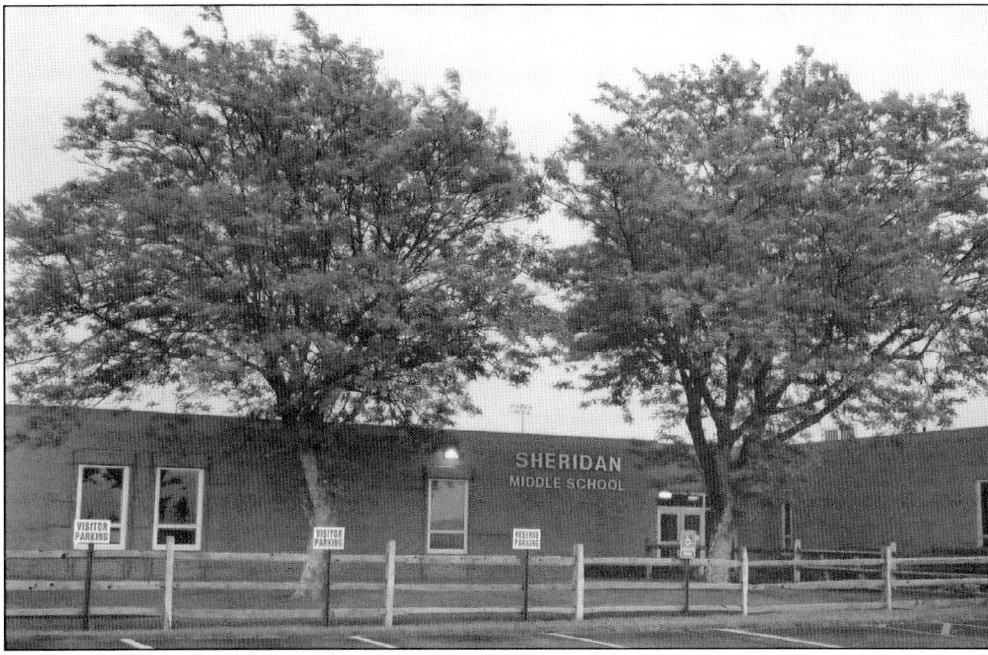

The current Sheridan Middle School, built in 1960, is on Sheridan Drive halfway between Thornville and Somerset. It served as the high school for Northern Local Schools until 2005.

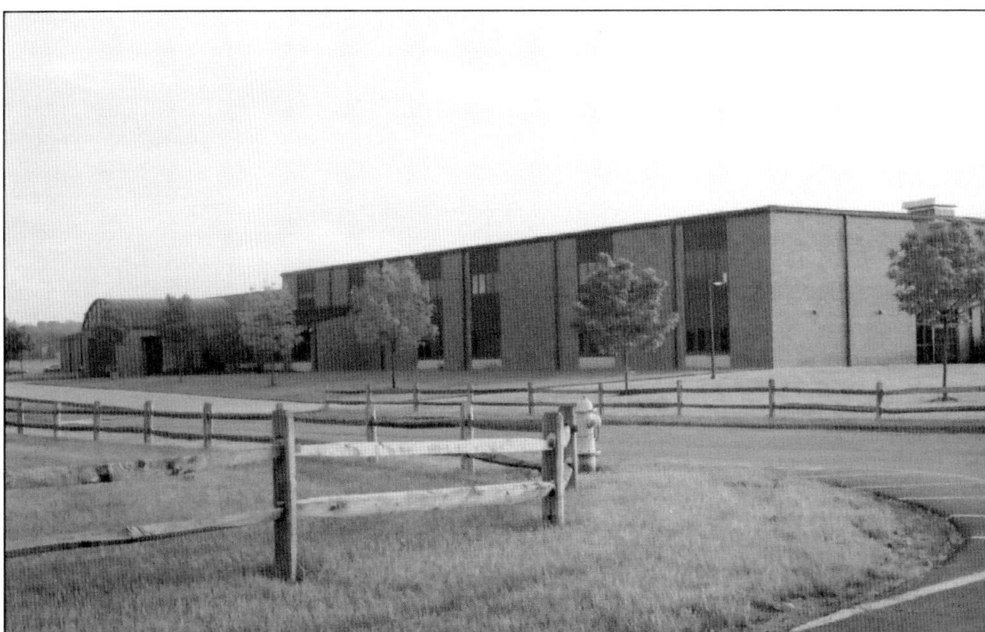
Sheridan High School, named for Somerset's Gen. Phillip Sheridan, sits across the road from the middle school. It was constructed in 2005.

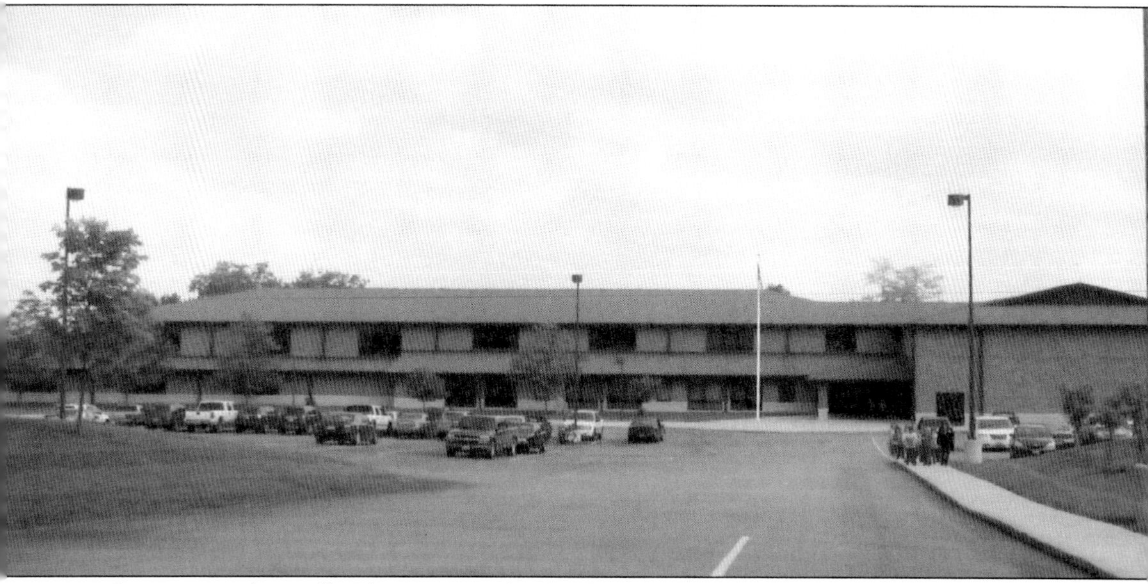

The current Thornville Elementary School, which houses kindergarten through fifth grades, welcomes students along Columbus Street.

Seven

TODAY AND TOMORROW

Life is a continuum of change, and certainly, here in Thorn Township, Perry County, Ohio, there is no exception. Buildings will be replaced with new and better ones. People will move away, and others will move into the township. In a few years, the schools will again need to be updated and improved. Businesses will close, and new ones will begin. People can always look back and see the way it used to be, but residents must now look forward and consider what it might be like tomorrow.

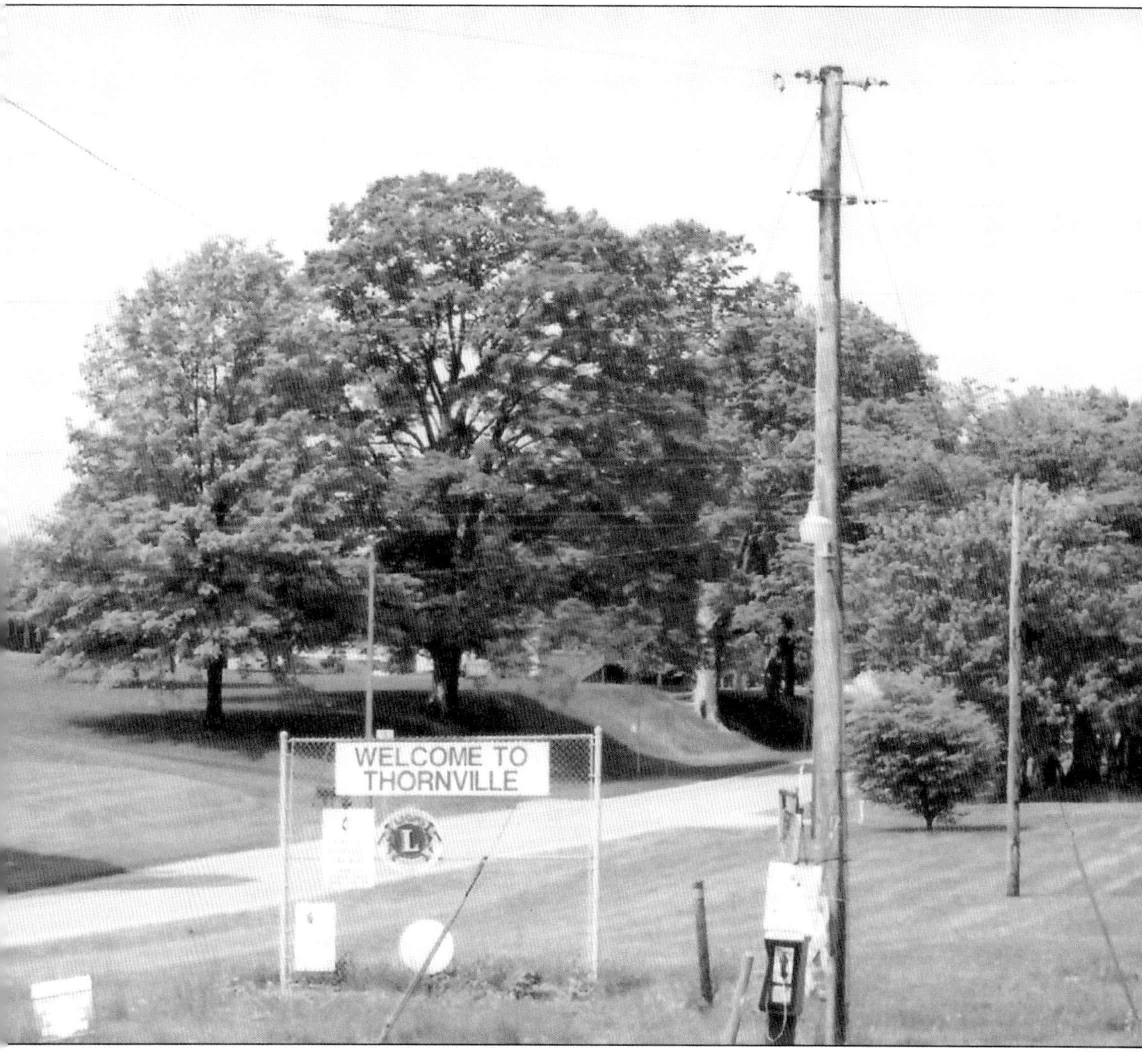

The Thornville Lions Club was organized in 1951 and has been involved with area activities ever since. Early events included Labor Day horse shows and fundraising events to benefit families in need, the high school band, vision screenings for students, and park improvements, including the baseball field, picnic area, bleachers, restrooms, and swimming pool. Following the recent 2011 tornado in the Plains, members passed out Kroger gift cards to those victims. Currently, they sponsor the Thornville Country Fair held every October in downtown Thornville.

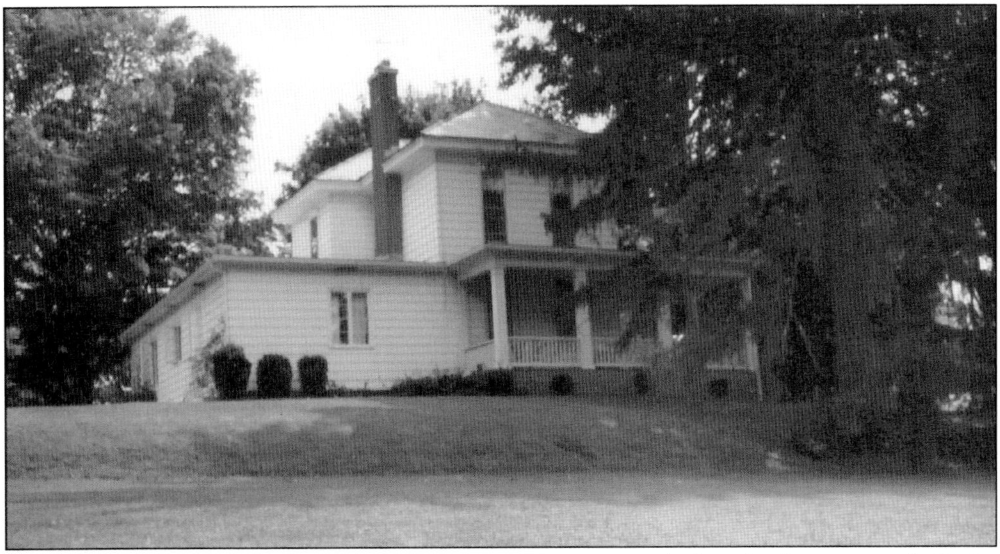

The local library has had at least three homes over the years, including the former town hall, the present town hall, and its current location at 99 East Church Street, the former Wilson-Chen house. C.V. Clum was president of the local library committee and gave financial assistance, as well as a collection of books. Harry Hite was also a benefactor.

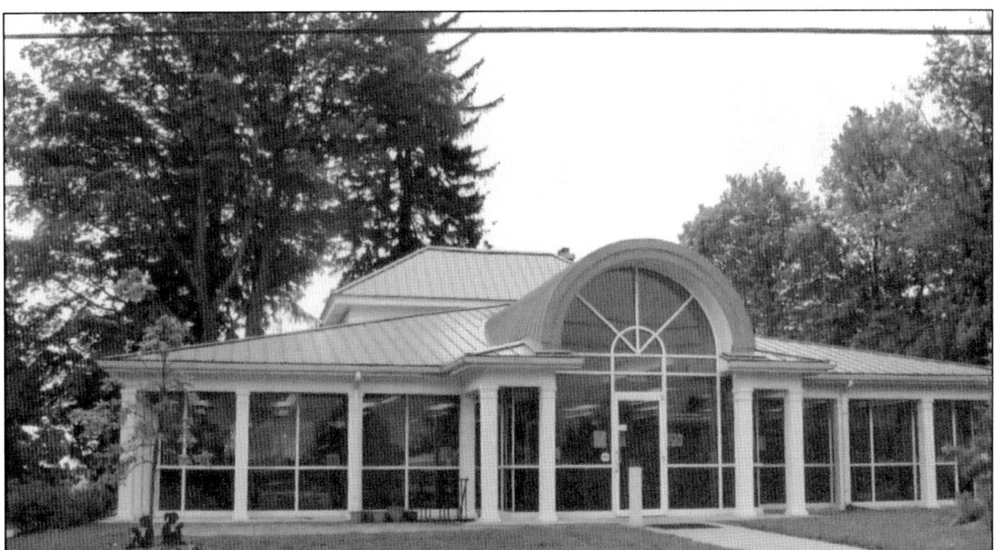

The rear view of the library welcomes visitors from the parking lot. In 2001, Thornville elementary students lined the street between the town hall and the new library and passed books from one to another until they were all safely shelved in the new library. The branch librarian is Sharon Chaffin.

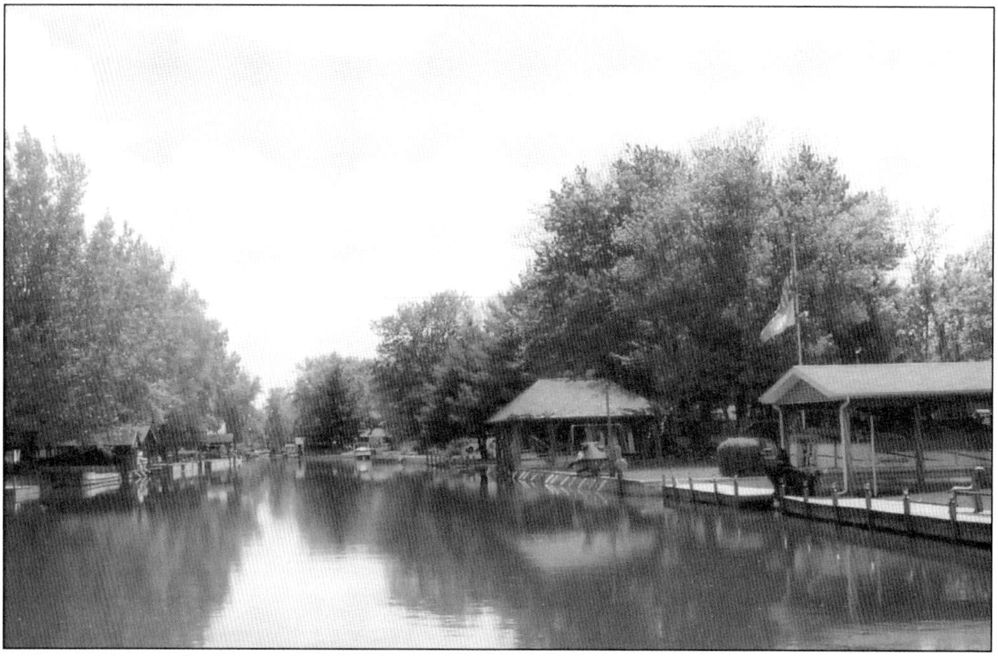

Many residents of Thorn Township live along the canals on the south shore of Buckeye Lake. While many people live year-round, some also have permanent homes elsewhere and spend their weekends and vacations enjoying the lake atmosphere.

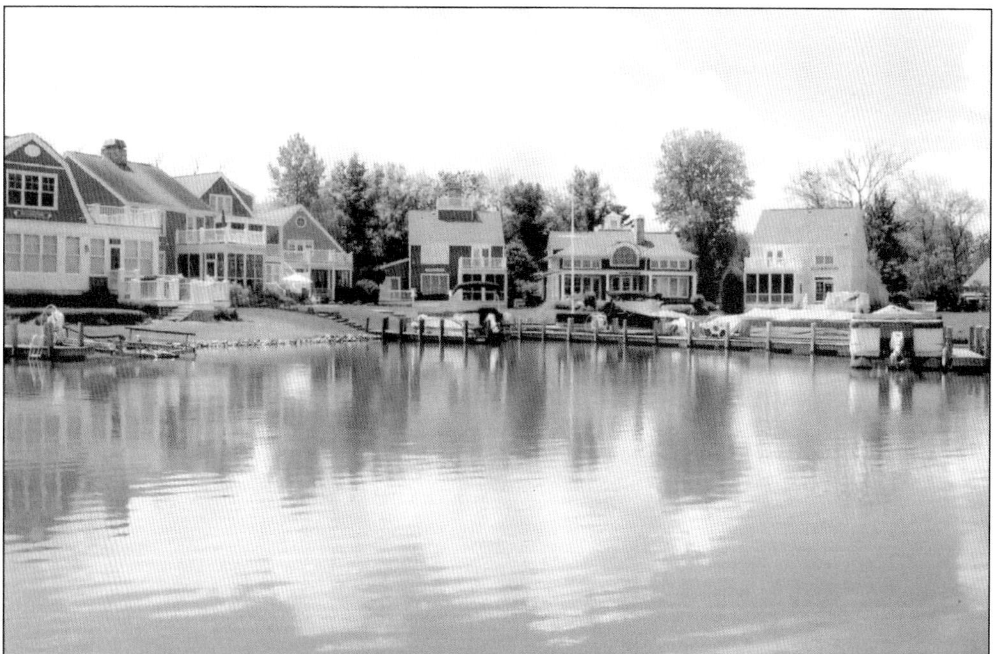

Most homes in Heron Bay were built to resemble New England architecture. The area is made up of bays, walking trails, and beautiful landscapes.

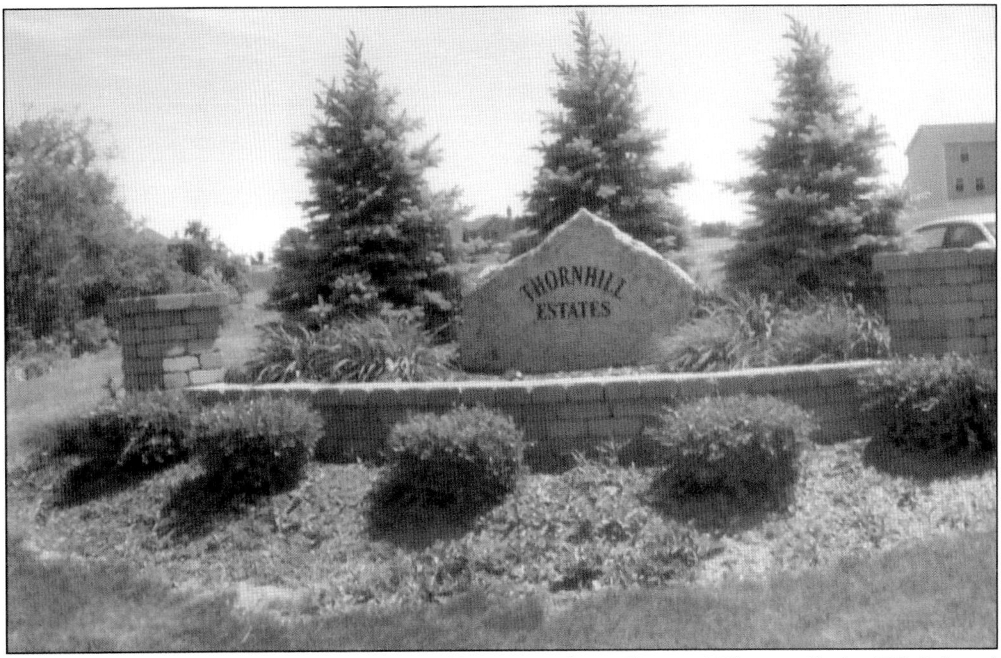

Thornhill Estates was a new housing addition to the village of Thornville by TDC Land Development in 2002.

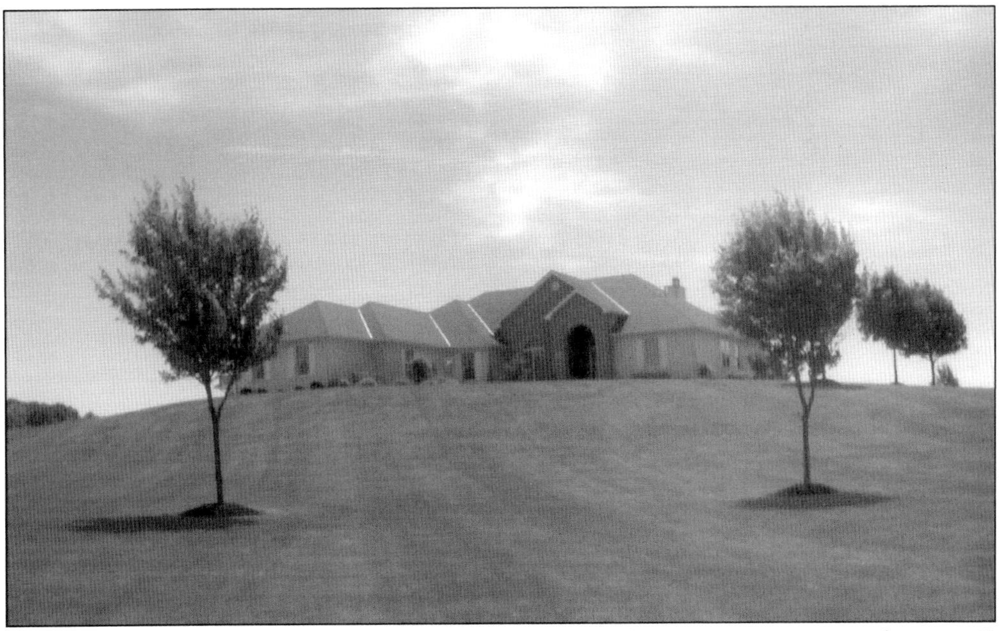
Homes were built on the knolls overlooking Bruno Road and Route 188. At present, there are 42 homes located there. (Courtesy of Thelma Crader.)

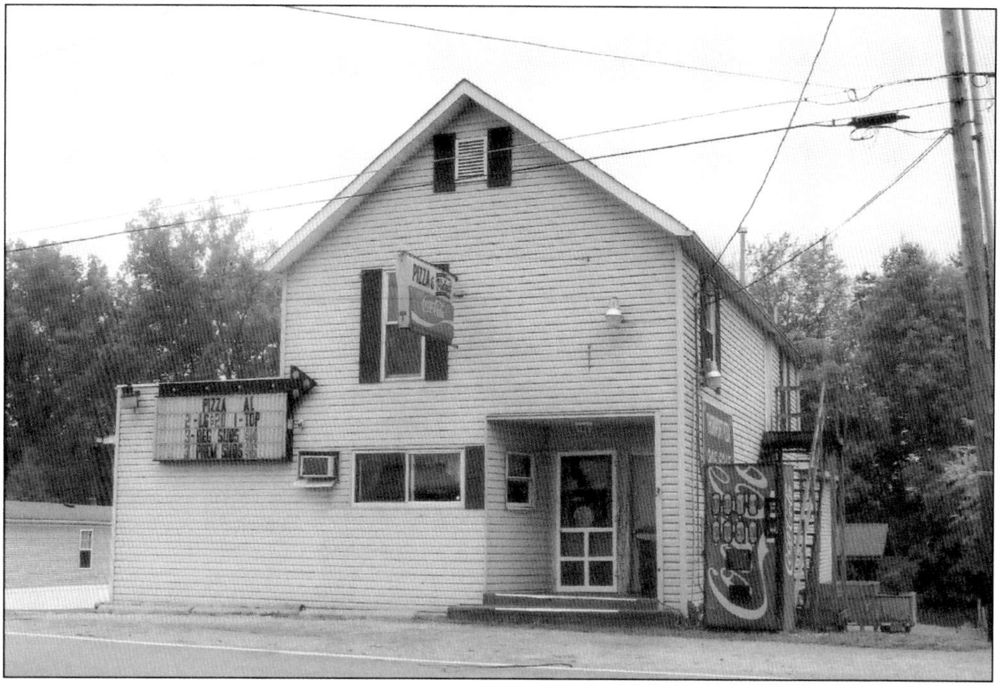

For many years, Bosen's General Store served the residents of Thornport; today, this building is the home of Thornport Pizza.

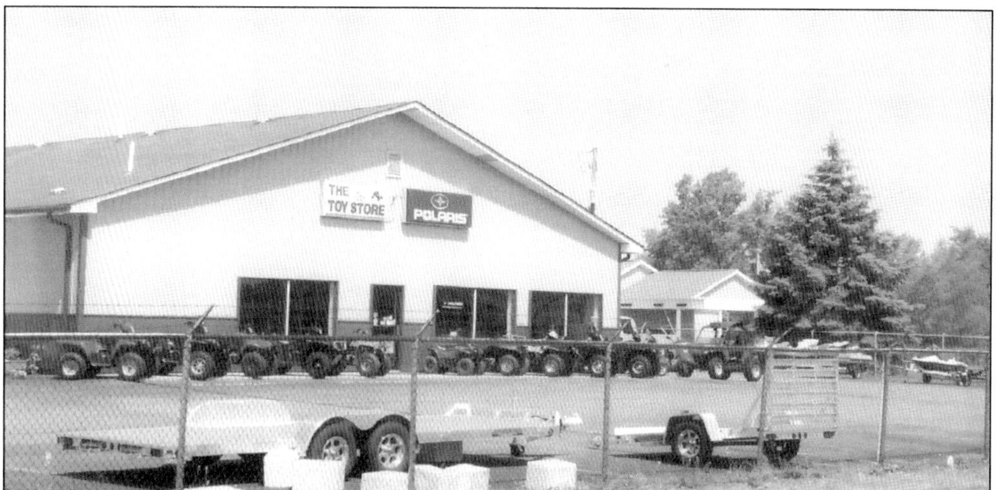

The Toy Store, once the Sand Castle Marine, is located on Route 13 in Thornport. Owner Frank Correll sells boating items, trailers, and off-road vehicles.

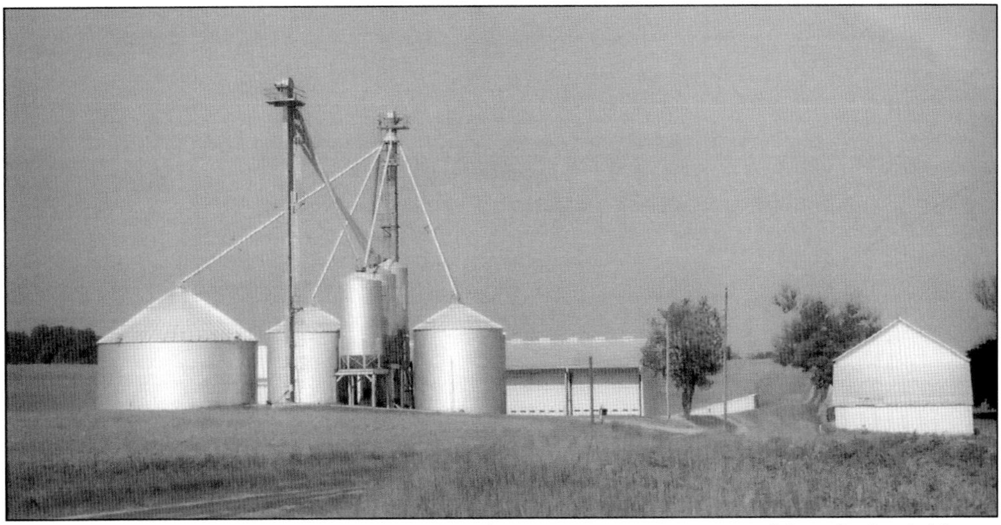

Thorn Township has remained as agricultural as it was 100 years ago, although the fields are much larger now, with corn and soybeans being trucked to granaries. Hearty yields have been created with improved mechanization, seed development, and better methods of fertilization and crop rotation.

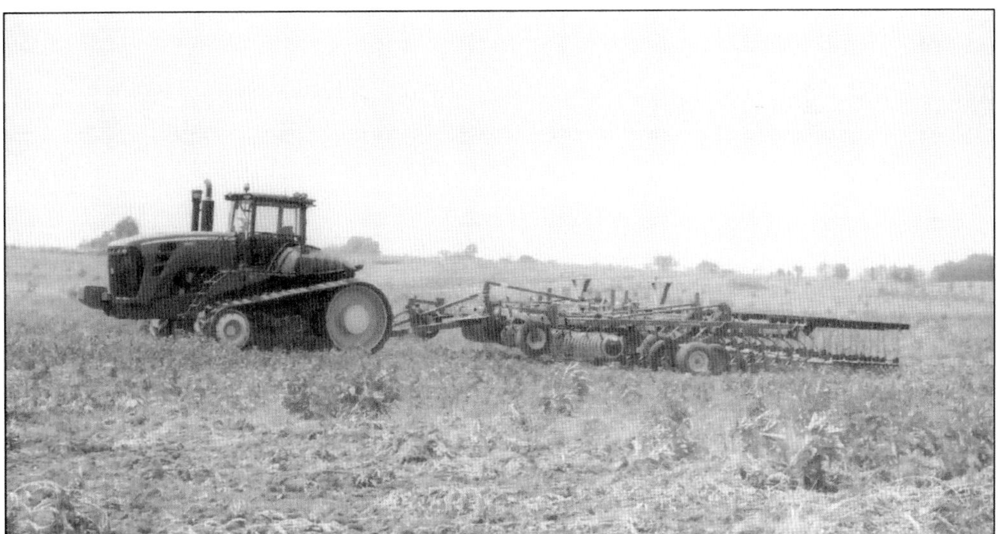

Planting, fertilization, and harvesting are done with air-conditioned diesel tractors rather than horses and plows. Many of the barns and outbuildings in the township have been torn down. Fencing, unless needed for livestock, is not seen anymore.

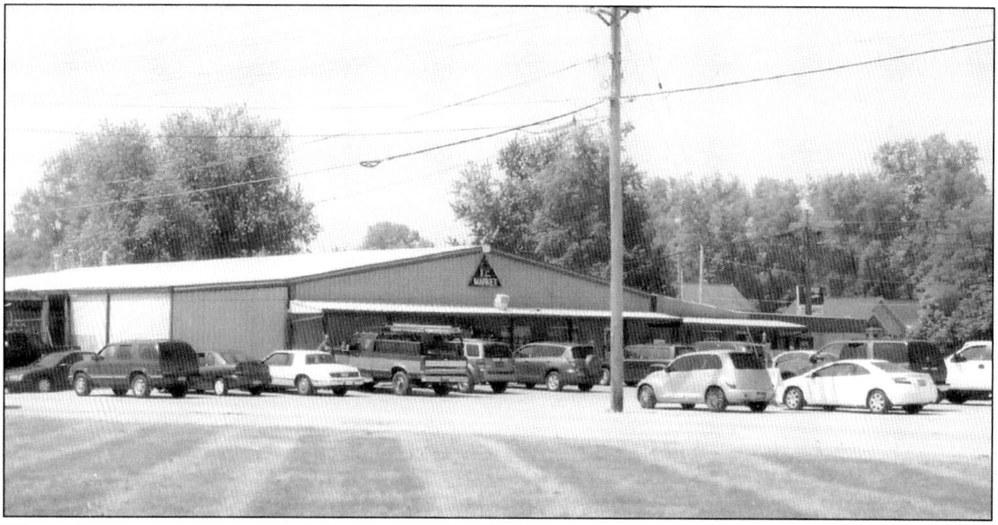

The only grocery store in Thorn Township is T.C.'s Market, owned by Tim Cotterman, in Thornport. The area was once a sawmill, a blacksmith shop, Tom's Union 76, and Hat's Gulf Station. An icehouse used to sit behind the store.

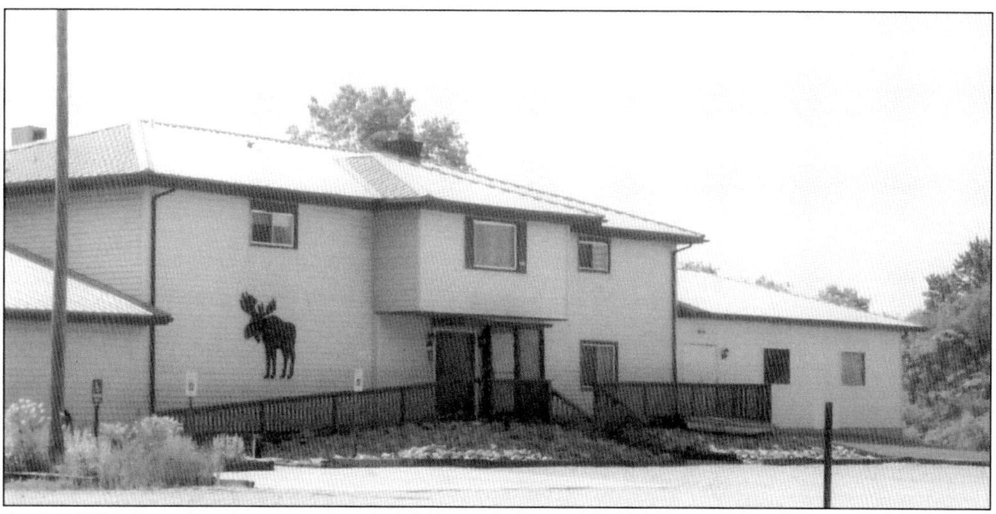

At 8985 Blackbird Lane near Thornport is the Buckeye Lake Moose Lodge. One of its primary service projects is the Special Olympics.

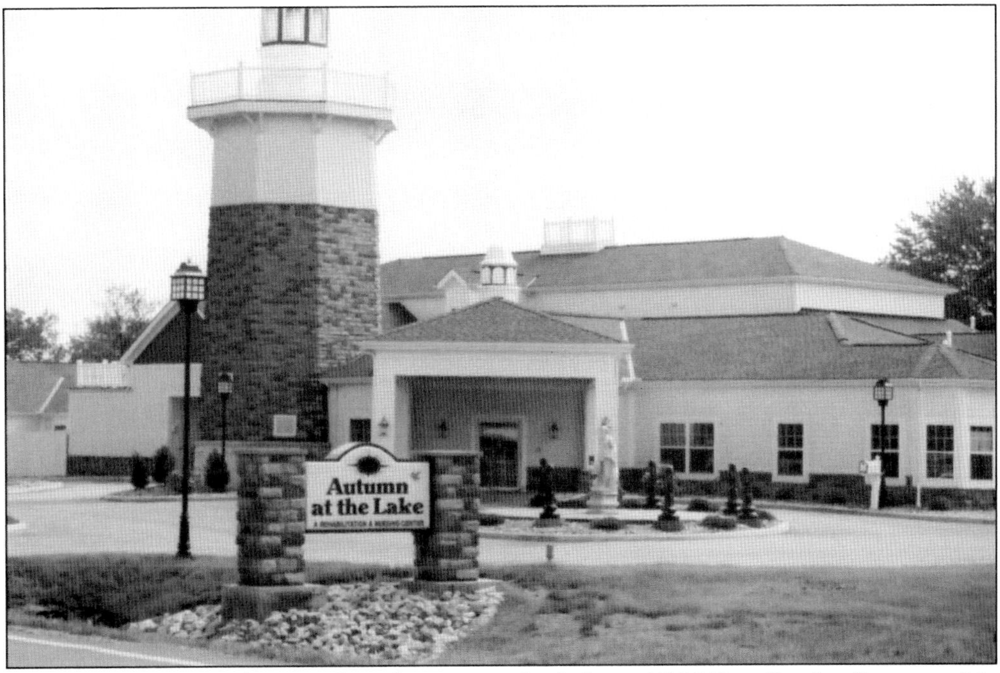

A recent addition to the township, Autumn at the Lake at 14100 Zion Road, offers township residents skilled nursing care, assisted living facilities, and a rehabilitation center.

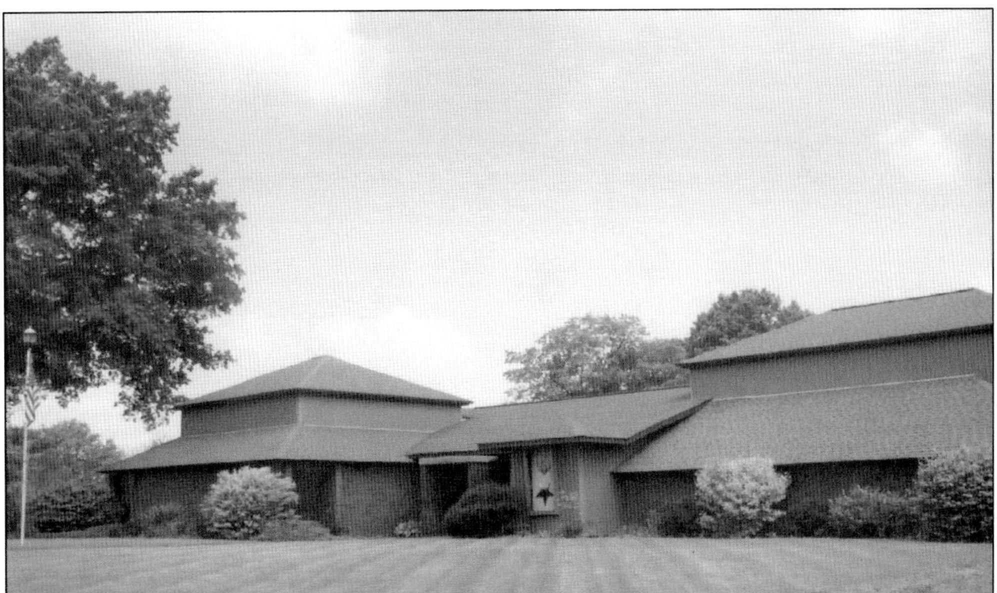

Harry L. Hite bequeathed his estate to various village organizations. The Masons used their share to build this new location at 44 East Columbus Street, which they share with the Eastern Star.

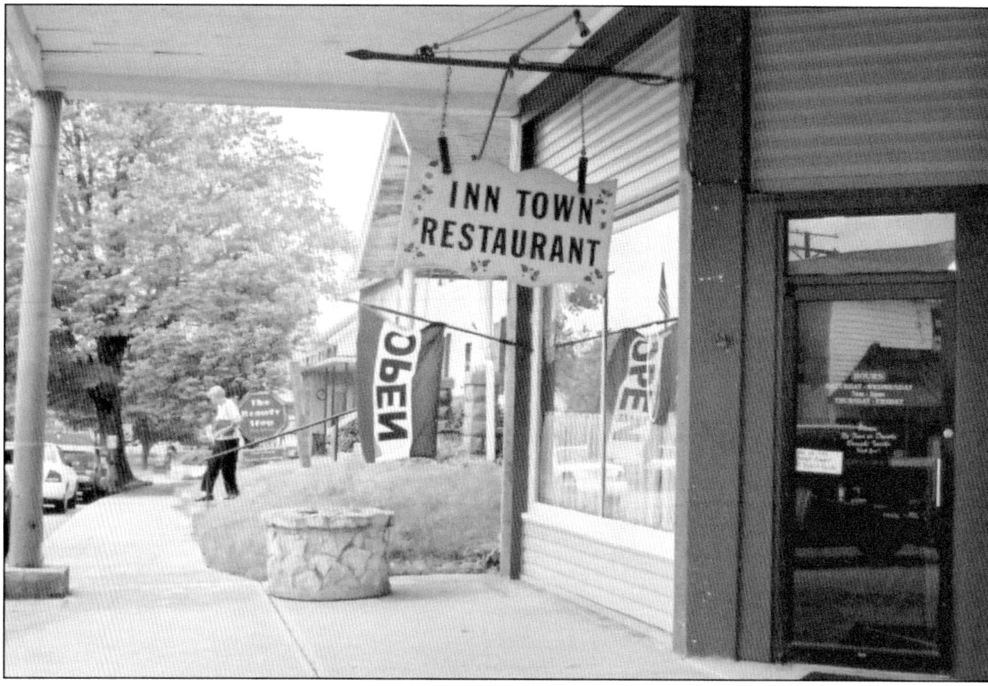

Formerly Buxton's Grocery and ice cream parlor and Inn Town Restaurant, this building just recently became the home of the Thornville Restaurant.

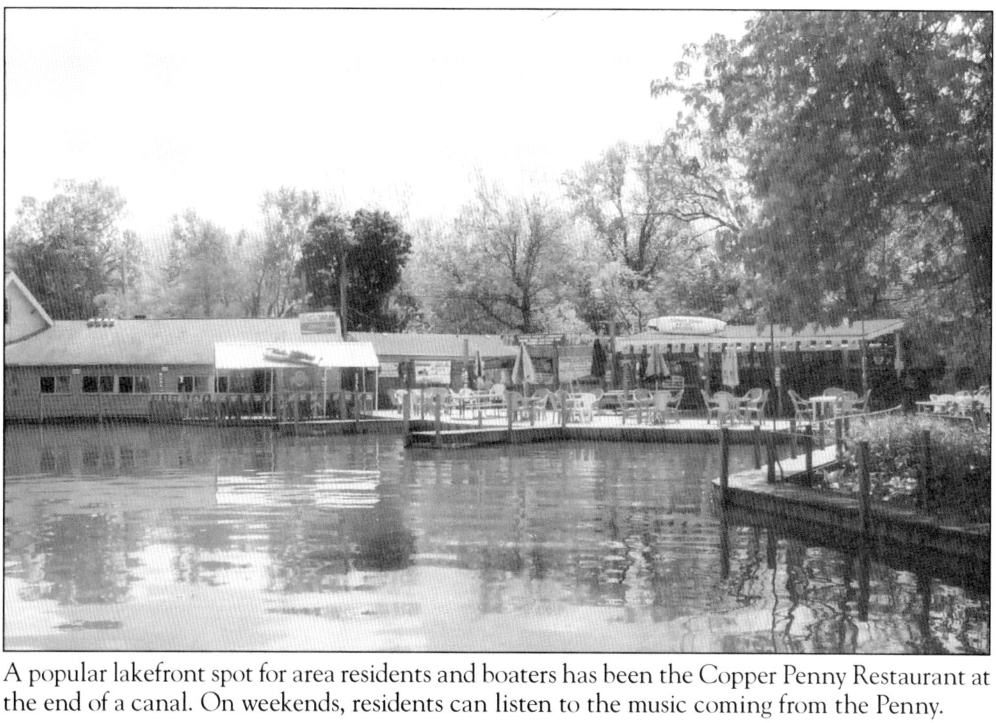

A popular lakefront spot for area residents and boaters has been the Copper Penny Restaurant at the end of a canal. On weekends, residents can listen to the music coming from the Penny.

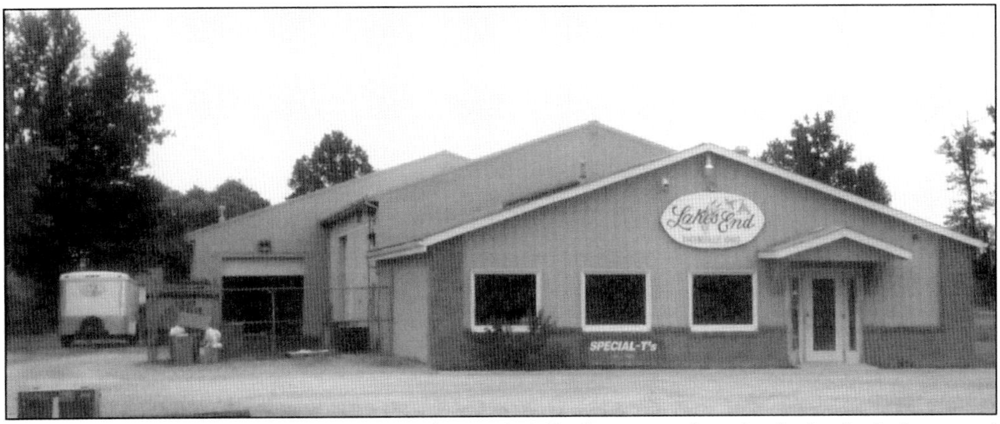

The only clothing store in Thorn Township, Lake's End, is a retail outlet for both clothing and shoes. It is located at the Licking-Perry county line and has been operated by Steve Dornon since 1988.

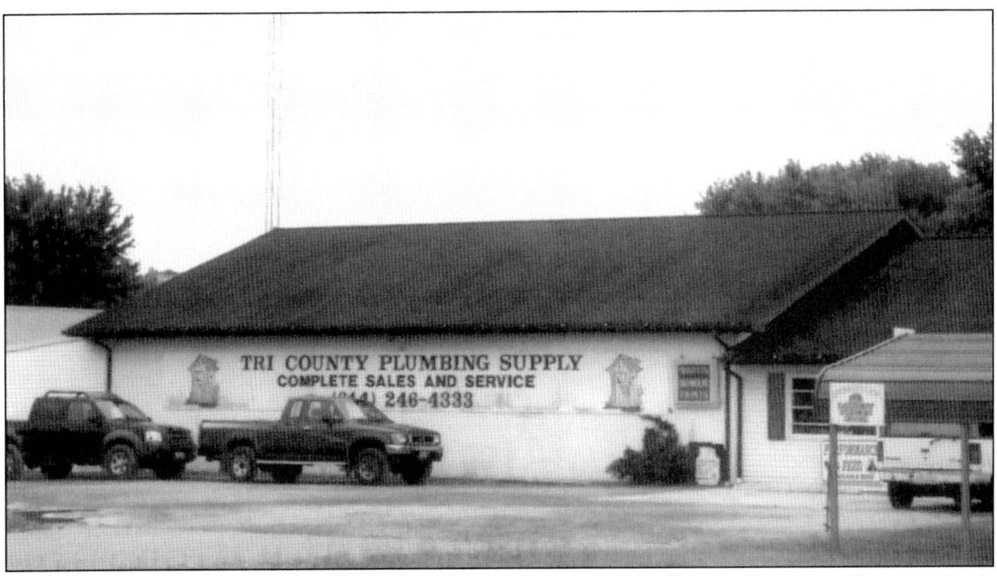

Replacing the Thornville hardware store when it closed was Tri County Plumbing Supply, which sits beside Lake's End at the Licking-Perry county line.

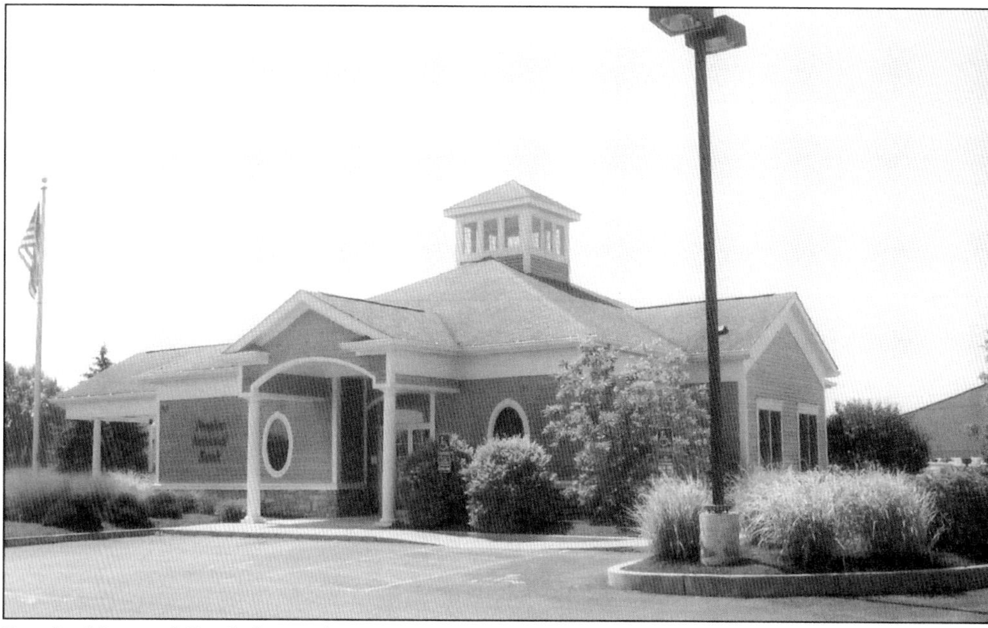

Peoples National Bank, located at 14806 Zion Road in Thornport, is one of two banks serving the township. It was built in 2002 to match the architectural style of the homes being erected in nearby Heron Bay. Dale DeRolph is branch manager.

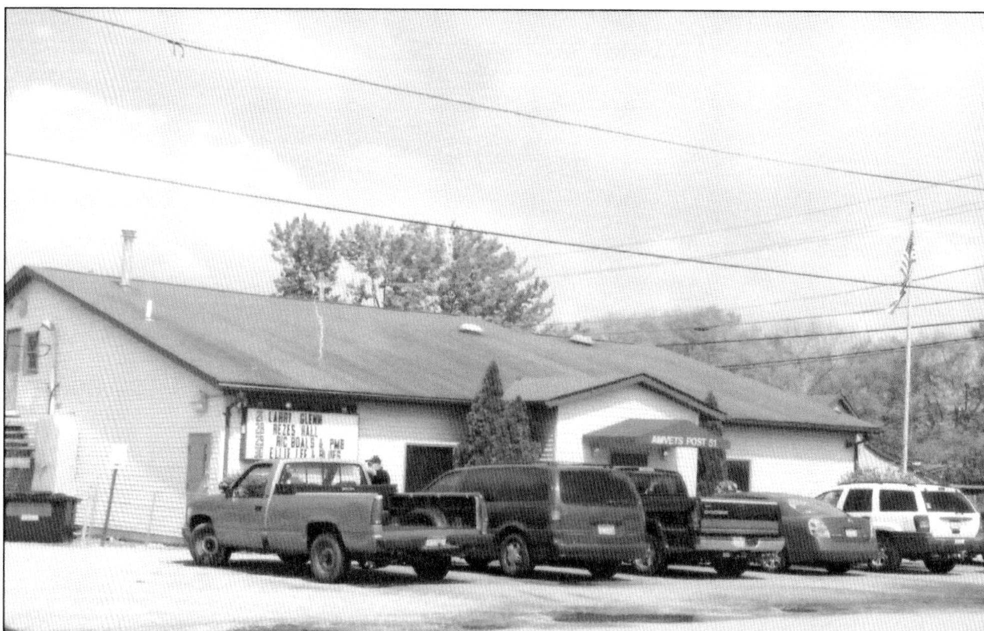

The AmVets Post 51 is located in Thornport. The American Legion building, which was on South Church Street, was demolished and replaced by All Starz Gymnastics, which is owned by Michelle and Scott Crane.

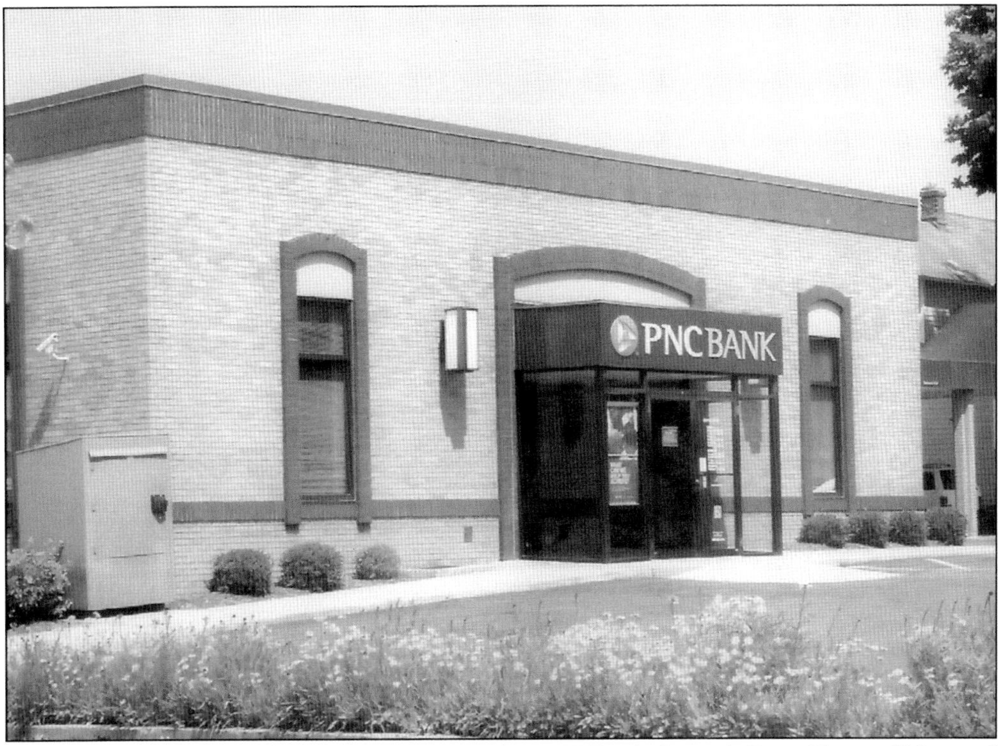

At the corner of Main and Columbus Streets is the PNC Bank, formerly BancOhio and National City. Kim Hannah is the branch manager.

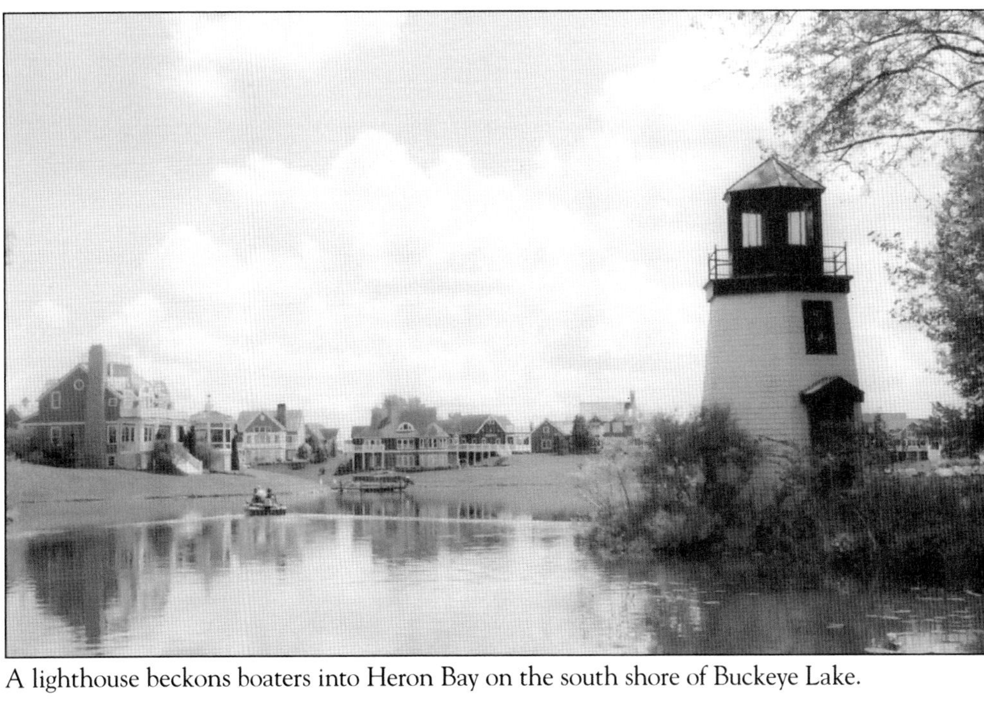
A lighthouse beckons boaters into Heron Bay on the south shore of Buckeye Lake.

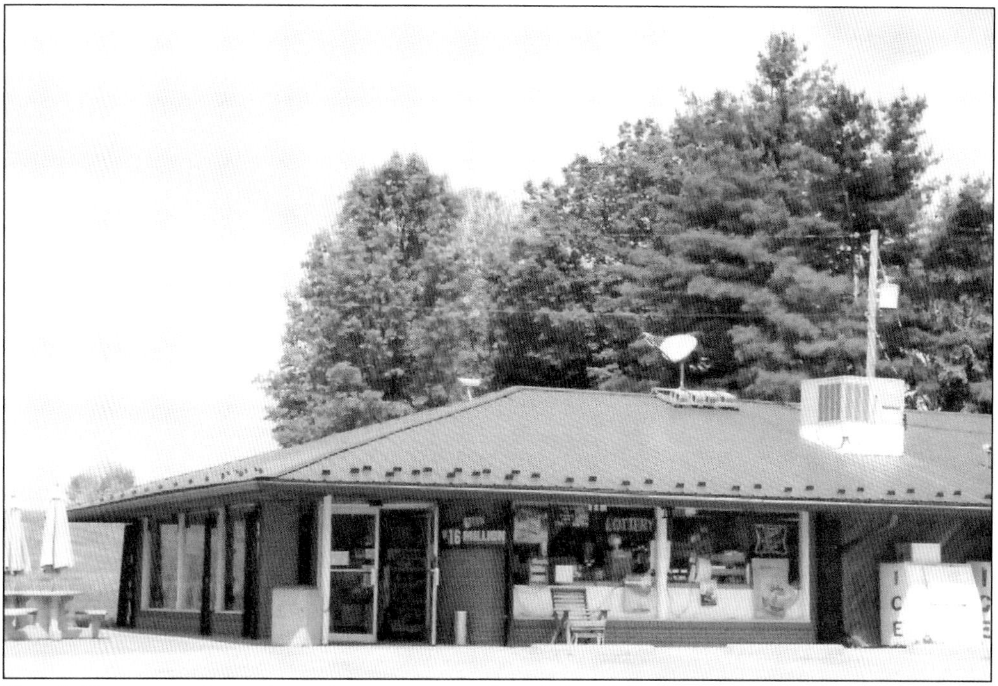

Coop's Corner was formerly a television repair shop. John Gillogly purchased the building at the corner of Routes 204 and 13 and opened a gas station and convenience store.

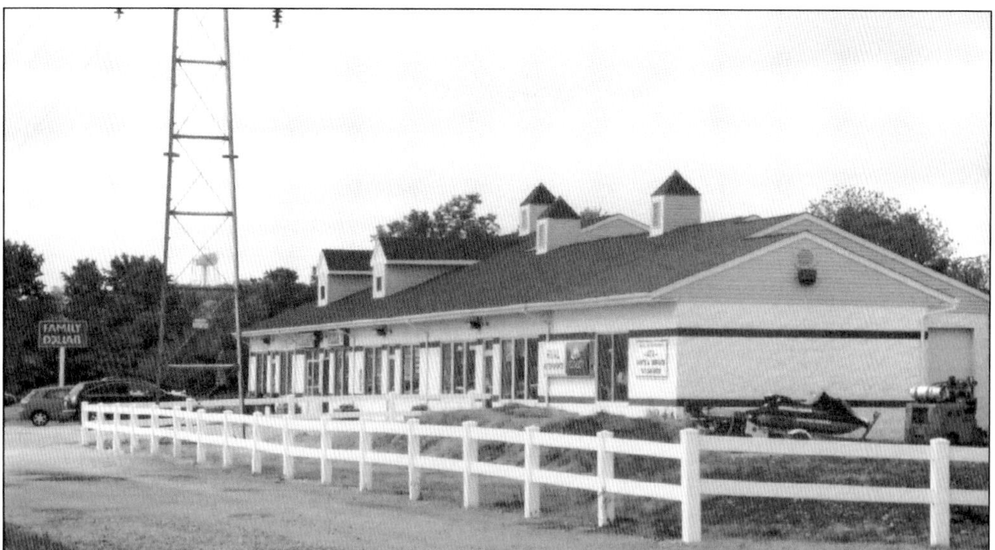

Some of the newest businesses in Thornport are Champs Pizza, the Dollar Store, Sopapilla Express, Hill Real Estate, and Rival Sports. Also, Thornport boasts a Subway restaurant, Thompson Insurance, Highpoint Taxidermy, and Beaches Beauty Salon.

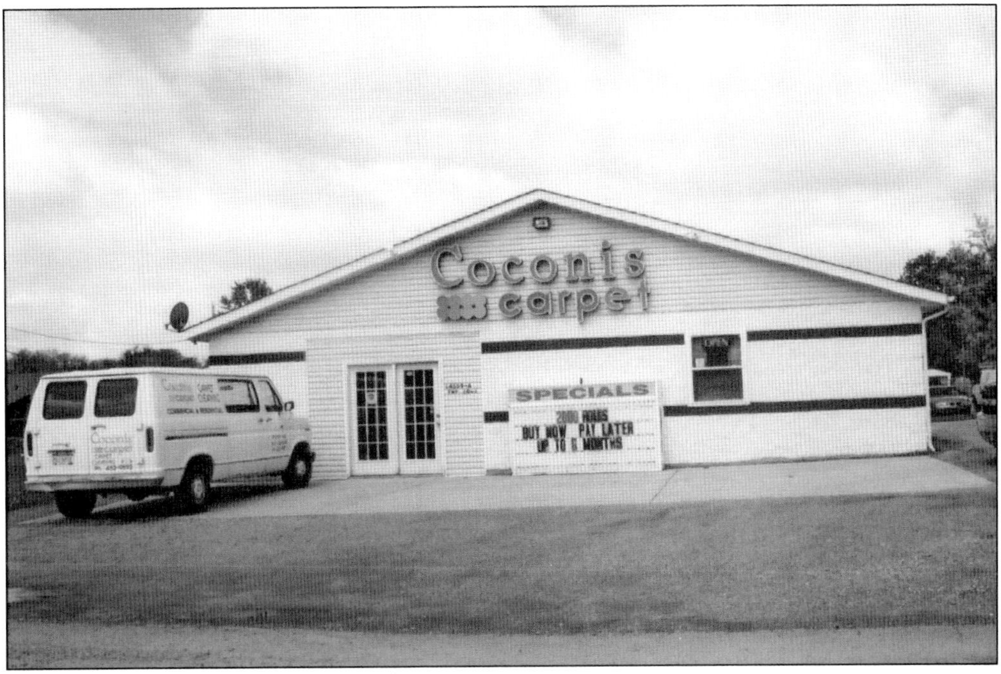

Coconis Carpet opened in 2010 in Thornport.

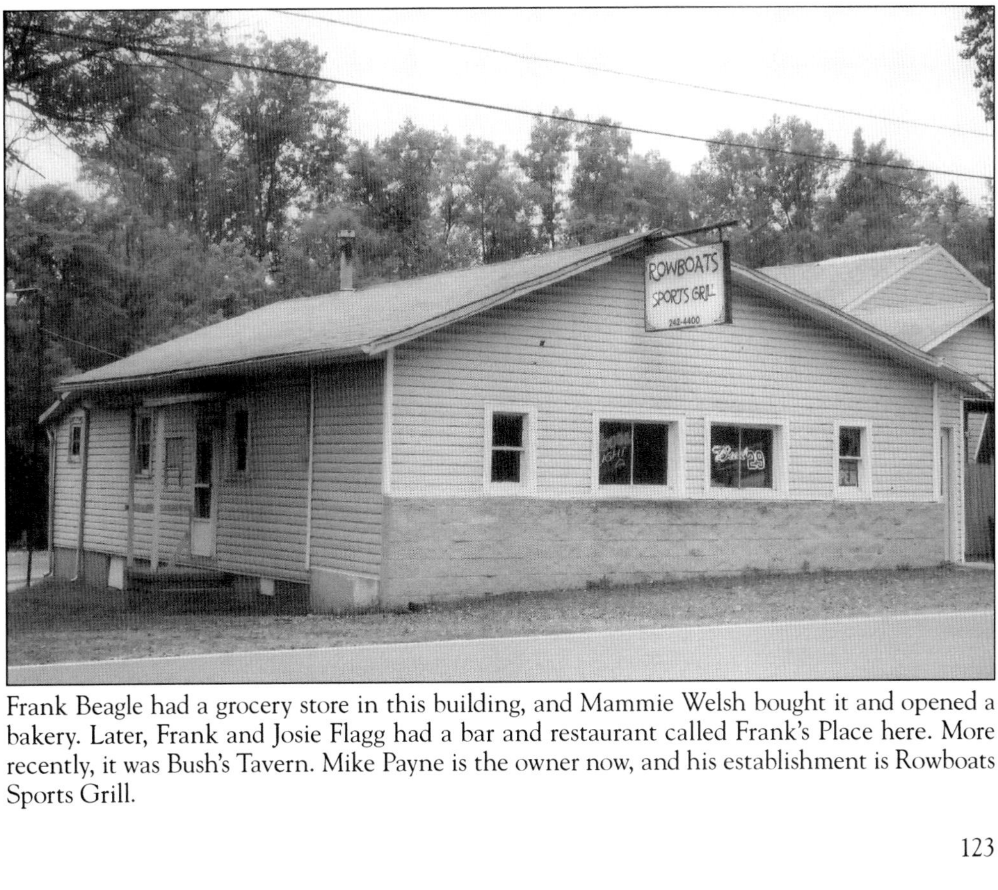

Frank Beagle had a grocery store in this building, and Mammie Welsh bought it and opened a bakery. Later, Frank and Josie Flagg had a bar and restaurant called Frank's Place here. More recently, it was Bush's Tavern. Mike Payne is the owner now, and his establishment is Rowboats Sports Grill.

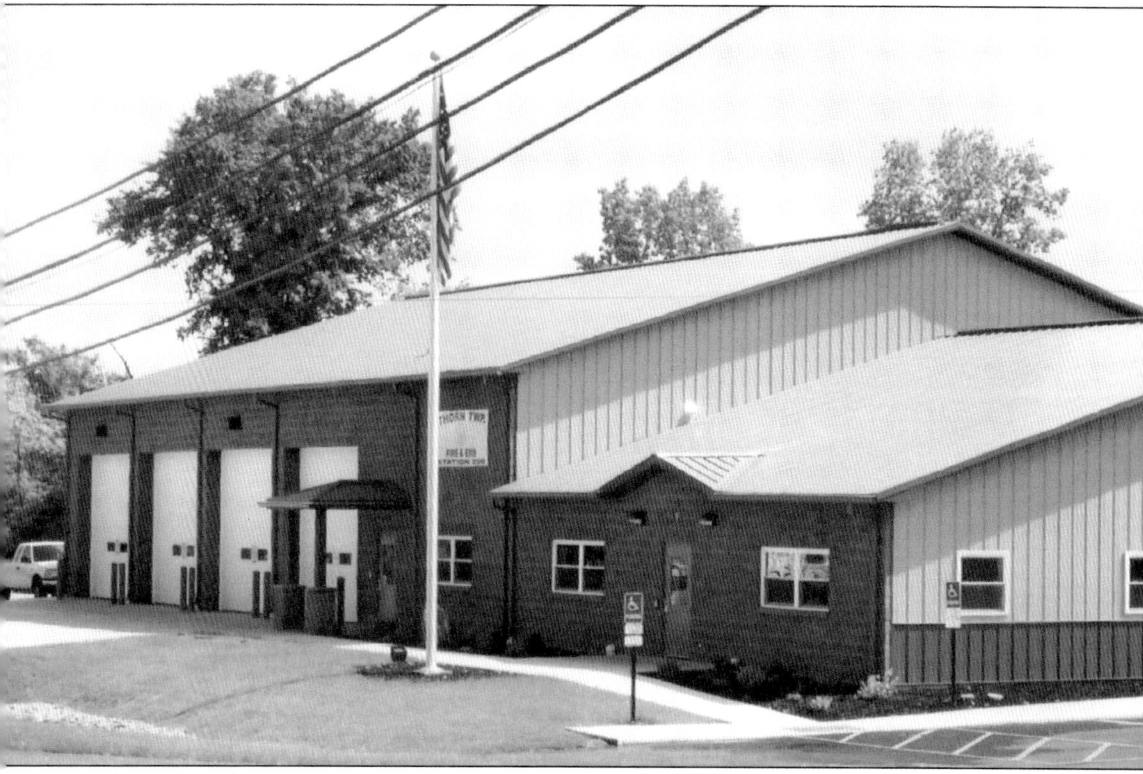

The earliest fire protection in the township was a bucket brigade. Each family owned one fire bucket for that purpose. There were also cisterns located between the village stores to hold water in case of fire. Later, six firemen pulled a hand-drawn pumper. Horse-drawn equipment came next. In 1923, the first motorized fire engine was purchased for the village. In 2010, the Thornville Volunteer Fire Department moved into this new facility at 13770 Zion Road.

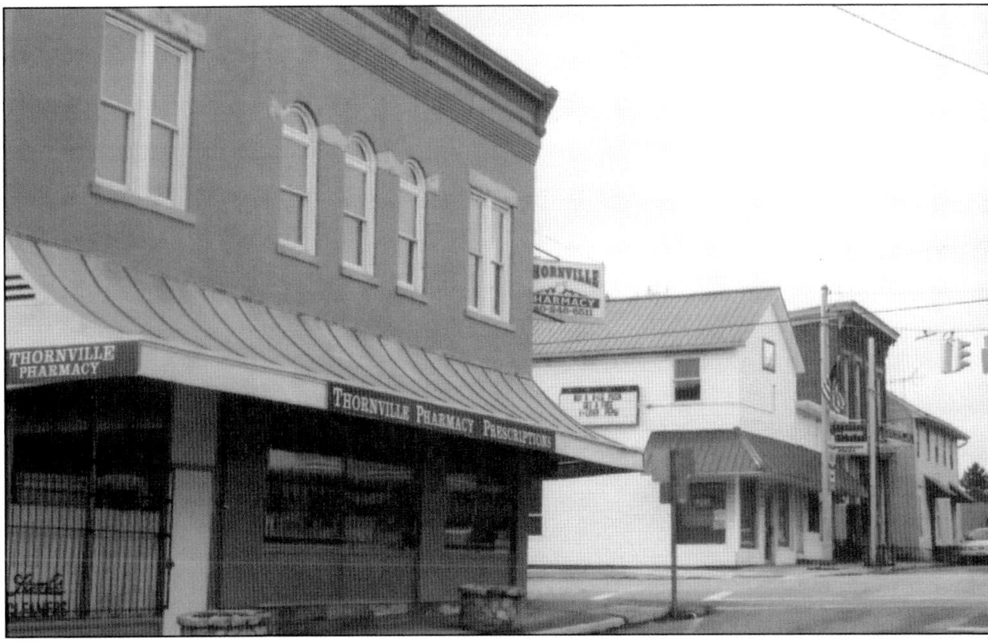

Dave and Linda Whetstone own the Thornville Pharmacy, which was purchased from Vesta and John Skinner. Dave has been the area's pharmacist since 1983.

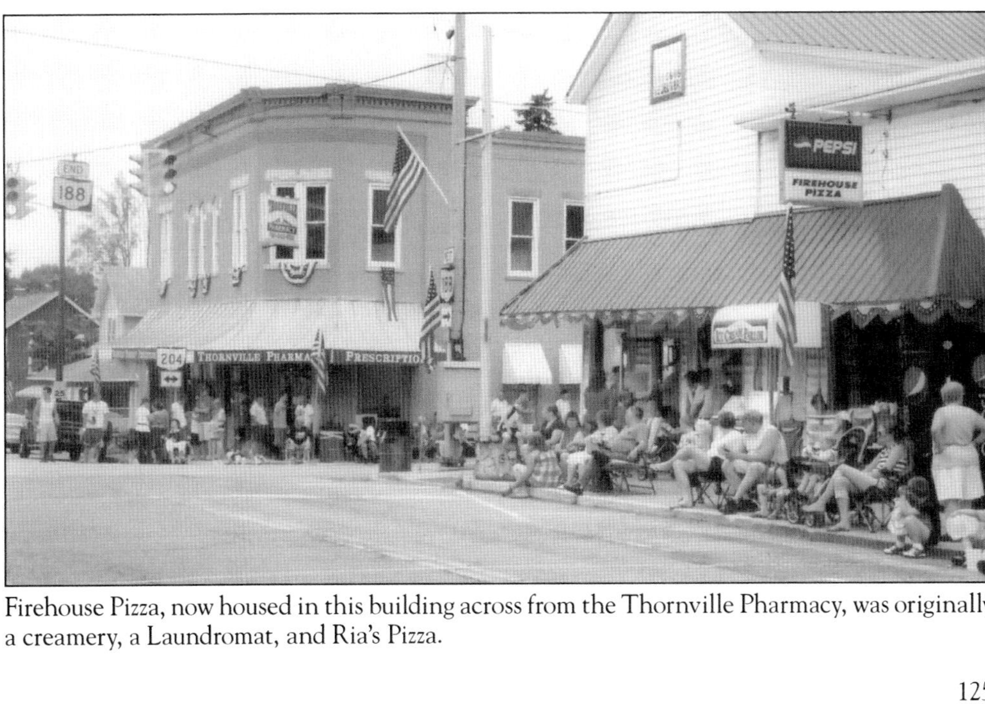

Firehouse Pizza, now housed in this building across from the Thornville Pharmacy, was originally a creamery, a Laundromat, and Ria's Pizza.

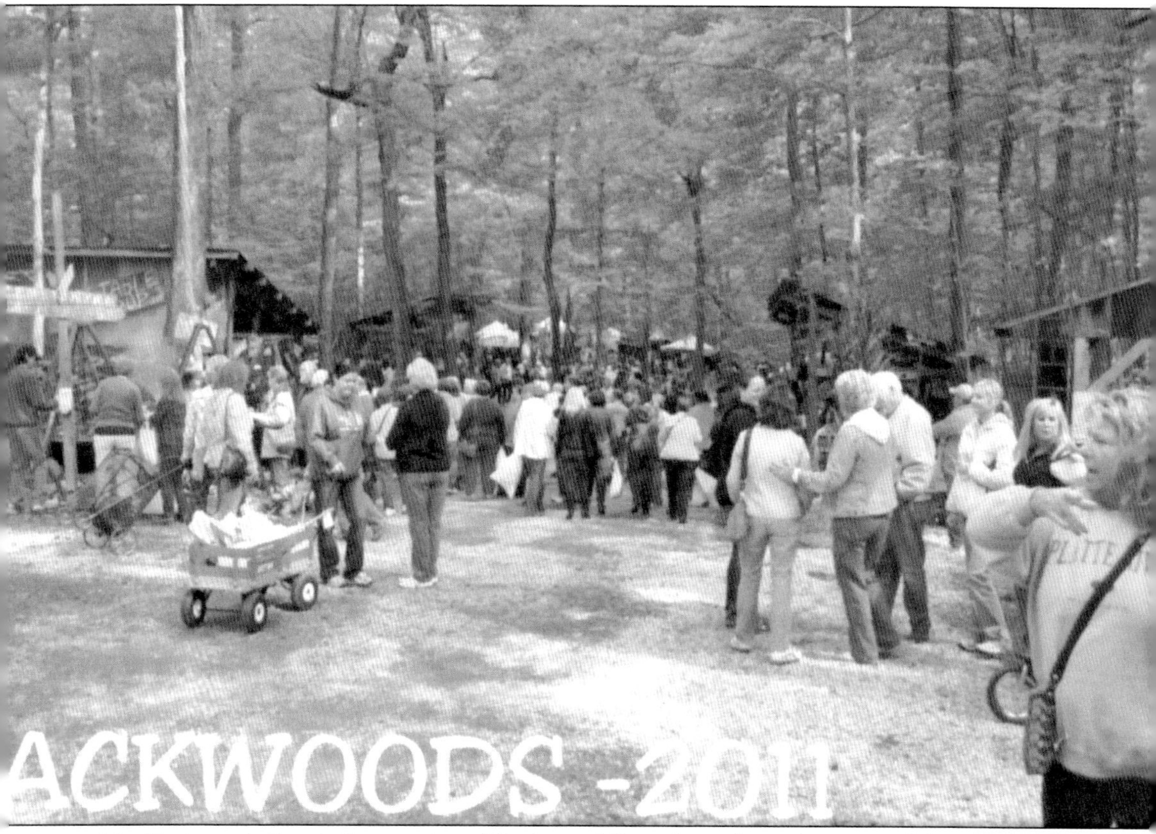

The Backwoods Fest is the creation of Kathy and Gene Launder and comes to Thorn Township every September. Thousands of people come for the shopping, arts and crafts, food vendors, music, and fun. (Courtesy of Kathy Launder.)

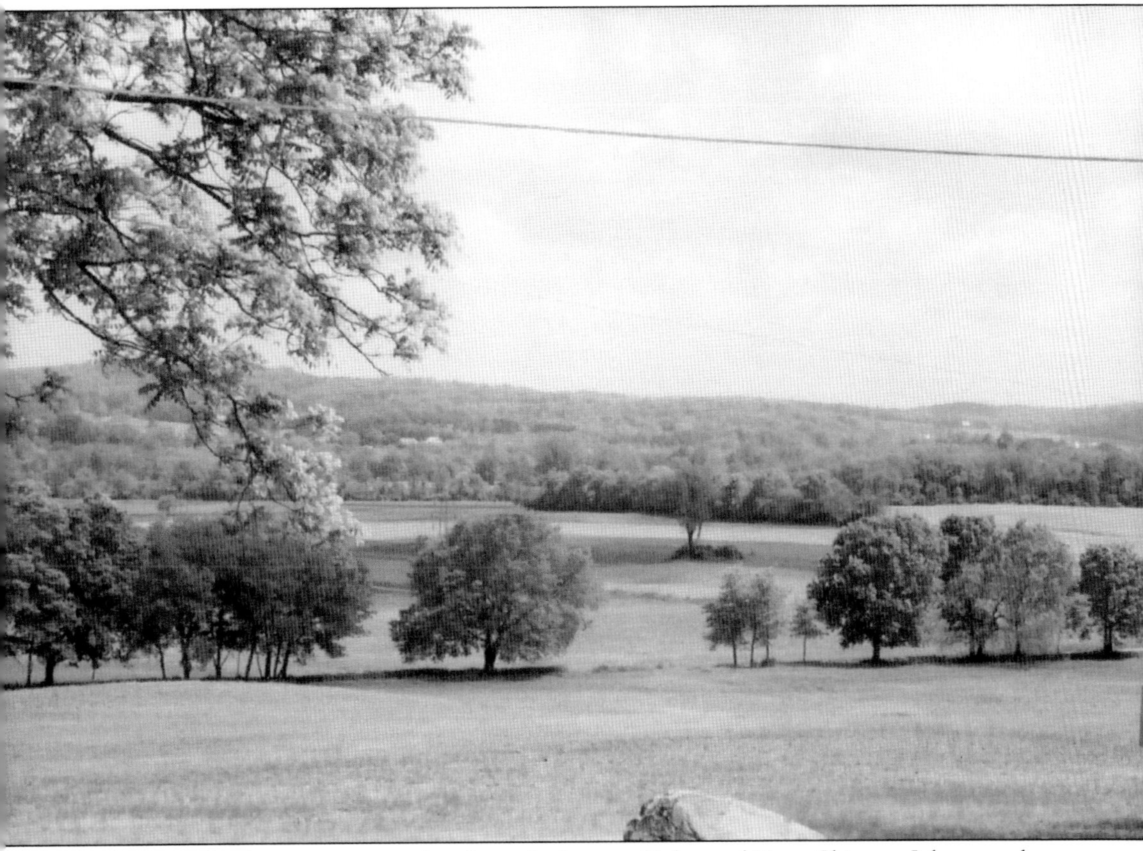

Looking north, this picture was taken from the home of John and Vesta Skinner. John says that, on a clear day, he can see trucks moving on Interstate 70.